◆ALTERNATIVES *is a series under the general editorship of Eric S. Rabkin, Martin H. Greenberg, and Joseph D. Olander which has been established to serve the growing critical audience of science fiction, fantastic fiction, and speculative fiction.*

Bridges to Fantasy

Edited by
George E. Slusser
Eric S. Rabkin
and
Robert Scholes

Southern Illinois University Press
Carbondale and Edwardsville

Library of Congress Cataloging in Publication Data
Main entry under title:

Bridges to fantasy.

"Written specifically for the Second Eaton Conference on Science Fiction
and Fantasy, held February 23–24, 1980, at the University of California,
Riverside"—Introd.
Includes bibliographical references and index.
1. Fantastic literature—Congresses. I. Slusser, George Edgar. II. Rabkin,
Eric S. III. Scholes, Robert E. IV. Eaton Conference on Science Fiction and
Fantasy Literature (2nd : 1980 : University of California, Riverside)
PN56.F34B7   809.3'876   81–13548
ISBN 0–8093–1043–0   AACR2

Contents

Introduction
George E. Slusser, Eric S. Rabkin, and Robert Scholes   vii

Clinamen: **Towards a Theory of Fantasy**
Harold Bloom   I

Form, Formula, and Fantasy: Generative Structures in Contemporary Fiction
Larry McCaffery   21

A View from Inside the Fishbowl: Julio Cortázar's "Axolotl"
Marta E. Sánchez   38

The Meeting of Parallel Lines: Science, Fiction, and Science Fiction
Arlen J. Hansen   51

On Realistic and Fantastic Discourse
David Clayton   59

The Audience in Children's Literature
Roger Sale   78

The Apparition of This World: Transcendentalism and the American "Ghost" Story
G. R. Thompson   90

Fantasy and "Forestructures": The Effect of Philosophical
Climate upon Perceptions of the Fantastic
Robert A. Collins   108

The Logic of Wings: García Márquez, Todorov, and the Endless Resources of Fantasy
John Gerlach   121

Power Fantasy in the "Science Fiction" of Mark Twain
David Ketterer   130

The Unconscious, Fantasy, and Science Fiction: Transforma-
tions in Bradbury's *Martian Chronicles* and Lem's
Solaris
George R. Guffey   142

Confronting the Alien: Fantasy and Antifantasy in Science
Fiction Film and Literature
Jack P. Rawlins   160

The Search for Fantasy: From Primitive Man to Pornography
Gary Kern   175

Notes   197

Biographical Notes   219

Index   221

Introduction

Toward a Theory of Fantasy:
Essays from the Eaton Conference

One of the most significant aspects of modern culture is the resurgence of interest in fantasy on all levels—as element of human thought, as constant factor in man's social and intellectual environment, as generator of form in art and literature. In all these areas the focus on fantasy as category of investigation promises to lead to important modifications in accepted critical patterns, indeed to reevaluation of the role and purpose of artistic activity itself.

The central problem in the study of fantasy, then, is not merely to define another genre, but to circumscribe the tools and methods needed to approach works of art from a new perspective. Each of the essays presented in this volume seeks to provide a coherent theoretical model for such an approach. The essays fall, roughly, into three groups—structures, contexts, and themes—which provide general "angles of definition." These are only starting points, however, and each study uses its particular angle not to confine a given text or problem, but rather to open it out. The goal, in each case, is to investigate particular ways in which these categories ultimately interact to produce a work of fantasy. By crisscrossing the literary and artistic landscape, then, from multiple directions, this set of essays provides a beginning to the theoretical study of a complex and elusive mode.

Bracketing the essays in this volume are two highly personal statements about the nature of fantasy which are diametrically opposed in their approaches: Harold Bloom's intense analysis of a single work, Lindsay's *Voyage to Arcturus*; and Gary Kern's wide-ranging "search" for a fantasy constant in disparate areas of literature across the ages. The other essays offer a mixture of theoretical stances on a sliding scale between these two poles. It is hoped that in this counterpoint of methods—with the focus on single works, periods, or national traditions constantly set against more general attempts to ground fantasy in Jungian archetypes, language structures, or philosophical systems—a theoretical balance is struck.

In the lead essay, "*Clinamen*: Toward a Theory of Fantasy," Harold Bloom, extending critical categories—Gnostic and Freudian in inspiration—developed in his *Anxiety of Influence* to literary fantasy, discovers the aesthetic dynamic of this "belated version of romance" to reside in "its ironic or allegorical conflict between a stance of absolute freedom and a hovering fear of total psychic overdetermination." In this perspective, Bloom asserts, it is the compounding of Narcissism and Prometheanism which produces the *clinamen*, or "swerve," that initiates literary fantasy. The next four essays, as a group, discuss from diverse and divergent angles the freedoms and limitations of this same fantasy process on the level of forms and structures. In seeking to define the generative system that informs the works of such diverse contemporary writers as Borges, Delany, Coover, and Italo Calvino, Larry McCaffery offers a model of literary creation which, while producing what might seem to be fantasy, in fact may actually obviate the concept of fantasy altogether. On the other hand, Marta Sánchez, arguing against Todorov's claim that the twentieth century has produced no fantastic literature, would recuperate fantasy as a formal category valid at least for non-European literatures. In her extended analysis of Cortázar's "Axolotl," she attempts to prove that its structures—which function, as in the works McCaffery discusses, also on a plane of linguistic experimentation—are fantastic, a transformation of the nineteenth-century form rather than its denial. From a different angle Arlen Hansen, in his essay on the closed, open, and looped structures of scientific fantasy, considers the implications—both liberating and requalifying—of the thesis that scientific as well as artistic propositions are "functional fantasies, not absolute truths," and concludes with a demand for a new look at science fiction as the contemporary literary form that most compels us to recognize that fantasy serves the ends of both science and art. Finally, David Clayton, beginning with the hypothesis that "fantastic discourse can be defined only by its differential relation—of conjunction and opposition—to another discourse and not to some extralinguistic reality," makes a sweeping examination of the interrelation of "noematic" and "fantasmatic" discourse, passing from linguistic categories to the models of structural psychoanalysis only to return to the study of individual texts and development in the historical context. Here, on this final plane, Clayton concludes that modern literature is not marked (as Todorov claims) by circumscription of the fantastic so much as by liberation of the fantasmatic "in its own right."

The next three essays examine the contextual parameters of fantasy. In "The Audience in Children's Literature," Roger Sale examines the possibility that children's literature, and, by extension, fantasy literature in general, are literary categories which more than any other define an audience rather than a subject, hence are areas where determining responses (that is, our receptivity as adults rereading what we read as a child) are clearest and most open. With G. Richard Thompson's essay, we pass from the rhetorical context for fantasy to broader national and intellectual ones. Asking why, in the age of Gothic fantasy, major American Romantic authors wrote so few out-and-out ghost stories, Thompson explores the relation of the Gothic in America to the dominant intellectual movement of the time—Transcendentalism—and contends that the absence of "straight ghosts" reflects this movement's uncertainties as to the apparitional nature of existence itself. Finally, Robert A. Collins sets as framework for fantasy creation the broad philosophical idea of "forestructures." Invoking Heidegger's concept of *Dasein*, Collins traces differences in contemporary perceptions of the fantastic to preconceptions, forestructures conditioned by the "philosophical climate" in which the critic or writer operates. He seeks to demonstrate, through analysis of the very different "grounds," or "worlds," of authors such as Ionesco, Tolkien, and Le Guin, that the difficulties in defining fantasy as a genre arise in large part from problems in defining the real, a category dependent on those preexistent structures that condition our perception of things.

The last block of essays deals with different thematic impulsions and restrictions which operate in fantasy literature and film. The first two essays make use of individual works or writers to raise general problems about the thematics of fantasy. John Gerlach considers the possibility both that the creation of fantasy may depend on certain themes and that these themes may have been "exhausted," may have lost their generative power. Through detailed analysis of a single story, García Márquez's "Very Old Man with Enormous Wings," a modern work which seems to have as its theme the impotence of fantastic themes themselves, Gerlach concludes that fantasy, if viewed as a linguistic process rather than as the result of that process, in fact has endless resources, becomes the "wings," or higher theme of language itself. David Ketterer, in his discussion of Mark Twain as author of proto–science fiction, uses the theme of power to demonstrate the difficulty of distinguishing between the genres of science fiction and fantasy on the basis of theme alone. He reveals how this thematic material shifts emphasis from one form to the other, showing a responsibility "in the cognitive sense" to reality in the more epistemological context of science fiction, an impulsion toward irresponsibility in the ethical context of fantasy. The last two essays in this group attempt to define the fantasy component in the thematic configurations of that particular genre often considered the rationalistic obverse of fantasy—science fiction. Applying Jung's distinction between "directed" and "fantasy" thinking to a series of statements by science fiction writers, George R. Guffey discusses the role of the unconscious in the creative process, then goes on to analyze the role of the unconscious "theme" of transformation in two works—*The Martian Chronicles* and *Solaris*—apparently opposite in their cultural contexts, scientific accuracy, and philosophical pretentions. He argues for the ubiquity of transformational elements in works of science fiction, hence for the fundamental fantasy nature, in the Jungian sense, of the genre. Jack Rawlins, finally, in "Confronting the Alien," seeks to clarify the terminological jungle of "science-fiction-and-fantasy"—and at the same time explain the confused reaction of many viewers to such films as *Close Encounters* and *2001*—by organizing readers' and viewers' responses around two antithetical thematic directions—what he calls "fantasy" and "antifantasy," inscrutability and knowability, nightmare and daylight reason. He hopes to demonstrate how these divergent impulses account for our perception of the alien, or "other," in these works either as metaphor (internal reality externalized) or as literal object, thus defining what may be two mutually exclusive perceptual systems.

Concluding the volume is Gary Kern's "Search for Fantasy," which traces the convolutions of the fantasy-reality relationship, and with it the relation of mind to world, art to chaos, from an imagined first instance of fantasy—primitive man's altering the tale's relation to real events by merely changing them at will, thus freeing mind from the tyranny of action and matter—through a series of reversals to the diametrically opposite vision of Dostoevsky, where it is now the human imagination itself, with all its unpredictable and insane thoughts, that is deemed reality, and fantasy become the literary act, the attempt to give such thoughts form. Kern ends with an indictment of today's "dead" forms of fantasy—pornography, for example, where both terms of this alternation, the fantastic and the real, have been rendered lifeless negatives—and a plea to free this process so that it may function anew, carve out new forms in the modern fields of relativity and uncertainty.

It is hoped, then, that this volume, in its organized diversity, will accomplish two things: that it will demonstrate the variety of fantasy forms and their pervasiveness throughout the ages; and that it will stimulate further study of these forms in the broadest theoretical manner.

All the essays in this volume are original, and all were written specifically for the second Eaton Conference on Science Fiction and Fantasy, held February 23–24, 1980, at the University of California, Riverside. The Eaton Conference, centered in the University Library's Eaton Collection of Science Fiction and Fantasy Literature, one of the largest and finest in the world, is an annual gathering of international scholars and writers devoted to discussion of problems concerning these literatures and, on a broader plane, science and fantasy in modern art and culture in general.

The editors would like to thank Vice Chancellor Eleanor Montague, University of California, Riverside, and Jean-Pierre Barricelli, Chairman of the Department of Literatures and Languages, University of California, Riverside, for their eager and untiring sponsorship of the Eaton Conference. We would also like to thank Dean David Warren, Vice Chancellor Michael Reagan, and Chancellor Tomás Rivera, all of the University of California, Riverside. Without their support, neither the conference nor this present set of essays would have existed.

Riverside, California   George E. Slusser
January, 1981   Eric S. Rabkin
                                  Robert Scholes

Bridges to Fantasy

HAROLD BLOOM

Clinamen: **Towards a Theory of Fantasy**

I intend to offer here only the opening move or swerve of what might become a theory of literary fantasy, or perhaps might join itself to some existent theories of that mode. As motto or epigraph I take from my personal favorite among modern fantasies the plangent sentence spoken by Nightspore to Krag over the corpse of the Promethean quester, Maskull: "Why was all this necessary?", to which Krag replies with his customary angry abruptness: "Ask Crystalman. His world is no joke." "All this" is nothing less than the most Sublime and spiritually terrifying death-march in all of fantastic literature, in some respects even overgoing similar journeys from Dante on to Browning's *Childe Roland to the Dark Tower Came*, David Lindsay's *A Voyage to Arcturus*, first published in 1920 in England, is a very unevenly written book, varying in tone from preternatural eloquence to quite tedious bathos. Yet I will assert for it a greatness that few contemporary critics might grant, and part of that greatness is the book's near-perfection in a particular kind of romance invention, as once it would have been called, that kind we have agreed to call fantasy.

I am moved by Eric Rabkin's insight when, in his recent anthology of fantasy, he places *A Voyage to Arcturus* together with *Alice in Wonderland* in his range (10) category of fantasy, meaning the outer limit of the mode, after which I suppose we would pass into a strange new Scripture, a revelation like that of the Gnostic Valentinus or of Joachim of Flora. The deepest affinities of Lindsay's mad sport of a book are with Lewis Carroll's apocalyptic release of fantastic energies and desires, though what emerges as purified wonder in Carroll manifests itself as horror and torment in Lindsay. Try to imagine *Through the Looking Glass* as it might have been written by Thomas Carlyle, and you will not be far from the verbal cosmos of David Lindsay.

I invoke Carlyle deliberately, because he is the tutelary spirit who informs Lindsay's frightening romance, which is a direct descendant of *Sartor Resartus*. Indeed Carlyle himself, I take it, is the perhaps unconscious model for the god or demi-god Krag, just as Walter Pater and his disciple Oscar Wilde served Lindsay as repressed models for Krag's adversary, Crystalman or Shaping. But I will postpone an account of the Carlyle-Pater agon in *A Voyage to Arcturus* until I have explored some opening aspects of my *clinamen* or ironic swerve into a beginning for a theory of fantasy. "Why was all this necessary?" is the question that, with Nightspore, we must put to the elaborate inventions of any particular fantasy, if we wish to apply those high standards of inevitability in figuration and design that traditionally have been applied to literary romance.

Fantasy is a literary sub-genre, by which I do not mean to deprecate it, but rather to state this formula: what is good in fantasy *is* romance, just as anything good in verse *is* poetry. Historically, the eighteenth century, and subsequently Romanticism, replaced the heroic genre by romance, even as the concept of the Sublime replaced theology. If Freud, as I now believe, extended and rationalized Romanticism rather than replaced it, we can aver that the literary element in dream, as expounded by Freud, is always romance. In the anxiety of belatedness that the eighteenth century waning of the Enlightenment passed on to Romanticism (and to Freud), can be found the repressed source of modern literary fantasy, because fantasy beckons as a release to any sense of belatedness.

The course of nineteenth century romance had to ensue in the submode of fantasy, first for children and then for adults, because romance, in reclaiming itself, discovered that it had ceased to be in competition with its Oedipal child, the novel. I would cite here not so much Novalis and Hoffmann, though I will say something of them later, but rather Hans Christian Andersen and Lewis Carroll, who seem to me the most inventive of nineteenth century romance fantasists. What releases itself in Andersen and Carroll is what I would call a natural Gnosticism, or perhaps only a natural religion that is a kind of gnosis.

Gnosticism, largely an Alexandrian invention, I take as being uniquely the religion of belatedness, and gnosis as a mode of knowing seems to me, as it did to Emerson, finally the knowing of what is oldest and so earliest in oneself, and so the true counterforce to a sense of having arrived too late. Prose romance, particularly in its late version of fantasy, attempts an end run around belatedness, and so must skirt the dangers of appearing childish and silly, just as the jealous child of romance, the novel, must skirt instead the dangers of appearing prosaic and expository. I am going to begin now upon a theory of fantasy by dividing the fantasy from the novel on the basis of Freud's two principles of mental functioning, yielding the reality principle to the novel, and claiming the pleasure/pain principle as the domain of fantasy. But I cannot effect such a division without first expounding and also criticizing the Freudian account of the two principles.

Though Freud assigns temporal priority to the pleasure/pain principle, I will discuss the reality principle first, precisely because of its high irrelevance to any theory of fantasy. Freud's principle of reality modifies, dominates and regulates the pleasure/pain principle, and so compels the human urges for fulfillment to go by detours and postponements, obstacles set by the external universe and by society. I would say that Freud, in his writing, takes up three very different rhetorical stances towards the reality principle: economic, topographical, and dynamic. In the economic tonality, free energy is transmuted into bound energy by the reality principle. From a topographical viewpoint, the reality principle finds its home in the preconscious-conscious system of the psyche, as opposed to the unconscious. To a dynamic stance, the reality principle relies for its enabling energy upon urges or drives supposedly in the service of the ego, a very dubious notion even in terms of Freud's own later ideas.

Clearly, such views of the reality principle are more consonant with the fictive universe of George Eliot than with that of Lewis Carroll, and Freud's pragmatic exaltation of the reality principle is a psychological version of the displacement of the romance by the novel. Freud needed to provide what no novelist could hope to invent, a rational account of how the pleasure/pain principle yielded its priority to the disenchantment of the reality principle. With marvelous significance for any theory of fantasy which is not content with mere formalism or structuralism, Freud hypothesized that as infants we begin by living in fantasy. But when fantasy ceases to bring actual satisfaction, then infantile hallucinations end, and the reality-principle begins to enter, together with a lengthening of attention-span, of judgment, and the first sense of memory. In this curiously genetic psychology, really rather uncharacteristic of Freud, the infant's cathexis or investment in his own freedom of fantasy is displaced, and energy begins to become bound. Yet the pleasure/pain principle retains its sway over fantasy, a word which for Freud refers to the unconscious and to its primary process workings.

It will be clear already that I dissent absolutely from those theorists of literary fantasy who wish to separate vigorously their subject from psychological processes of fantasy, but a theorist of influence anxieties and of agonistic misprisions takes up Freudian stances towards fantasy only with some strong misprisions all his own. Freud himself tells us that the drive for ego-preservation provides the dynamic for the onward march of reality-testing, but that the sexual drives are educated by reality only partially and belatedly, thus making for an apparently thoroughgoing dualism between the ego and the unconscious. But Freud, though the greatest and most adroit of modern explainers, cannot explain why as infants we don't all just choose to stay hallucinated. Nor can he explain ever precisely what reality-testing is, which leads me to surmise that finally it is Freud's own displaced version of a kind of Platonizing transcendentalism, a moral vision masking itself as an evidentiary science. We all live and are trapped in time, so I am in no way impressed by the anti-Freudian shibboleth that Freud's "reality" is only a limited nineteenth century Darwinian or Helmholzian scientism, but I am very disturbed that Freud's reality-principle may be only an idealized and idealizing good in itself, one more thing-in-itself that Nietzsche's dialectic can destroy with great ease. Do we possess the Freudian reality-principle as we possess art, only in order not to perish from the nihilizing truth?

No such question is tempted by the pleasure/pain principle, which Freud usually called just the Pleasure Principle, but which in fact he had begun by naming the Unpleasure Principle. It is difficult to quarrel with a purely economic principle, since it defines pleasure as a reduction in the quantities of any excitation, and pain as an increase in such quantities. These perfectly and outrageously minimalist definitions Freud never sought to modify, yet he could not ever fix the pleasure/pain principle in regard to the rest of his theories. Temporality as to pleasure and pain alike baffled him, nor could he work out the qualitative differences between pleasure and pain upon his own reductive premises. Yet Freud could not let go of the pleasure/pain principle because uniquely it worked for both conscious and unconscious psychic agencies. Still, this shrewdest of all modern theorists never clarified the relation even between the pleasure/pain principle and his cherished principle of constancy: ought energy to be maintained at a minimal level or at a constant level to avoid unpleasure? The rather desperate attempt to identify the constancy and pleasure/pain principles is the opening move in Freud's beautiful exercise in catastrophe theory, *Beyond the Pleasure Principle*, which I will cite at the end of my discourse, but here I want to turn to consider Freud's own anxieties about fantasy, both personal and literary, by way of his essay on Hoffmann's magnificent story, *The Sandman*.

As one of the strongest literary fantasies, *The Sandman* simply casts off the economics, topography and dynamics of the reality principle, and I pause here to cast off, with amiable simplicity, the theory of fantasy set forth by Todorov. We do *not* hesitate between trope and the uncanny in reading Hoffmann or David Lindsay or Lewis Carroll or *The Tin Drum* and indeed we can say that here the reader who hesitates *is* lost and *has* lost that moment which is the agonistic encounter of deep, strong reading. Where literary fantasy is strong, the trope itself introjects the uncanny, as Freud rather involuntarily both sees and shows in his anxiously strong reading of *The Sandman*.

Freud's *Sandman* is unquestionably his strongest reading of any literary text, but its strength is in its allegorization of the story as being an overwhelming instance of repetition compulsion, of the castration complex, and most complexly as the Freudian version of the Sublime, which is the "uncanny." As I have remarked in some earlier discourses, on Freud, the concerns of Hoffmann are thus swerved into what is at once the great strength and the great weakness of literary fantasy: anxieties when confronted with anterior powers. Though Freud hardly could or would acknowledge it, these were his anxieties also, in him specifically anxieties relating to authority and to transference. Uncanniness in Hoffmann is related to the narcissistic belief in the "omnipotence of thought," which is aesthetic terms *is* the Miltonic and High Romantic faith in the power of the mind over the universe of death. *Das Heimliche*, the canny or homely, is identified with its merely apparent opposite, *das Unheimliche*, or as Freud says, "this uncanny is in reality nothing new or foreign, but something familiar and old-established in the mind that has been estranged only by the process of repression."

As a formulaic reading of Hoffmann's literary fantasy, this could have been superb, yet Freud applied it rather oddly. Canny and uncanny, familiarity and estrangement are dialectical entities, rather than ambivalent dualities, but Freud reads a pattern of psychic ambivalence right through the story. Coppelius becomes the castrating bad father who destroys the good father, and who ruins every erotic possibility for Nathanael. Fixated upon Coppelius as the representation of the dead father, the psychically castrated Nathanael is incapable of loving a woman. But surely Freud cannot, as a reader, persuasively give us a *Sandman* whose pattern is at once dialectical and self-contradictory, at

once Sublime and castrating. I think though that we can learn from
Freud here, as everywhere, because Freud has stumbled brilliantly, in
one of his errors that are also grand insights. What he has uncovered is
what I would name as the *clinamen* or opening Lucretian swerve of a
theory of literary fantasy, and I phrase it in this formula: *fantasy, as a
belated version of romance, promises an absolute freedom from belatedness, from the anxieties of literary influence and origination, yet this
promise is shadowed always by a psychic over-determination in the
form itself of fantasy, that puts the stance of freedom into severe question.* What promises to be the least anxious of literary modes becomes
much the most anxious, and this anxiety specifically relates to anterior
powers, that is, to what we might call the genealogy of the imagination.
The cosmos of fantasy, of the pleasure/pain principle, is revealed in the
shape of nightmare, and not of hallucinatory wish-fulfillment.

My formulaic swerve, and immediate subsequent remarks may
give the impression that I am deprecating literary fantasy or at least
describing its apparent strength as its implicit weakness, but my intention is exactly the reverse; I speak descriptively, but indeed of fantasy's
true strength and of its use for the literary mind in our belated age. To
illustrate my formula and the role of fantasy as a belated Sublime, I
turn at last to David Lindsay's *A Voyage to Arcturus*, recalling as I turn
that the Sublime originally meant a style of "loftiness," of verbal power
conceived agonistically, against all rivals. But in the Enlightenment,
this literary idea was psychologized negatively, into a vision of terror
in both art and nature, an oxymoronic terror uneasily allied with plea-
surable sensations of augmented strength and indeed of narcissistic
freedom. This freedom is what Emerson was to call the American
stance of "wildness' and what Freud named "the omnipotence of
thought," the narcissistic illusion at its height. Freud's own Sublime
constituted his true narcissism, the pride of an originator who could say
"I invented psychoanalysis because it had no literature," or even more
ironically: "I am not fond of reading."

Criticism begins in the lived experience of a text, meaning both
the fondness of reading, and the ambivalences that fondness calls forth,
including those ambivalences that play through relationships between
texts in many of the ways they play through human relationships. In
regard to Lindsay's *A Voyage to Arcturus*, I have experienced a relationship marked by a wild fondness and an endless ambivalence, itself
productive of my own first attempt at literary fantasy, published in 1979
as *The Flight to Lucifer*, a book very much in the Arcturan shadow.
Shadow is the great closing trope of Lindsay's book, as Nightspore, the

pneuma or spark of the dead Promethean, Maskull, confronts the Demiurge Crystalman, from the standing-point of a tower beyond death:

> The shadow-form of Crystalman had drawn much closer to him, and filled the whole sky, but it was not a shadow of darkness, but a bright shadow. It had neither shape, nor colour, yet it in some way suggested the delicate tints of early morning. It was so nebulous that the sphere could be clearly distinguished through it; in extension, however, it was thick. The sweet smell emanating from it was strong, loathsome, and terrible . . .

This demiurgic shadow has a profound literary anteriority, and historically can be identified with the Aesthetic Movement in England (circa 1870–1900), which we associate with Swinburne, Whistler, Beardsley, the young Yeats, but above all others, with Pater and Wilde. Crystalman's bright shadow, with its delicate tints of early morning, has its clear source in the high purple of Pater's vision of the Renaissance, as here in the famous "Conclusion":

> To such a tremulous wisp constantly reforming itself on the stream, to a single sharp impression, with a sense in it, a relic more or less fleeting, of such moments gone by, what is real in our life fines itself down. It is with movement, with the passage and dissolution of impressions, images, sensations, that analysis leaves off—that continual vanishing away, that strange, perpetual weaving and unweaving of itself.

It might well be a more powerful and subtle version of Lindsay's Crystalman or Gangnet speaking to Maskull, as they wait for the blue sun of Alppain to rise, bringing Maskull's death. Lindsay, like Pound and Stevens, must have read Pater's first essay *Diaphaneite*, where the artist is called a crystal man, transparent and Apollonian, more than human in his perfection. Against Crystalman as Paterian Demiurge Lindsay sets his most imaginative creation, the grotesque but stalwart god of redemptive pain, strikingly named Krag in what I take to be a tribute to Carlyle's isolated hill farm in Dumfriesshire, the rugged Craigenputtoch, where *Sartor Resartus* was written, it being the book from which the religious vision of *A Voyage to Arcturus* is quarried. In *Sartor Resartus*, the post-Calvinist Lindsay found most of the ingredients of his Gnostic myth, presented by Carlyle however with his characteristic German High Romantic irony and parodistic frenzy of despair. Carlyle's outrageous ontological fable has the humor that Lindsay could not attain, yet it lacks the final frenzy of absolute literary fantasy, which past all opening swerves must stage its own death-march beyond the pleasure/pain principle. We can cite here Carlyle's own Professor Teufelsdröckh's quotation from Friedrich von Schlegel: "*Fantasy* is the organ of the Godlike," and on that basis prepare to turn again to Lindsay's quest for fantasy's simultaneous stance of freedom and over-determination.

Carlyle had insisted that the poet's work was to *see*, a willed seeing that would dissolve the cosmos of the pleasure/pain principle for the sake of the high purpose of bringing the reader under the reign of the reality principle. But Pater, and Wilde after him, subverted Carlyle's and Ruskin's moral, post-Calvinist emphasis upon willed seeing as a royal road to reality. Pater's Aesthetic or Crystal Man swerves away from a seeing that is a reality-testing to an Epicurean perceptiveness that dissolves external realities into a concourse of sensations. David Lindsay, following the Northern vision of Carlyle, oddly achieves a fantastic world that indeed is Crystalman's or Pater's flux of sensations, but this is a world that Lindsay loathes, and names Tormance, a sado-masochistic amalgam of torment and of romance. The Carlyle-like demigod Krag remarks, with his customary bitterness, that once and for all there is nothing worth seeing upon Tormance, an amazing remark that belies both the reader's experience of the book and also Lindsay's fantastic achievement. This paradox between disavowal and representation, in my own view, actually constitutes the aesthetic dynamism of literary fantasy.

Indeed this discursive paradox, at once exalting the *design* of romance, and yet rejecting all romantic *designs*, seems to me a clinching version of my formulaic swerve that begins a theory of literary fantasy by stating the simultaneous presence and absence of freedom, or the rhetorical stances of freedom, and of absence and presence of bondage, of an all but total psychic overdetermination. Other readers, friends and students, whom I have urged to read *A Voyage to Arcturus*, have tended to be severely divided in their reaction to the book, and to literary fantasy in general. When, in my disappointment, I have probed the negative reactions of readers I trust, I have found that they do center uncannily on what I take to be the true critical issue here: why do books promising aesthetic freedom (and I know no fantasy wilder than *A Voyage to Arcturus*) seem to labor under such apparent aesthetic bondage? Why might a sensitive reader come to believe that Lindsay's book is a vivid nightmare, at best, rather than the absolute vision that I keep discovering in it?

A Voyage to Arcturus begins rather weakly, I would concede, as a kind of parody of science fiction, more or less in the mode of Jules Verne. Yet even in that hopeless first chapter, "The Séance," the Uncanny enters the book with the leaping advent of Krag. Still, it is not until Chapter VI, when Maskull wakes up on Tormance, that the Sublime proper begins, as in this book it must: by, through and in suffering. Shelley suggested, as Longinus had, that the Sublime existed in order to induce the reader to abandon easier pleasures for more difficult pleasures. In Lindsay's savage fantasy, the Sublime has passed through Carlyle's Everlasting No and Centre of Indifference, leapfrogged over his Everlasting Yea, and then culminated by turning his Natural Supernaturalism inside out, to produce a Supernatural version of a Darwinian Naturalism. Lindsay seems to have invested himself in the most peculiar chapter of *Sartor Resartus*, "Symbols," and to have taken literally Carlyle's grand injunction there:

> A Hierarch, therefore, and Pontiff of the World will we call him, the Poet and inspired Maker; who Prometheus-like, can shape new Symbols, and bring new Fire from Heaven to fix it there . . .

That Fire from Heaven Lindsay names Muspel-fire, taking the name "Muspel" I suspect from *Sartor Resartus* again, where Carlyle writes of "the Adam-Kadmon, or Primeval Element, here strangely brought into relation with the *Nifl* and *Muspel* (Darkness and Light) of the antique North." Carlyle's juxtaposition is of the Kabbalistic Primal Man with the Niflheim or mist-home, the Northern night, and with Muspelheim or bright-home, the Southern realm of light. Lindsay reverses these mythological *topoi*, in one of his many instances of a kind of natural Gnosticism. It may be, though, that here Lindsay followed Novalis, who in Chapter 9, "Klingsohr's Tale," of *Heinrich von Ofterdingen* placed the realm of King Arcturus in a northern region of light. Maskull lands on Tormance in its south, and always goes due north, but dies just before the gateway of Muspel, which he then enters in his spritual form as Nightspore. But that raises the issues both of quest and questers in this daemonic fantasy, and I need to remark on these issues before I can relate the narrative patterns of *A Voyage to Arcturus* to my incipient theory of literary fantasy.

Novalis and Shelley are the two greatest masters of High Romantic fantasy-quest, and Lindsay descended from both of them, like the James Thomson of *The City of Dreadful Night* who called himself "Bysshe Vanolis." Writing to Friedrich Schlegel, Novalis described his own *Klingsohr's Fairy Tale* in terms precisely applicable to Lindsay's book:

> The antipathy between Light and Shadow, the yearning for clear, hot, penetrating aether, the Unknown-Holy, the Vesta in Sophia, the mingling

of the romantic of all ages, petrifying and petrified Reason, Arcturus, Chance, the spirit of life, individual strokes merely as arabesques,—this is the way to look upon my Fairy Tale.

This would also be the way to look upon Lindsay's fantasy, except that Lindsay's remorseless death-drive is so much darker than anything in Novalis, even than the *Hymns to the Night*. Shelley is the closer prototype for Maskull's drive beyond the pleasure/pain principle, a prototype that begins in *Alastor*, proceeds through *Prometheus Unbound* and *Epipsychidion*, and culminates in *Adonais* and *The Triumph of Life*. The protagonists of Shelleyan quest are all antithetical beings, set against nature and every merely natural value or affection. I venture the surmise that Shelley's verse-romances had much to do with establishing the theoretical pattern for most of the prose-fantasies that move in the Promethean tradition from Mary Shelley's *Frankenstein* on to Lindsay's *Arcturus*. I would call this pattern a Narcissistic one, in both the Ovidian and the Freudian sense, because the assimilation to one another of the unlikely duo of Narcissus and Prometheus is central to this internalized kind of fantastic quest-romance. Indeed, that curious assimilation, ensuing in a narcissistic Prometheus or Promethean narcist, is the direct cause of what I have been calling the *clinamen* or opening swerve, or ironic reaction-formation, of a theory of literary fantasy. The aggressivity of Promethean quest, turned quite destructively inwards against the self, results from a narcissistic scar, a scar inflicted by nature upon the questing antithetical will. One consequence of this scar is the aesthetic bafflement of literary fantasy, its ironic or allegorical conflict between a stance of absolute freedom and a hovering fear of total psychic over-determination. Shelley's Poet in *Alastor*, like his wife's Victor Frankenstein, is haunted by his *daimon* or dark double, in Frankenstein's case the creature he has made. The Shelleyan wandering Poet, and Frankenstein, and Lindsay's Maskull are all unable to get beyond self-destruction because their profound Narcissism is indistinguishable from their Prometheanism. Like Ovid's Narcissus, every protagonist of fantasy, even the greatest among them, say Don Quixote and Lewis Carroll's Alice, conclude by crying out: "my image no longer deceives me" and "I both kindle the flames and endure them." To state this another way, the Shelleyan quester, the Don, Alice, Maskull, Frankenstein, any true hero or heroine of literary fantasy discovers at last that the only fire they can steal is already and originally their own fire.

I offer this as a theoretical defense of fantasy and science fiction

alike, against the eloquent strictures of the philosopher Stanley Cavell
in his recent masterwork, *The Claim of Reason*:

> Dr. Faust's descendant Dr. Frankenstein is generally more childish, or
> more patently adolescent, in comparison with his ancestors. This is due,
> it would seem, to his more superficial narcissism, and his more obvious
> sense of guilt, as well as to his assumptions that what you know is fully
> expressed by its realization in what you can make. . . . It would be nice
> to understand, in connection with the declension from the damnation of
> Faust to the damnable Frankenstein, why there is a parallel declension in
> the genres they have inspired—why one of them is the subject of one of
> the great poetic epics of the modern world and the other is a classic, even
> a staple, of the literature (I include cinema) of the fantastic . . . we . . .
> need to articulate the difference between what we might call a thought
> experiment and what we might call a piece of science fiction . . . a fic-
> tional tale is a history over which the teller has absolute authority, call it
> the power to stipulate the world from beginning to end . . . I . . . assert
> my sense that science fiction cannot house tragedy because in it human
> limitations have from the beginning been by-passed. . . .

What Cavell does not see is that Frankenstein, as a Shelleyan,
High Romantic quester, has a Narcissism more profound than Faust's,
and a sense of guilt not so much obvious as it is Promethean. The
compounding of Narcissism and Prometheanism produces the swerve
that begins literary fantasy, a swerve that calls into question Cavell's
notion that a fictional tale is a history over which the teller has absolute
authority. Neither narcist nor Promethean can transcend human limitations, and the story of Narcissus is as much the tragedy of human sexuality as Prometheus is of human aspiration. Technically, of course,
Cavell is correct, because Milton's Satan is doubtless the paradigm of
Narcissus confounded with Prometheus, and Milton does not allow Satan to become a tragic figure. But fantasy *can* become a tragic mode, if
we shift perspectives, and yet again I turn back to read *A Voyage to
Arcturus* as a fantasy that triumphantly becomes a narcissistic yet Promethean tragedy.

All through this discourse I keep verging upon an entrance into
Lindsay's Tormance, and find great difficulty in negotiating that thresh-
old, so I will allow myself to become more personal even than usual,
in order to account for my difficulties on a cognitive as well as an
affective basis. Reading Lindsay's book (and I have read it literally
hundreds of times, indeed obsessively I have read several copies of it
to shreds) is for me at once an experience of great freedom and of
tormented psychic over-determination or nightmare. I know of no book

that has caused me such an anxiety of influence, an anxiety to be read
everywhere in my fantasy imitating it, *The Flight to Lucifer*. I have a
vivid recall still of the surprise and shock I felt when it was republished
in 1963, and my friend John Hollander gave me the book to read,
quietly telling me it was written for me. Repeated readings have confirmed my initial sense that no other fictional work inflicts such spiritual
violence upon its audience. E. H. Visiak, himself the author of a violently effective fantasy in his *Medusa*, accurately observed this strange
tonality of *A Voyage to Arcturus*:

> This effect, whatever may be the cause of peculiar subconscious energy
> that was involved, is violently disturbing. The reader's very intellect is
> assailed; his imagination is appalled . . .

I would go a step further than Visiak, and say that Lindsay's violence directly assaults what Freud called the bodily ego, the self's or
personality's investment of libido in its own ego, which perhaps by
such investment creates the Narcissistic ego. Like Blake's, Lindsay's
aim is precisely apocalyptic: our relation to the natural world and to
ourselves as natural men and women is to be broken, once and for all.
No book, be it Blake's *Jerusalem* or *A Voyage to Arcturus*, can achieve
so Sublime an aim; our natural defenses properly are aroused, and we
resent so palpable a design upon us. It is Lindsay's astonishing achievement that, like Blake, he can persuade many attentive readers of the
universal aspect of his personal nightmare. And, after many palpable
evasions, I now will devote the remainder of this discourse to Lindsay's
terrifying fantasy, except for a coda upon my anxious misprision of
Lindsay in my own first venture into fantasy fiction.

The four central beings of Lindsay's narrative are Krag, whose
hidden name is Surtur; Crystalman, whose other name is Shaping; Maskull, the Promethean quester; and Nightspore, who so mysteriously is
Maskull's friend upon earth, but who on Tormance cannot come into
existence until Maskull dies. As a fourfold, these have their rather precise equivalents in the mythologies of Blake, Shelley, Yeats and Freud,
and to list the equivalents is highly instructive. Krag is Blake's Los, or
what Yeats in *A Vision* calls Creative Mind, or Freud the achieved Ego,
beyond the narcissistic investment, and so in touch with the Reality
Principle, or what Shelley's Prometheus will become only after he is
unbound. Crystalman is Blake's Satanic Urizen, or Yeats's Will, the
Freudian Superego or the Jupiter of *Prometheus Unbound*. Maskull is
Blake's Orc, and rather fascinatingly his name in Yeats's *Vision* is also
the Mask, at once the Freudian narcissistic libido and the Shelleyan

Promethean. Nightspore, perhaps Lindsay's most surprising personage, is akin to the driving instinctual force or urge that Blake calls Tharmas, Yeats the Body of Fate, Shelley Demogorgon, and Freud the Id, agency of the Unconscious. But further allegorization of Lindsay's narrative must wait until I have clarified its weird shape as narrative.

Yeats, in the note he added to Lady Gregory's *Cuchulain of Muir-themme*, in 1903, spoke of that traditional element in romance where "nobody described anything as we understood description" because all was figurative: "One was always losing oneself in the unknown, and rushing to the limits of the world." This is certainly the world of Torm-ance, where every antagonist to Maskull's Promethean quest is only another pleasure, another rejected otherness that ensnares Maskull briefly, intensely, and to no purpose. A narrative that is nothing but a remorseless drive to death, beyond the pleasure/pain principle, can pro-ceed only by a systematic assault upon the reader's sensibilities, be-cause the reader *is* the antagonist, whose motive for reading at least begins in pleasure, and desires to end in pleasure. Lindsay audaciously sets as many obstacles for the reader to break through as his master Carlyle did, but the reader who persists will be rewarded, albeit some-what belatedly.

After the rather unconvincing opening séance, the narrative is puz-zlingly inconclusive until the moment that Maskull wakes up in the Arcturan night, to find his companions gone. He will never see Night-spore again, because Nightspore is his own spiritual form, who cannot function upon Tormance until his natural aspect, embodied in Maskull, has died. And there is not the slightest doubt but that Maskull is doom-eager, in the mode of Shelley's Poet in *Alastor*, or of Ovid's Narcissus. He is also astonishingly violent, and awesomely capable of enduring the really unbearable climates, regions and beings of the accursed world of Tormance. The typical inhabitant of Tormance is summed up in the description of one particular ogre as someone "who passed his whole existence in tormenting, murdering, and absorbing others, for the sake of his own delight." Since Maskull is hardly interested in his own delight, but only in his own possible sublimity, a very curious narrative principle goes to work as soon as Maskull starts walking due North upon Tormance. It is that singular kind of nightmare some of us dream obsessively, in which you encounter a series of terrifying faces, and only gradually do you come to realize that these faces *are terrified*, and that *you* are the cause of the terror. Maskull himself is at once the most remarkable and most frightening consciousness upon Tormance, and Maskull after all is technically a lost traveller, cut off in space and time. His truest precursor, as I will suggest later, may be Browning's Childe Roland, who is himself far darker than the dark tower he searches out.

Lindsay's narrative thus has the shape of a destructive fire seeking for a kindlier flame, but finding nothing because it burns up everything in its path. As we discover only in the book's last scene, after Maskull is dead, there is no Muspel or divine flame anyway, because Nightspore's true encounter with the Sublime, beyond death, results in his beautiful realization "that Muspel consisted of himself and the stone tower on which he was sitting. . . ." By then, the exhausted reader has transferred his identification from Maskull to Nightspore, from Prometheus-Narcissus to what Blake called "the real Man the imagination." It is the progressive exhaustion of the reader, through violence and through identification with Maskull, which is the true plot of Lindsay's narrative, as I will demonstrate by breaking into the text at Chapter XIV, which is Maskull's third morning on Tormance.

By then, Maskull has had a career of endless catastrophe, having suffered four murderous enchantments the previous day, and having been instrumental in at least four murders. Once away from the beings completely entranced by Crystalman, the Pater- or Wilde-like aesthetes Panawe and Joiwind, Maskull plunges into the problematic world of Ifdawn, where he breaks the neck of the hideous Crimtyphon, fails to prevent the murder of Oceaxe by Tydomin, is saved by Krag from being sorbed by Tydomin, himself sorbs Digrung, and then needlessly executes Tydomin and Spadevil. This sequence of disaster is followed by Maskull's vision in the Wombflash Forest, where he sees himself murdered by Krag, and then is shocked unconscious when he attempts to follow Nightspore. When the reader stands with Maskull in the subsequent idyll of the encounter with the gentle fisherman Polecrab and his uncanny wife, Gleameil, then the reader, like Maskull, badly needs a rest. And, for a very few pages, we are rested, but only to be set up for an extraordinary violence, unlike any other narrative effect I have known. With daemonic cunning, even a kind of narrative cruelty, Lindsay introduces children for the first and only time in his book, and they are presented as being the least narcissistic beings upon Tormance, in another reversal of earth-psychology. Each child's ego seems wholly unparanoid, and in no way formed by the self's narcissistic investment. Confronted by children who have never known a narcissistic scar, and whose reactions to their mother's voluntary departure and almost certain death are so much more dignified than any earthly child could manifest, the reader is lulled into an ontological security, a delusive sense that the book's worst violence is past.

This sense is literally detonated upon Swaylone's Island, where the Paterian dictum that all the arts aspire to the condition of music is answered by a vision of music as the most destructive of all the arts. After Earthrid's music has murdered Gleameil, and failed to rid Tormance of Maskull, the quester from earth plays his own music upon the circular lake called Irontick. Maskull forces the Muspel-light to appear, but strains too hard to contract it into a solid form. His intention is to compel Surtur, the true or alien God who actually is Krag, to appear, but if he were successful, surely he would materialize Nightspore, his own spark or *pneuma*, as the Gnostics would have said. Despite the dangerous power of his extraordinary will, Maskull's success is limited. His music kills Earthrid, yet his fire destroys the lake, Earthrid's instrument. When the Muspel-light vanishes, it is because the waters of the lake have fallen through, thus breaking the instrument, the waters in their descent having met Maskull's fire. The category of the aesthetic and the reader's response to the final pastoral element in the narrative have been broken together. Maskull, and the reader, are left exhausted, waiting for the fourth daybreak upon Tormance.

That exhaustion, and the textual violence provoking it, are the uncanny or Sublime splendor of Lindsay's book, and place the book, I would argue, at the very center of modern fantasy, in contrast to the works of the Neochristian Inklings which despite all their popularity are quite peripheral. Tolkien, Lewis and Williams actually flatter the reader's Narcissism, while morally softening the reader's Prometheanism. Lindsay strenuously assaults the reader's Narcissism, while both hardening the reader's Prometheanism and yet reminding the reader that Narcissism and Prometheanism verge upon an identity. Inkling fantasy is soft stuff, because it pretends that it benefits from a benign transmission both of romance tradition and of Christian doctrine. Lindsay's savage masterpiece compels the reader to question both the sources of fantasy, *within the reader*, and the benignity of the handing-on of tradition. Fantasy is shown by Lindsay to be a mode in which freedom is won, if at all, by a fearful agon with tradition, and at the price of the worst kind of psychic over-determination, which is the sado-masochistic turning of aggressivity against the self.

Reluctantly, I forbear further commentary upon Maskull's misadventures, and move on to the instructive moment of his death: instructive, particularly in regard to a theory of fantasy, but highly problematic as to its meaning in the book. The ultimate romance model is certainly the curious wasting-away into death of Shelley's Poet in *Alastor*, yet that death seems a less equivocal triumph than Maskull's ebbing-away into sublimity. With Crystalman barely disguised as the Oscar Wildean Gangnet on one side of him, and the glowering Krag hammering away on the other, Maskull stands for the dignity of the Promethean human caught between contending divinities. But Lindsay negates the Promethean by an occult triumph, crucial for his dialectic:

> "What is this Ocean called?" asked Maskull, bringing out the words with difficulty.
> "Surtur's Ocean."
> Maskull nodded, and kept quiet for some time. He rested his face on his arm.
> "Where's Nightspore?" he asked suddenly.
> Krag bent over him, with a grave expression.
> "You are Nightspore."
> The dying man closed his eyes, and smiled. Opening them again, a few moments later, with an effort, he murmured, "Who are you?"
> Krag maintained a gloomy silence.
> Shortly afterwards a frightful pang passed through Maskull's heart, and he died immediately.
> Krag turned his head round. "The night is really past at last, Nightspore. . . . The day is here." Nightspore gazed long and earnestly at Maskull's body.
> "Why was all this necessary?"
> "Ask Crystalman," replied Krag sternly. "His world is no joke. He has a strong clutch . . . but I have a stronger. . . . Maskull was his, but Nightspore is mine."

I quoted the end of this great passage at the beginning of my discourse, and come full circle back to it now, but in I trust the finer tone of a *clinamen*, a swerve into the start of a theory of literary fantasy. What kills Maskull? In an earlier vision, he had seen Krag murdering him, whereas Krag, at the start of the final voyage, prophesies that Crystalman as Gangnet will be the cause of Maskull's death. Lindsay equivocates, as he has to. Every other corpse in this book of endless corpses has the vulgar Crystalman grin upon it, even that of the beautiful High Romantic Sullenbode, who has died for love of Maskull. But Maskull's corpse disappears, without our knowing what final expression it carried. Krag speaks two utterly contradictory truths: to Maskull: "You are Nightspore," and to Nightspore: "Maskull was his." In death, Maskull becomes Nightspore; in life the Narcissus in him kept him

Crystalman's. The discursive contradiction is at the heart of the fantasy mode: Promethean freedom or striving for freedom implicates quester, writer, and reader more deeply in the bondage of Narcissus, and a form that promises under-determination takes on both the strength and the nightmare quality of over-determination.

I cannot leave *A Voyage to Arcturus*, even for the brief coda of a glance at my loving but uneasy tribute to it in *The Flight to Lucifer*, without a few words of sheer praise for a book that has affected me personally with more intensity and obsessiveness than all the works of greater stature and resonance of our time. Nothing else in English since Blake and Shelley, that I know of, has found its way back so surely to that early romance world where gods and men meet and struggle as equals or near-equals. It is Lindsay, about whom C. S. Lewis was ambivalent, rather than George Macdonald, who justifies the odd principle as to literary fantasy that Lewis brought forth on behalf of Macdonald:

> The texture of his writing as a whole is undistinguished, at times fumbling. . . . But this does not dispose of him even for the literary critic. What he does best is fantasy—fantasy that hovers between the allegorical and the mythopoeic. . . . It begins to look as if there were an art, or a gift, which criticism has largely ignored. It may even be one of the greatest arts; for it produces works which give us (at the first meeting) as much delight and (on prolonged acquaintance) as much wisdom and strength as the works of the greatest poets. . . . It gets under our skin, hits us at a level deeper than our thoughts or even our passions, troubles oldest certainties till all questions are reopened, and in general shocks us more fully awake than we are for most of our lives . . .

I am not certain that Lewis is making a critical statement, but I do recognize the reading experience he describes, except that I know it far more strongly from *A Voyage to Arcturus* than from *Lilith* or *Phantastes* or *At the Back of the North Wind*. And that is where I would locate Lindsay's great power, strangely akin to that of more genial masters of fantasy: Carroll, Andersen, Borges, and related also to Kafka's preternatural gifts. Carroll's Alice is after all as much a compound of Narcissus and Prometheus as Maskull is, because that "evilly compounded, vital I" as Wallace Stevens called it, is the ego of the hero or heroine of belated romance or literary fantasy. Lewis hints at a mode that strikes us beneath the level of discursive contradictions, because like our fantasy lives it eddies between the polarities of bondage and freedom, total psychic over-determination and total changeling-like independence of the family romance, which is after all finally indistinguishable from

romance itself, or its belated but beautiful child, the literary fantasy of
the nineteenth and twentieth centuries.

I turn, as a personal coda, to my own book, *The Flight to Lucifer:
A Gnostic Fantasy*, which had its genesis in my obsession with Lindsay's book, just as my fantasy-in-progress, *The Lost Traveller's Dream*,
has a double genesis in my inability to get my broodings away from
two remarkable semi-fantasies or realistic romances, the Elizabethan
Thomas Nashe's *The Unfortunate Traveller* and Nathanael West's
apocalyptic *Miss Lonelyhearts*. I recall that Allen Tate once wrote an
essay on his own *Ode to the Confederate Dead*, and called it *Narcissus
as Narcissus*. I will attempt to be consistent wtth my own theory, and
so I will try to be both Prometheus *and* Narcissus as I comment briefly
on the theoretical aspects of *The Flight to Lucifer*.

I don't know how many narratives have had their genesis in a
reader so loving a story that a sequel is desired, and not found, and so
the reader proceeds to write the lacking sequel. If my own theories
about influence anxieties are at all relevant or useful, then any really
intense love for a story or a poem has its ambivalent elements, however
repressed they may be. Psychic ambivalence, as Angus Fletcher re-
minded us in his superb, path-breaking book, *Allegory*, does *not* mean
mixed feelings but rather a mixture of diametrically opposed feelings,
usually related to a concept of taboo. If the extreme degree of ambivalence is, as Fletcher said, irony *or* allegory, we need to remember that
for Freud the masterpiece of psychic ambivalence was the Oedipal conflict. This conflict emerged for Freud most vividly both in the taboo
and in the psychoanalytical transference, but I think that Freud always
repressed his rather shady basing of the structure of the transference
upon the structure of the taboo. Fletcher acutely notes the presence of
heightened emotive ambivalance in the literary Sublime, in Gnosticism, and in the Freudian dialectic of Negation, and also in really fierce
satire. I quote Fletcher at his most sublimely illuminating:

> In a way Freud's term "negation" names the process by which, uncon-
> sciously, the mind selects terms to express its ambivalence. Extreme
> dualism must cause symbolic antiphrases. One gets the impression some-
> times that the most powerful satirists are dualists, users of "negation," to
> the point that they become naive gnostics. They, like Gnostics, hover on
> an edge of extreme asceticism which can drop off absolutely into an ex-
> treme libertinism. . . .

As I think Fletcher implies, it is aesthetically superior to be a
"naive gnostic" than it is to be a Gnostic proper, which is only one of

many reasons why *A Voyage to Arcturus* is a much more powerful literary fantasy than its anxious imitation, *The Flight to Lucifer*. Lindsay probably did not even know that he was creating a kind of gnostic heresy all his own, despite *his* anxious debts to Carlyle. The hapless author of *The Flight to Lucifer* set out to assimilate Lindsay's characters and narrative patterns to the actual, historical cosmology, theology and mythology of Second Century Gnosticism. But being a disciple of Walter Pater, and not of Thomas Carlyle, he sought to exalt Narcissus as well as Prometheus, or more simply to accept psychic over-determination as fantasy's price for freedom. Though a violent narrative, freely plagiarized by misprision of endless fantasy-sources, from Spenser to Kafka, *The Flight to Lucifer* has too much trouble getting off the ground, not because it knows too well what it is about, but because it is rather too interested in the ground, which is to say, too interested in the pleasure/pain principle. If *A Voyage to Arcturus* reads as though Thomas Carlyle was writing *Through the Looking Glass*, then *The Flight to Lucifer* reads as though Walter Pater was writing *Star Wars*.

Still, I do not deny the book *all* merit. It does get better as it goes along, and towards its close can be called something of a truly weird work, as its protagonist Perscors engages in a final battle with the Demiurge himself. But I wish to conclude by using the book not as a finality in itself, but as another commentary upon the mode of fantasy, another step towards a critical swerve into a more comprehensive theory of fantasy. Clearly I am neither formalist nor structuralist, nor would any psychoanalytic critic accept me as a brother. I write a kind of Gnostic or Kabbalistic criticism even as I write a Gnostic narrative, or as I would now say, I am a fantastic or Romantic critic of fantasy. For here also, in criticism as in story, the uncanny identity of Narcissus and Prometheus asserts itself. The stance of freedom, critical or creative, is not more nor less catastrophic than the stance of fate, of critical as well as creative psychic over-determination. Literary fantasy, creative or critical, is the mode where pleasure/pain principle and reality principle become most inextricably blended, even as the mode appears to proclaim a negation of the reality principle. As taboo and transference mutually contaminate one another in Freud, even so, literary fantasy contaminates fate and freedom in its own texts. Perscors, my American version of Maskull, goes into battle against Saklas, the ancient Gnostic version of Crystalman, convinced that he fights as Prometheus against Narcissus, but his pathos is that he is mistaken, and he dies in the Ovidian Narcissistic or high Shelleyan vision that always beautifully deludes the hero of fantasy:

The will to follow the maimed Demiurge ebbed in Perscors. He felt neither pain nor desire but only the peace of exhaustion. After a few moments, a fire broke forth from his own loins. When he realized that it was indeed his own fire, he smiled in contentment. Triumph was his final thought as his head became the fire.

LARRY McCAFFERY

Form, Formula, and Fantasy: Generative Structures in Contemporary Fiction

> It may be that men ceaselessly re-inject into narrative what they have known, what they have experienced; but if they do, at least it is in a form which has vanquished repetition and instituted the model of a process of becoming.
>
> Roland Barthes, *Image—Music—Text*

> The Poet, without being aware of it, moves in an order of *possible* relationships and transformations. . . . Here is the final and noblest game of skill and hazard, the wager against odds, number and calculation versus chance and probability.
>
> Paul Valéry, *Aesthetics*

I

In "The Library of Babel" Jorge Luis Borges creates an image of writing and of the universe which haunts the contemporary literary imagination. The universe, Borges suggests, can be compared to an unthinkably large library filled with mysterious texts. The organizing principles underlying the library's structure of the books contained within it are rigidly determined: "Five shelves correspond to each of the walls of each hexagon; each shelf contains thirty-two books of a uniform format; each book is made up of four hundred and ten pages; each page, of forty lines; each line, of some eighty black letters" (the letters themselves consist of twenty-five orthographic symbols).[1] The library contains one—but only one—of each combination of symbols that can be generated from this set of orthographic symbols, meaning that every possible book of this format is contained within the library somewhere. Thus, although the number of volumes contained in the library is not

21

infinite (the library can be shown to contain precisely 25 [1,312,000] volumes), for all practical purposes the combinatory possibilities are endless. Naturally, however, most of the books contained in this library appear to be nonsense, random arrangements of symbols which fail to produce any sense of order or pattern. These combinations, then, remain maddeningly inscrutable, useless from any practical sense, aesthetically displeasing to all but the most fervent Dadaists.

The allegory implicit in this tale is obvious: the universe, like Borges's library, is composed of a near-infinite number of elements which combine to create "shapes" that mankind attempts to decipher. From an ontological standpoint, all such combinations are equal, since all have been generated from precisely the same set of elements; but, because man has devised certain useful but arbitrary methods of imposing order upon the chaos—the methods of language, myth, game, mathematics, scientific and judicial laws, and so forth—various "constellational patterns" which assist man in navigating through life have gradually emerged. In his desire to uncover hidden patterns and meanings in the jumble around him, man is quite naturally tempted to hang on desperately to any sense of order that mysteriously emerges, lest it disappear once more into the flux. Still, one comforting thought that does arise from this view of the universe is the idea that, given the workings of eternity, other patterns, other meaningful sequences are bound to emerge if we are patient—sequences of greater beauty, of greater utility, of greater power to excite our senses and delight our aesthetic tastes than those we previously admired. In Italo Calvino's *Castle of Crossed Destinies*, a story which explores, in miniature, a similar view of the generative potential of life and literature, Faust provides a striking summary of this outlook:

> The world does not exist . . . there is not an all, given all at once; there is a finite number of elements whose combinations are multiplied to billions of billions, and only a few of these find a form and a meaning and make their presence felt amid a meaningless, shapeless, dust cloud; like the seventy-eight cards of the tarot deck in whose juxtapositions sequences of stories appear and are then immediately undone.[2]

I shall return to Calvino's remarkable book near the end of my discussion, but for now let us consider the view that literature is a sort of generative game in which a limited number of elements, subjected to fixed rules of association, combine to produce literary texts. Yet, because writers who adhere to this model for the creation of literary forms are often labeled "fantasy" writers, perhaps we must first consider the relation of this generative structure to the various models currently proposed to define fantasy as a mode or genre. In the context of Borges's library, it is obvious that the "reality" against which fantasy, in the most naive sense, sets itself and exists by declaring itself other, is a referential category whose privileged ontological status is arbitrarily determined. Less obviously, but still patently referential, are the more sophisticated categories of recent theoreticians of the fantastic. In distinguishing between the "fantastic" and "fantasy," W. R. Irwin states that it is the former which involves an opposition of the "anti-real . . . against an established real," whereas the latter must be understood as a rhetorical strategy, a "game of the impossible" where "narrative sophistry" is deployed to make nonfact appear as fact.[3] Yet, even on this level of game, the system of fantasy creation is still defined by reference to ontological absolutes: nonfact, impossibility. What I am proposing here—the substitution of a generative for a relational system—will, I hope, shed light on the inadequacy of the concept of fantasy as it currently exists as a tool to define the nature and purpose of much contemporary literature tagged with the label. Thus even where, as in the case of fantasy's most subtle commentators, the model proposed may seem generative, it may not actually be so. Eric S. Rabkin's system, for instance, based on the reversal of "ground rules" and narrative expectations, appears relativistic. And yet, in its exclusion of such categories as the "irrelevant," it opens the way to a reinvestment of the relational model on a different plane. For, if we accept that all the works in Borges's library, however inscrutable to us and indifferent to our aesthetic codes (and Rabkin affirms that, "as Gestalt psychology teaches us, there is no narrative world, any more than there is a physical world, without a set of ground rules by which to perceive it"),[4] then the statement that "the truly irrelevant has nothing to do with ground rules"— indeed the a priori assertion of a "true" irrelevance—merely reinstates an external "other" as privileged category, oddly enough as the "reality" against which fantasy now becomes the guarantor of narrative relevance. Our generative model, on the other hand, by recuperating the irrelevant, better describes the formulas and forms of such contemporary literature; more importantly, it also defines a mode of creation which, while appearing to be fantastic, may actually obviate the concept of fantasy along with that of realism by refusing all such privileged perspectives sanctioned by the humanist tradition, all limits which seek, in one subtle way or another, to restore the referential axis.

The hypothesis of literature as generative game, of course, is hardly unique to Borges or Calvino; it was explored almost a century ago by Mallarmé and Valéry and has been recently more systematically developed by such structuralist critics as Roland Barthes, Brémond, Greimas, Propp, and Todorov.[5] Although the specifics of applications differ, these critics all agree with the idea that all narratives are expressed by means of a finite narrative code—a process characterized by the insistent, paradoxical interplay between the uniformity of the system and the variety of its specific manifestations.[6] The full range of implications of this view of literature lie far beyond the scope of this paper, but, on a very basic level, the structuralist hypothesis strikes at the heart of the Romantic myth of the creator's producing an absolutely unique work as a result of certain inner motives and experiences to which he has absolute privilege.[7] Just as the fact that all books have already been written in Borges' library makes all writing plagiaristic, so too does the idea that all discourse can be analyzed in terms of a finite number of elements suggest that all works are *already* implicit within the generative potential of its elements—it simply remains the project of writers to choose certain alternatives and explore them, for, as Valéry remarked, "Formally the novel is close to the dream; both can be defined by consideration of this curious property: *all their deviations form part of them*."[8] In actual practice, of course, this reduction of literature to a sort of "verbal algebra" (in Borges's terms)[9] does not automatically destroy the value or utility of artistic production, for not only does the potential number of narratives which can be generated by this process approach infinity, but obviously there also remain various means by which individual narratives can be judged. As Calvino explains in a recent essay, even though "the writer is already a writing machine," this does not imply that all narratives are equal:

> Yes, literature is a combinatory game which follows the possibilities implicit in its own material, independently of a personality of the author, but it is a game which at a certain point is invested with an unexpected significance and which puts into play something of supreme importance to the author and the society to which he belongs.[10]

The key phrase in Calvino's commentary is his contention that literary games are capable of possessing "an unexpected significance . . . something of supreme importance to the author and society." for the question immediately arises as to how this process occurs. What "significance" do these literary narratives have and how is this significance transferred from the realm of a formal game to the real world? This question has been pondered by writers, scholars, and readers for centuries; it also has direct bearing on the more general issue of the relationship between *any* system of signs—such as is found in logic, mathematics, science, and the novel—and the outside world. In the case of the novel, the traditional emphasis on mimesis seemed to solve the problem: fiction could be "significant" to the extent that it "mirrored the world"; its truths resulted from the writer's ability verbally to re-create or imitate actual conditions in the world. Insofar as fiction successfully duplicated these conditions, it could reproduce the truth functions that existed in the world. Much the same case, we might recall, was made by Wittgenstein for logical propositions in the *Tractatus:* language, in the form of logical propositions, could lead man to truths about the world to the extent that the words contained in the propositions corresponded to (or "pictured," to use Wittgenstein's famous analogy) elements in the world.

As is evident today, however, major problems arise if we accept this view of fiction or this view of language's general ability to picture reality. Eventually, Wittgenstein completely overhauled his view of language's functioning, and mimesis was shown to be merely a narrative convention. Indeed, it is no accident that Wittgenstein's later theory of language employs exactly the same metaphor—that is, language *games*—as Calvino uses in the passage cited above, for both suggest that the meaning of a given discourse, whether it be personal conversation, logical theorems, or a literary text, derives not from its correspondence with any state of affairs in the world, but from an ongoing dynamic transformation of basic elements on the basis of certain arbitrary but fixed rules. Roland Barthes explains the basic flaw in the mimetic view of narrative:

> In all narrative imitation remains contingent. The function of narrative is not to 'represent', it is to constitute a spectacle still very enigmatic for us but in any case not of a mimetic order. The 'reality' of a sequence lies not in the 'natural' succession of the actions composing it but in the logic there exposed, risked, and satisfied. . . . Narrative does not show, does not imitate; the passion which may excite us in reading a novel is not that of a 'vision' (in actual fact, we do not 'see' anything). Rather it is that of meaning, that of a higher order of relation which also has its emotions, its hopes, its dangers, its triumphs. 'What takes place' in a narrative is from the referential (reality) point of view literally *nothing*; 'what happens' is language alone, the adventure of language, the unceasing celebration of its becoming.[11]

Obviously, the overthrow of such notions as mimesis, absolute truth (except in a tautological sense), and substance had a profound effect on all fields which relied, in one way or another, on narrative discourse—

and, as Robert Coover recently commented, "Even a formula is a type
of sentence."[12] This growing understanding of the way narrative principles functioned in various disciplines was very liberating: there no
longer being any "higher truth" to appeal to, intellectuals in many fields
were forced to examine the accepted paradigms from new perspectives.
This self-reflexive examination of the processes and forms of disciplines, rather than of their *content* per se, is evident in the proliferation
of metadisciplines, the dominance of linguistic analysis in philosophy,
and the emergence of metafiction and the various structuralist applications.

The plight of fiction writers during this period of reevaluation is
evident: people reading fiction, indeed, all people responding to coded
systems, have traditionally preferred systems which masquerade as part
of the natural world. As Roland Barthes puts it, "The reluctance to
declare its codes characterizes bourgeois society and the mass culture
issuing from it: both demand signs which do not look like signs."[13] If
fiction loses its direct representational ability, where does its "significance" and "importance to the author and the society" reside? Closely
related to this issue was the question of the viability of certain fictional
conventions—elements like plot, character, causality, the use of mythic
patterns, and so on. One of the most obvious results of this self-ques-
tioning process was the outburst of a certain type of highly self-conscious, nonrealistic fiction which Robert Scholes has designated as
"fabulation."[14] Another development in the turn away from mimetic
norms was a renewed interest in literary modes which had never
claimed verisimilitude as their primary goal—modes such as science
fiction, fairy tales, and mythological stories. A wide range of writers
began to perceive that realistic fiction had been naively and rigidly
structured on the basis of certain questionable, anthropocentric norms
(chief among these is the view that the world and the people who inhabit it can be analyzed on the basis of causal, empircally determinable
operations). But these principles are by no means revealed truths; they
are merely conventions that have been greatly undermined as this century has moved forward. Consequently, it is not surprising that writers
have been drawn to science fiction and other literary approaches which
are, in Darko Suvin's terms, "a mapping of possible alternatives" to
reality.[15] In his *Metamorphoses of Science Fiction*, Suvin also suggests
that science fiction's movement can be seen as shifting "from a basic
direct model to an indirect model"[16]—a movement which, as I have
indicated, is evident in all such "fabulation" as well. Suvin later admits

that, although science fiction is defined by having the reality it describes be "interpretable only within the scientific or cognitive horizon,"[17] the realm of literature is theoretically much larger:

> But besides the "real" possibilities there exist also the much stricter—though also much wider—limits of "ideal" possibility, meaning any conceptual or thinkable possibility, the premises and/or consequences of which are not internally contradictory.[18]

If literature is viewed as a game, governed primarily by *internal* rules of consistency rather than by allegiance to outer laws or conditions, it becomes quite natural for writers to wish to explore literary games which can be played with fresher, more vital rules. One consequence of this spirit of formal exploration, evident in writers such as Barth, Coover, Hawkes, Pynchon, Delany, Zelazny, and Calvino, was a revival of interest in ancient mythic patterns and in prenovelistic fictional forms—older games, long ignored because of the popularity of the realistic novel, but which possessed fascinating, intricate rules all their own. At the same time, wholly original formal approaches were being pursued, and new myths and new patterns of perception were developed. In the remainder of this paper, I would like to examine briefly several representative works which illustrate these tendencies. Although these works are formally somewhat different, they all abandon realism in favor of more blatantly artificial approaches and thus convey a shared distrust of previous literary patterns and structures (a distrust which typically becomes a metafictional self-commentary within the text); more centrally, they all tend to approach prior literary forms, myths, and conventions purely as formal elements which can be freely manipulated to generate new shapes. I begin with Samuel R. Delany's *Einstein Intersection*, for here is an acknowledged classic of science fantasy which quite literally "deconstructs" its genre. In his novel Delany does not create a structure where "ground rules," either those of our referentially verifiable world or those of an agreed-on set of narrative conventions, are reversed. Rather, he gives us a narrative where the generative patterns of the very referential system that determines this reality-fantasy axis are themselves explored. Significantly, Delany's "aliens" are seeking to become human by adopting the myriad and contradictory norms and codes which constitute that field of investigation Michel Foucault calls *science humaine*—that closed system of generative functions in which man has traded ontological status for a role as problematic element in an interacting set of "human" models.

Delany's figures, then, are neither the victims of this world nor the masters of some other, fantasy realm, but rather energy in search of form.

2

Mythological patterns, like scientific paradigms, offer man a comprehensive, understandable image of the world around us, telling us what our universe looks like and where we belong in it. Yet, like all other systems for organizing our experience, myths possess the dangerous potential for controlling us. In *The Einstein Intersection*, Delany develops this view of the oppressive nature of myth as a means of exploring the more general issue of man's relationship to all prior patterns which have lost their freshness and utility. In the process the book becomes a metafictional inquiry into man and the fiction-making process itself, and exhibits the popular contemporary tendency to manipulate prior literary and mythic formulas in order to undercut the hold which their content might have on us.[19]

Set on earth in some undetermined future, *The Einstein Intersection* tells the story of young Lo Lobey's journey in search of the murderer of his beloved Friza. Lobey's race has arrived on Earth from some unspecified region in outer space after mankind's departure (either literally or metaphorically); they are currently trying to use our legends, myths, and stories as models from which to structure their own experiences on this alien planet. Their central problem, of course, is that mankind's patterns and myths are not necessarily appropriate for Lobey's race: not only have thousands of years passed since man left the earth but, more fundamentally, Lobey's race is not even human, thus making their appropriation of man's perceptual structures a problematic venture. As the Dove, a sort of futuristic reincarnation of Jean Harlowe, tells Lobey near the end of the novel, "We have tried to take their forms, their memories, their myths. But they don't fit. It's an illusion."[20] This opinion that past methods of ordering existence are inadequate to deal with present realities is expressed in one way or another by most of the figures encountered by Lobey on his odyssey. For example, Lobey's most important guide, Spider, explains to him the novel's key concept of "difference" as follows:

> Some people walk under the sun and accept . . . change, others close their eyes, clap their hands to their ears and deny the world with their tongues. Most snicker, giggle, jeer and point when they think no one else is looking—that is how humans acted throughout their history. We have taken over their abandoned world, and something new is happening to

the fragments, something we can't even define with mankind's leftover vocabulary. You must take its importance exactly as that: it is indefinable; you are involved in it; it is wonderful, fearful, deep, ineffable to your explanations, opaque to your efforts to see through it. . . .

The response required of Lobey to this sense of the present moment's "difference" would appear to be obvious: he must abandon mankind's myths and other principles of organization and pursue his own vision, create new stories and legends which better serve his current needs. As the story concludes, this is what Lobey does, for he castrates cross-hung Green-Eye (the image of mankind's resurrection) and vows to leave Earth for the stars—a realm which he knows will be different. Along the way, however, Lobey must first work his way through various prior patterns and ways of dealing with things before he can break free of their constricting power. Thus Lobey's pursuit of "difference" is ironically portrayed as a series of archetypal reenactments of mythical and literary conventions: the pastoral journey-to-the-city convention, the initiation motif, the descent into the labyrinth, several ritualistic encounters with death and sexuality, and many others. The logic of this process is provided by PHAEDRA, who explains, "You have to exhaust the old mazes before you can move into the new ones," and by the Kid, who says, "We have to exhaust the past before we can finish with the present. We have to live out the human if we are to move on our own future."[22] The point here seems to be that the structural elements of mythic experience may retain a sense of validity even though their specific applications may no longer be useful. Myths, as Lévi-Strauss constantly points out, can be useful only insofar as they provide the basis for active regeneration of their arguments; to the extent that myths insist on an ontological equivalence with the real, they hinder our ability to use them. Thus, in a recent discussion of the role of myth in the modern novel, Eric Gould comments that

> myths are hugh interlocking systems of transformational variants, exhibiting the same intentions to ask "ultimate" questions, and to answer them as factually as possible by referring to concrete events in the natural world, which are instigators rather than objects of myth. With a particular myth, we always deal with a hypothetically comprehensive narrative, a compromise text because the strength of that myth is its logical persistence to tend to a conclusion, to be a self-evident truth, even though we know that it cannot be a final statement.[23]

It is this potentially dangerous quality of myths "to tend to a conclusion, to be a self-evident truth" that Lobey is constantly warned against.

Lobey's journey, then, contains the seeds of a universal quest for an authentic personal vision freed from the outmoded constrictions of previous methods of organizing perceptions. Yet Lobey is also an artist figure as well as a quester whose machete plays music as well as it kills; thus his journey also portrays the difficulties contemporary artists always face in attempting to define their art in relation to artistic conventions of the past. When Lobey announces, "I'm tired of the old stories, their stories. We're not them; we're new, new to this world, this life," he anticipates dozens of similarly phrased expressions of dissatisfaction voiced by authors and characters recently (for example, Barthelme's Snow White, who exclaims, "Oh I wish there were some words in the world that were not the words I always hear!").[24] The artistic issue is central to contemporary fiction: how to escape from stale conventions and exhausted story lines while yet acknowledging that certain fundamental patterns remain essential to the artist in defining our existence. The parameters of this conflict between the desire to seek the new, completely outside prior patterns and the belief that the new can only be defined in terms of the past are clearly delineated in an important conversation between Lobey and Spider:

> [Lobey] "The stories give you a law to follow—"
> "—that you can either break or obey."
> "They set you a goal—"
> "—and you can either fail that goal, succeed, or surpass it."
> "Why?" I demanded, "Why can't you just ignore the old stories? . . . I can ignore those tales!"
> "You're living in the real world now," Spider said sadly. "It's come from something. It's going to something. Myths always lie in the most difficult places to ignore. They confound all family love and hate. You shy at them on entering or exiting any endeavor."[25]

Since "myths always lie in the most difficult places to ignore," it is not surprising that one of the most common structural approaches employed by contemporary writers is to adopt directly a mythic framework as an organizing method. However, various factors mitigate against the use of myth except in an ironic, highly self-conscious manner.[26] Thus in most recent works which employ overtly mythic materials—Barth's Giles Goat Boy and Chimera, Barthelme's Snow White, Pynchon's works, Zelazny's Lord of Light, Steve Katz's Creamy and Delicious— there exists a central tension between the mythic framework's tendency to organize and rigidify its elements into teleological wholes and the ambiguous, fragmented nature of contemporary experience, which refuses to yield to formulas and patterns. The result is usually a sense that the textual elements are struggling against their roles, threatening to break out of the preset patterns in order to open us up to new constructive possibilities.

A good example of this tendency can be found in the "Mythologies" sections of Steve Katz's *Creamy and Delicious*, in which Katz, like Delany, aims at exploiting the transformational possibilities of myth. Katz, however, develops a more radical formal method of allowing prior mythic and literary materials to generate new fictional shapes. Roland Barthes has claimed that "the very end of myths is to immobilize the world; they must suggest and mimic a universal order which has fixated once and for all the hierarchy of possessions."[27] Katz, on the other hand, seeks to disrupt any sense of myth's universality, fixated order, and immobilizing power by introducing new and actively disruptive elements into the system. In each of his "Mythologies," Katz begins by selecting a name which will be certain to evoke a rich series of associations from his audience. These names are "mythic" in the sense that they suggest specific story lines and clusters of other narrative elements. But in addition to the usual names (Faust, Achilles, Hermes, Goliath, Apollo), Katz devotes equal time to more recent mythological characters (Nancy and Sluggo, Wonder Woman, Plastic Man, Ghandi, and Nasser). Once the stories begin, however, Katz defiantly divorces the names from their traditional associations—as when Nancy and Sluggo are revealed to be a gay cowboy and a "terrible gulch-riding bandit," respectively[28]—and goes about the business of creating pure narrative adventures. The "Faust" mythology, for example, begins:

> Don't believe any of those stories you had to read in college about Faust, the big scientist who wanted to know all the shit in the world, so he turned on with the devil. Don't believe all that. It's big put-on, and maybe some of it is almost true, but none of it is really true, and if you fall for it you deserve to be pasted on the wall like a wall-paper pattern.[29]

The remainder of the story has nothing to do with the Faust legend; rather, it tells of Faust, a farmer "who loved girls better than he loved his daily chores," his amorous adventures with one notorious Lulu, and a later encounter with a "befouled beauty" named Margaret. The Katzian Faust story, then, turns our expectations—which have been aroused by Katz's use of the coded signal "Faust"—upside down as he pursues a completely new story line. Since all received versions of the past have been fundamentally falsified in their transmission, Katz implies, the contemporary writer should feel free to invent whatever variations he chooses; indeed, Katz even suggests as the story concludes that "telling the truth" about Faust interferes with the storytelling impulse:

> It is a bitch to really tell the truth about Faust, as you can guess. Even
> this story fudges a little bit. Faust couldn't have got his farm farmed ever
> if he carried on like this, even if he farmed like the devil. You can't seem
> to say anything about Faust without lying.[30]

If Katz is intent on defying all the mythic patterns, we might ask ourselves, why use the name at all? The answer appears to be that Katz uses the name purely as an arbitrary formal departure point—it immediately establishes a context of meaning and story structure which Katz can disrupt (thus creating a sort of dialogue with the earlier text) while freely inventing a narrative line all his own.

Another, more rigidly controlled generative approach to fiction can be found in various fictions collected by Robert Coover in *Pricksongs and Descants*. In most of these stories Coover is clearly interested in using prior literary and mythic material as formal elements which he can rearrange into new, harmonious designs. As the title of the collection suggests, one useful way to view many of these fictions is as variations or "counterpoints" (a "pricksong" or "descant") to the basic line of the familiar mythic or literary "melody." Several of these stories use the simple method of retelling familiar stories from unfamiliar points of view. For instance, in "The Brother" and "J's Marriage," Coover takes biblical material which clearly is selected for its familiarity and its power to evoke a cluster of responses from us: he then creates a series of new revelations about this material by refocusing our angle of vision on it. In "The Brother," the more successful of the stories, Coover tells the story of Noah's Ark, not from the perspective of the holy survivor of God's wrath, but from the point of view of one of the flood's victims—Noah's brother. From this angle Coover can capitalize on many dramatic ironies by presenting the frightened "other side's" position—a position we probably had never considered before. Told in an unpunctuated Joycean monologue that uses an incongruously modern-sounding idiom, the story quickly wins our affection for Noah's unnamed brother. Much of the early material in the story is comical: before the storm Noah is seen as a ludicruous, helpless figure, "him who couldn't never do nothin in a normal way just a hugh oversize fuzzyface boy."[31] We also see the bemused attitude of the brother and Noah's neighbors as they watch the building of the huge ark on the top of a hill and the not so amused reactions of Noah's wife to his activities. But because we know the eventual pattern of the events, our laughter is strained. After it begins to rain, the brother swallows his pride out of concern for his pregnant wife and runs to the ark to seek Noah's help. If our perspective of these events is not yet transformed, it surely is changed by Noah's cold refusal of aid. Since Coover has deliberately left out one element crucial to the biblical story—the biblical logic justifying Noah's actions—we are forced to view the situation from a purely human standpoint. The story ends with the narrator precariously perched at the top of a hill, soon to die, his wife already dead. The story is typical of the way contemporary writers are capitalizing on the *forms* of prior literary material while undercutting the hold their content has for us.

Coover achieves much the same effect with a different formal approach in a series of related fictions that I have elsewhere described as "cubist" in structure.[32] In many ways the sensation created by these stories is similar to watching film rushes of the same scene shot from several different angles, with the "action" moving slowly forward because of so many retakes. Basically, Coover assembles all the elements of a familiar literary or mythic situation—the characters, setting, symbolic motifs, plot structure—and then starts the story on its way. But as soon as any pattern or design begins to assert itself, he stops the action, retraces his steps, and allows other plot lines to develop. The result is a sort of miniature version of Borges's famous hypothetical novel, *The Garden of the Forking Paths*, which was designed by its creator, Ts'ui Pen, to present all possible variations of a given fictional context.

A good example of this method can be found in "The Gingerbread House," a tale which takes as its primary structural components the elements of the Hansel and Gretel fairy tale. Coover builds this story out of forty-two short sections, many of which are only one or two lines in length, to present a fragmented variety of possible outcomes to the story. In the process Coover allows parts of the original tale to mix freely with other possibilities rather than simply create a single alternative pattern, as he did with "The Brother." Thus "The Gingerbread House" is a good example of the way Coover deliberately undercuts, reverses, obscures, and builds upon the familiar associations we may have brought to the story. For instance, Coover freely introduces plot or character elements which are extraneous or even contradictory to the original story (as with the appearance of an old man and a dove). At other times he suddenly switches the symbolic or allegoric implications that we are familiar with from the original: rather than having the black witch (who should represent evil, experience, the adult world) kill the dove (purity, grace), Coover has the young Hansel figure perform the task. Even the basic opposition between the two innocent children and the evil witch is undercut by a variety of hints that there is a willing sexual connection between them.

In addition to such manipulations and reversals, Coover also plants an overabundance of familiar images and symbols (doves, butterflies, flowers, colors, and so on), but deliberately refuses to allow them to link up and establish a single meaningful pattern. We probably notice, for example, that some sort of color imagery is being employed, since specific colors recur in section after section. But if we seek to establish a consistent "meaning" for this color imagery, we find our analysis is futile; like the whiteness of the whale in *Moby-Dick* or the white found in Poe's *Narrative of Arthur Gordon Pym*, the final "meaning" of certain colors is denied. If we approach Coover's story aware of the usual associations of "white"—"white suggests purity," for example—we will feel on solid ground at the early mention of the girl's "white petticoats" and at the appearance of the "lustrous white dove," for these are narrative codes that have assumed a conventional meaning over the years; but what are we to make of the witch's "ghostly white leg," or the fact that the old man who takes the children to the witch has "white hair" and a "white jacket"?[33] As the readers-critics we are placed in much the same position as Lobey in *The Einstein Intersection* as we attempt to apply previous patterns of meanings to new, fragmented, ambiguous material. And, of course, this is precisely Coover's intent: because the materials refuse to cohere or develop into single, mutually exclusive patterns, the reader is forced to acknowledge the possibility that all fictions, including the fiction we call reality, is composed of discrete elements which can be manipulated into a wide variety of shapes. The result is a structural emphasis on literature as a formal design rather than as an imitation of something exterior to itself—an emphasis which establishes the freedom of the artist, the exemplary fiction maker, to alter preexisting patterns whenever the old ones have lost their vitality and usefulness.

The last and most complex example of recent generative approaches to be discussed here is Italo Calvino's remarkable work, *The Castle of Crossed Destinies*. As with Coover's cubist stories, *The Castle of Crossed Destinies* unmasks literature as a kind of "combinatory game"[34] whereby the author combines narrative elements into pleasing, often revealing shapes on the basis of certain "ironclad rules."[35] As Calvino explains it, his role as author is really that of "a juggler, or conjurer, who arranges on a stand at a fair a certain number of objects and, shifting them, connecting them, interchanging them, achieves a certain number of effects."[36] In both of the novellas which constitute the book, Calvino creates a framing story which brings together a group of travelers who find themselves unable to speak; being thus frozen in the mysterious, atemporal realm of literary generation—"suspended in a journey that had not ended nor was to begin"[37]—the travelers are forced to resort to telling their respective stories with the aid of tarot cards, which the narrator proceeds to interpret for us with the assistance of certain facial and bodily gestures displayed by the travelers. The tarot cards themselves are reproduced in the margin of the text, and, since there are only a limited number of cards (seventy-eight in all), the players are forced to construct their stories so as to intersect with cards that have been played earlier. Eventually the reader, together with the narrator, discovers that

> the stories told them from left to right or from bottom to top can also be read from right to left or from top to bottom, and vice versa, bearing in mind that the same cards presented in a different order often change their meaning, and the same tarot is used at the same time by narrators who set forth from the four cardinal points.[38]

As with Coover's shuffling of literary elements into various possible narrative sequences, the structure of *The Castle of Crossed Destinies* implies that fiction arises from the transformational possibilities inherent in minimal narrative units being operated upon by fixed laws of association. The seventy-eight tarot cards can be compared to the "minimal units or fictional universals of narrative"[39] that recent structuralist critics have postulated as lying at the basis of all fiction. In his afterword to the book, Calvino comments that the "tarots were a machine for constructing stories" and that "the game had a meaning only if governed by ironclad rules" at first appear to undercut the author's (and the reader's) freedom in relationship to the text.[40] But as is suggested by the narrator's startling discovery that the stories can be read in different sequences, Calvino's text possesses the same freedom that all texts do: they can be read from an infinite number of perspectives, just as Borges's story "Pierre Menard" demonstrates. Thus new games with new rules and new meanings can always be imagined. Just as importantly, the possibility always exists for new combinations of the old material: when the castle's mistress-maidservant, the final storyteller of the first novella, finishes her tale of her new husband's betrayals, she redirects her attention:

> And now she is setting a table for two, awaiting her husband's return and peering at every movement of the foliage of this wood, at every card

drawn from this pack of tarots, every turn of events in this pattern of tales, until the end of the game is reached. Then her hands scatter the cards, shuffle the deck, and begin all over again.[41]

Her shuffling has effectively destroyed the existence of the previous stories, of course, but it also anticipates the laying out of new sequences, just as the shuffling of any deck of cards signals the conclusion to the previous structure of relationships, but also demonstrates the possibility that new combinations can be played out.

The Castle of Crossed Destinies, like *The Einstein Intersection* and the other generative narratives I have examined, also portrays the artist as the archetypal creator of vitalizing patterns. As Lo Lobey learned in his journey to the city, the raw materials of life may be limited, but their meanings are not; it is the artist's duty to recombine these meanings into patterns more suitable to the demands of the current age. Calvino's book clearly insists that the symbols which comprise narratives—and reality—are not isolated units with fixed meanings assigned to them. "Each new card placed on the table," Calvino comments, "explains or corrects the meaning of the preceeding cards";[42] thus stories are built of elements which acquire meaning only as a result of their relationship with other elements in the narrative code. By extension, the entire process whereby meaning arises in the world is dependent on specific structures of meaning—games which produce meanings on the basis of certain coded sequences of interplay. As with each of the works examined, *The Castle of Crossed Destinies* demonstrates that fixed patterns are a sham, that meaning and truth make sense only within specific contexts, that the potential always exists for new combinations, new insights, new fictional patterns which can free us from exhausted perceptual systems. Appropriately, then, Calvino compares the role of the poet to that of the Jester, or Fool, who enlightens his master by ridiculing all venerated systems:

> It is an ancient and wise custom at courts for the Fool or Jester or Poet to perform his task of upsetting and deriding the values of which the sovereign bases his own rule, to show him that every straight line conceals a crooked obverse, every finished product a jumble of ill-fitting parts, every logical discourse a blah-blah-blah.[43]

In conclusion I would like to suggest that, from the contemporary standpoint, the fiction writer or the poet, like all men, inhabits a realm which greatly resembles Borges's Library of Babel—a world in which all order is but a fragile sequence of combinations which emerges briefly from the torrent of chaos and then disappears. Still, such order does emerge in the best of our music, poems, and fictions, in the most satisfying scientific laws and mathematical systems, even in absurd but magnificently developed structures such as medieval scholasticism and the system employed by our nation to select presidential candidates. Yet to call this creation of order simply another form of fantasy is as misleading as it is impoverishing. For the generative structure I have described is the opposite both of the closed Tolkienesque mode of fantasy—where the "other" world created bears continuous metaphorical relationship to something we have absolutely and yet arbitrarily designated "our" world—and of the so-called open-ended extrapolations of science fiction earlier described by Darko Suvin, where apparently metonymic shifts from "real" to "ideal" possibilities still conceal a metaphoric relationship founded on closure by fiat, the positing of a real and an ideal. By redirecting our attention, however, to structures that remain genuinely open-ended, by reformulating our perceptions of previous narrative elements, writers such as Delany, Katz, Coover, and Calvino reward the reader with a view of the world as a narrative (that is, fictional) construct and publicly perform what Roland Barthes calls narrative's "adventure of language, the unceasing celebration of its coming."[44]

MARTA E. SÁNCHEZ

A View from Inside the Fishbowl: Julio Cortázar's "Axolotl"

In the climactic passage of Julio Cortázar's short narrative "Axolotl," the reader undergoes a startling discovery. The reader learns the tale is told by a salamander, and not, as had been presumed all along, by a man who visits a modern museum in Paris. The salamander is an axolotl who, with the consciousness of a man, comments on our world from inside a fishbowl.[1]

A reading of "Axolotl" raises a question as to the validity of Tzvetan Todorov's claim in *Introduction à la littérature fantastique* that the twentieth century has produced no fantastic texts.[2] Those of us interested in debating Todorov's contention may ask why this leading theoretician of the nineteenth-century fantastic as a genre finds no evidence for a modern fantastic. One reason why Todorov reaches this conclusion is that he applies to twentieth-century writings formal criteria adduced from nineteenth-century European and North American fantastic literature.[3] A second reason is that he limits his vision to Europe, England, and the United States. While even students of Anglo-American and European letters may choose to challenge Todorov's denial of the presence of fantastic literature in these countries, those of us in non-European literatures will find that his geographical focus is too narrow, making no allowances for the possible existence of fantastic literature elsewhere in the world.

In the discussion to follow, I formulate an argument that accounts for a fantastic literature within a twentieth-century setting. Specifically, I use Cortázar's "Axolotl" to propose that the fantastic in the twentieth century has not disappeared, but has undergone a transformation.[4] In formulating this argument, I rely on Todorov's formal and historical definition as a useful starting point, but I also try to enlarge his definition.

Cortázar's "Axolotl" approximates the formal criteria argued by Todorov to constitute the fantastic par excellence, but it also distorts his criteria. The essence of Todorov's "pure" fantastic text is the "hesitation," or "ambiguity," experienced by the reader as he or she tries to decide between a natural or supernatural explanation for the events in the narrative.[5] The reader's perception of the events narrated in Gérard de Nerval's *Aurélia*, a work which constitutes for Todorov "an original—and perfect—example of the ambiguity of the fantastic,"[6] remains ambiguous to the end. The reader is left vacillating between believing the "rational" narrator's or the "demented" character's interpretation of events. Cortázar's "Axolotl" fits Todorov's definition of hesitation, or ambiguity, because it sets up two diametrically opposed viewpoints which are both equally true: "man is man"; "man is axolotl." The reader is thus forced to vacillate between the affirmation of one viewpoint and its explicit denial.

Though ambiguity is an essential ingredient to both Todorov's and Cortázar's fantastic, the important difference is in the kind of ambiguity. Whereas the ambiguity in Todorov's examples relates to events taking place in the outside world, causing the reader to hesitate about *what has happened*, in Cortázar's "Axolotl" it is the question of *who speaks* that is ambiguous. In *Aurélia* the reader's uncertainty results from not knowing which set of perceptions is true: the "sane" narrator's or the "demented" character's. However, the reader is never in doubt about who is uttering the words of the text. In Cortázar's "Axolotl" neither the man-character nor the reader ever doubts *what* the man sees inside the fishbowl. Rather, the uncertainty is felt at the level of *who* is speaking—the man outside the fishbowl or the axolotl within the fishbowl?

A second modification in Todorov's classification concerns the direction of each narrative's movement. Cortázar's fantastic stories are like structural distortions of the nineteenth-century fantastic tale. Where Todorov's texts move in a linear and irreversible direction, Cortázar's "Axolotl" moves in a nonlinear and reversible pattern.[7] This difference may also be expressed in terms of an opposition between metonymic and metaphoric, or diachronic and synchronic. Cortázar's "Axolotl," in other words, inverts the typical structure of the nineteenth-century fantastic text.

Considering the emergence of the fantastic in relation to its historical framework, Todorov states that the fantastic sprang from an age that was caught between the real and the imaginary. "The nineteenth century transpired . . . in a metaphysics of the real and the imaginary, and the literature of the fantastic is nothing but the bad conscience of this positivist era."[8] For Todorov, then, the fantastic is the product of an ambiguous moment, emerging in an era when the powers of the feudalistic imagination were giving way to the positivities of modern science. The powers of the magical and supernatural remained sufficiently alive to haunt nineteenth-century culture. The fantastic writer could call upon the magical and supernatural to transgress the ascending social group's portrayal of the world as a secular and objective totality. He could portray taboos that haunted it, not in empirical and rational terms, but by ojectifying them in the forms of demons, ghosts, and monsters.

The narrative mode of the late nineteenth century was primarily a mimetic mode of presentation. The events of the "real" world corresponded to the literary norms of realism, which formed the frame against which the supernatural or magical mode operated in disconcerting vacillation. Just as Todorov's fantastic, in the form of the magical and supernatural, challenges and denounces the norms of realist writing, so too Cortázar's fantastic denounces these same norms. "Axolotl" is set against the background of the assumed model of the realist-mimetic text, but for purposes of inverting and ultimately subverting it. Unlike Todorov's fantastic writer, Cortázar can rely on modernistic narrative techniques to attack nineteenth-century realism. Consequently, his fantastic constitutes a more fundamental and radical attack on the mimetic mode.

Dissociation and fragmentation, typical of twentieth-century writing, form the basis of Cortázar's attack. In the Cortazarian narrative, individuals are no longer the center of their world or the subjects of their history. They are no longer the significant totalities of the traditional novel or story who can transform their human existence. Cortázar's characters are more like pawns manipulated by some exterior power than like autonomous units. They become sole objects among the mass of objects vulnerable to the impersonal rhythm of a hostile or even indifferent society.[9]

The equivalent gesture in Cortázar's narrative to the magical and supernatural mode in Todorov's fantastic is linguistic experimentation. The uncertainty in "Axolotl" centers on the ambiguous usage of the personal pronouns and the binary oppositions. The secure and stable place of the narrating subject in Todorov's fantastic "slips" in "Axolotl." Cortázar's fantastic captures the breakdown of the security of the subject.

It's All in the Pronouns: The Problem of Énonciation

"Axolotl" devalues the material historical referent—actual concrete reality—and makes language the new "object" of its discourse. We are asked to notice now not so much *what* is being said, but *how* it is said or communicated. Or, to borrow from structuralist terminology, we are directed to read a text not at the level of the *énoncé* (what a story says, or its content), but at the level of *énonciation* (how it is presented, or its form).[10] By so doing, Cortázar's stories reverse the realist model which subordinates *énonciation* to *énoncé*.

What we experience in "Axolotl" is a certain placelessness of language, by which I mean that the signifiers of language (words themselves) seem to be isolated from what they signify. Specific personal pronouns (*Yo, él, nosotros, ellos*) are manipulated so that an ambiguous relationship is established between them and their referents. The pronouns are not restricted to one object of reference, nor are they to be thought of as "static," or "glued," if you will, to the words. They indicate the place of the sender of the message (that is, who is speaking); and yet, every so often their objects of reference shift. By using them inconsistently, this story points to and plays upon the linguistic function of pronouns as shifters, to use Roman Jakobson's term.[11] We begin reading the story thinking that the pronoun *Yo* ("I") refers to the man. No sooner do we come to the third sentence, "Ahora soy un axolotl" ("Now I am an axolotl"), but we learn that "I" also refers to the axolotl.[12] In "Axolotl" we are not certain who or what is speaking.

The setting of "Axolotl" is Paris. One spring day, a man, the supposed narrator, goes to the *Jardin des plantes* to see the animals and accidentally comes across the axolotl, a rare species of larval fish, rosy little bodies, resembling small lizards (about six inches long). Three rosy springs grow on each side of their triangular heads (the gills), constricting and relaxing in a steady rhythm every ten to fifteen seconds. Their very thin feet end in "tiny fingers with minutely human nails."[13] They have eyes like pinheads and are a transparent gold color. Once having seen them, the man, captivated and even obsessed by them, presses his face against the aquarium glass every day for long hours, watching the one axolotl he has isolated from the colony of nine, gazing into its eyes, and every day he feels more and more that he and it are one, until, finally, he "becomes" the axolotl of his gaze.

The discourse of "Axolotl" is presented as a subtle sliding between two viewpoints: the first-person singular (*Yo*, or "I") and the first-person plural (*nosotros*, or "we"). The first-person singular represents the man speaking of the axolotl as "other": "There were nine specimens"; "Mentally I isolated one"; "I saw a rosy little body."[14] The first-person plural is the voice of the axolotl community, as in the following sentence: "It's that we don't enjoy moving a lot, and the tank is so cramped—we barely move in any direction and we're hitting one of the others with our tail or our head."[15] In places the two viewpoints are mixed in the same sentence, a device which is sure to confuse and even jar the reader on a first reading. Note the following: "The axolotls huddled on the wretched narrow (only I can know how narrow and wretched) floor of moss and stone in the tank."[16] The "I" would seem to refer to the man who is outside the aquarium tank, since we assume the equation "I-man" from the story's outset. Yet in this sentence the "I" must refer to someone who is someone "inside" the tank. When we read that "the axolotls" were pressed together in the confined space of the aquarium, the referent is clear, or so we think; but then when the viewpoint shifts suddenly within the parenthesis, we are forced to think that "I," otherwise the man, also refers to the axolotl. Who is speaking? Who is the subject of the discourse? The man or the axolotl? Or is it both?

Indeed, sometimes the viewpoints of the man and the axolotl are juxtaposed so closely that the pronouns would seem to be equally applicable to both the man-narrator and the fish-narrator: "Above all else, their eyes obsessed me. In the standing tanks on either side of them, different fishes showed me the simple stupidity of their handsome eyes so similar to our own."[17] Three times this passage refers to the axolotl as "other": "*their* eyes"; "either side of *them*"; *their* handsome eyes." But when the phrase "so similar to *our own*" is suddenly inserted at the end, the ambiguity is heightened (my italics). If it is the man-narrator, the plural "our own" would have to refer to all humankind for the passage to make sense; but, since previous uses of the first-person plural insinuate a fish-narrator, "our own" could very well refer to the axolotl community, too. Again we ask, who is speaking? Who *really* is the referent of the pronouns?

The sentences corresponding to the first-person singular (man) affirm our belief in the narrator's nature as man: "I left my bike against the gratings and went to look at the tulips."[18] The sentences which follow in the narrative corresponding to the first-person plural (axolotl) undermine our confidence in that nature, and our perceptions become suspect: "the most sensitive part of our body."[19] In the end the discourse achieves the transference of viewpoint from that of the man to that of the fish. The discourse moves from the apparent certainty that the "I-man" point of view is the controlling point of view of the story, into a field that undermines that certainty ("I-man" or "I-axolotl"?), and from there into a field that negates the initial disjunction between the two opposites—man and animal.

The story transforms man into animal, but, significantly, not at a material, physical level.[20] The man does not "become" an axolotl, or the axolotl a man, in the same sense that transformations occur in nineteenth-century fantastic stories. There the transformation takes place at the level of the *énoncé*, meaning that we are to imagine a man *actually* transformed into a demon or a ghost. In Cortázar's story the man's and the axolotl's bodies, or the "containers" of their consciousnesses, as it were, remain stationary and fixed. It is at the level of *énonciation*, or at the linguistic level of the personal pronouns, that man is transformed into fish. The story shifts the linguistic identification between "I-man-narrator" and "I-fish-narrator" in a continual back-and-forth movement until the latter identification takes priority over the first and is firmly in place. Since the grammatical identification of "I-man-narrator" is undermined in favor of "I-fish-narrator," the human consciousness associated and attributed to the first is also undermined in that it has been transferred to the fish. The man's and the axolotl's consciousnesses, represented by the movable pronouns, seem fluid and presumably "pass" through the glass into one another's bodies: the man's consciousness into the axolotl's body, and the axolotl's consciousness, by implication, into the man's body. The transformation states the following: "I, a man, have the consciousness of the axolotl, and I, an axolotl, have the consciousness of the man."

It is this deceptive vacillation between the affirmation of one viewpoint and its explicit denial that produces the ambiguity in Cortázar's *cuentos fantásticos* and allows us to classify them within Todorov's definition of hesitation, or ambiguity.[21] But here the story's thrust does not cause the reader to hesitate in the face of the ambiguous relationship of natural to supernatural. The reader's hesitation centers on the insecure relationship between personal pronouns and their referents. The story articulates an uncertain relationship between words and their referents in that we are no longer to perceive the two as indissolubly joined. The pronoun becomes in some sense a "free-floating object." All this has implications for the reader's relationship to the text as well, for even the reader must change his or her vantage point in relation to the speaker of the text, sometimes perceiving events from the vantage point of the man, sometimes from that of the fish. The secure relationship we once enjoyed with a text has been threatened (secure in the sense not only that we knew what was going on, but also that we knew someone was interpreting events for us, as the narrator of those nine-teenth-century fantastic texts analyzed by Todorov).

Man-Fish Duality: The Binary Opposition

A second special characteristic producing a second level of ambiguity in Cortázar's text is the ambiguous treatment of the binary oppositions that frame and restrict the narrative. "Axolotl" is a laying bare of its own underlying structures or rules, or those specific binary oppositions that control and define it. The basic binary opposition constituting its framework is that of "man" versus "animal." Throughout the story these two terms are opposed dialectically in that their relationship involves a tension between identity and difference. No sooner does the text estab-lish the identity of "I" as "man" than it sets out to deny this identity and to affirm its direct opposite: "I" is "axolotl," or animal.

The third sentence of the story announces the two conflicting poles framing the narrative: "Ahora soy un axolotl" ("Now I am an axolotl").[22] As readers we automatically identify the "I" as "man-nar-rator," habituated as we are to make this identification by the reading rules of realism. But our perceptions immediately become confused at reading that "I" is "axolotl." Throughout the story we will be aware of having to identify "I" as "man" and simultaneously having to differen-tiate it as its opposite, "axolotl." In fact, one term is never present without reference to the other term, as if we could know "man" only insofar as we perceived it as different from "animal." This is the idea behind the binary opposition. We derive "a sense of the identity of a given element . . . solely from our awareness of its difference from other elements, and ultimately from an implicit comparison of it with its own opposite."[23]

The handling of the simple binary opposition, "man" versus "ani-mal," becomes more complex as the narrative gradually moves to gen-erate a second binary opposition, of which the two terms are relational possibilities of those contained in the first binary opposition. We can illustrate by diagram the working out of these oppositions on A. J. Greimas's "semantic rectangle."[24] Although this model does not permit us to grasp the full significance and subtleties of a text such as "Axo-lotl," the "semantic rectangle" does allow us to sketch out the elemen-tary pattern of relationships defining the narrative.

The story's initial binary opposition is the following:

$$S \text{ ---} -S$$

man   animal

If then, in Greimas's model, S represents "man," the presumed narrator, and $-S$ represents its opposing term, or "animal," the other two terms can be derived by following the "gaze" between man and fish.

The gaze is the only line of communication between man and fish, since the aquarium glass proscribes smell, touch, and even hearing: "It was useless to tap with one finger on the glass directly in front of their faces; they never gave the least reaction."[25] The man gazes into the eyes of the encased axolotl and they gaze back into his. From first sight of the axolotl, the man becomes obsessed with them: "I stayed watching them for an hour and left, unable to think of anything else."[26] The next day the man returns to the *Jardin*, and then he goes every day, sometimes "morning and afternoon," and always taking the same position: "I would lean up against the iron bar in front of the tanks and set to watching them"; on the other side of the glass, the nine axolotls, pressing their heads against the glass, look back "with their eyes of gold at whoever came near them."[27] The axolotl's eyes, above all else, obsess him.

> And then I discovered its eyes, its face. Inexpressive features, with no other trait save the eyes, two orifices, like brooches, wholly of transparent gold, lacking any life but looking, letting themselves be penetrated by my look, which seemed to travel past the golden level and lose itself in a diaphanous interior mystery.[28]

The man mentally isolates one axolotl to observe and detail its physical characteristics. Though he knows that the axolotl's physical appearance is totally unlike the human form, he makes a human assessment, comparing it to a human body: "On both sides of the head *where the ears should have been*, there grew three tiny sprigs red as coral, a vegetal outgrowth, the gills, I suppose" (my italics).[29] The human component is further developed when he interjects that the minute finger nails of the axolotl's feet are *human* and that their golden eyes communicate to him a *secret will*. The end result of his "logic" is "They were *not animals*" (my italics).[30] With this last phrase he contradicts the term "animal" of the initial binary opposition and asserts the axolotl's nature as nonanimal:

The gaze between man and axolotl continues: "Their blind gaze, the diminutive gold disc without expression and nonetheless terribly shining, went through me like a message: 'Save us, save us.'"[31] Their gaze convinces him that they possess a mysterious humanity. Though acknowledging this "humanity," he insists that "they were *not human beings*" (my italics). Now he contradicts the other term of the original binary opposition, "man," and asserts the axolotl's nature as nonhuman:

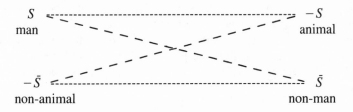

In the same sentence in which he has reached this conclusion, he contradicts it: "They were not human beings, but I had found in no animal such a profound relation with myself."[32] The story's consciousness now returns to the original opposition of "man" versus "animal." It reasserts simultaneously both the axolotl's nature as animal and its own identification with them: "but I had found in no animal such a profound relation with myself."

So far, then, the narrative has set up the basic opposition, contradicted the axolotl's animal nature ($-\bar{S}$), gone on to contradict their humanness ($\bar{S}$), then affirmed that they *are* animal ("but I had found in no animal" [$-S$]), while at the same time claiming that the narrator's life is intimately bound up with these animals (S). The narrative goes through the major poles never really fixing itself at any one of them: it is always off-center with one or another pole because there is always the implication that the axolotl is both man and animal. They are not animals—but many details used to describe their bodies indicate that they are. They are not human—but the narrator feels they were linked, "that something infinitely lost and distant kept pulling us together."[33]

This "off-center" quality about the text's "rotating" identity suggests an unstable, ambivalent consciousness unable to fix itself firmly at any one of the poles. The consciousness "jumps" around, shifting from pole to pole, and our own association with the identity must also keep shifting, now somewhere within the simple opposition "man-animal," now somewhere in between their contradictory poles "nonanimal" and "nonhuman," and then somewhere within the original opposition once again.

The final transformation occurs when the consciousness of the man is permanently transferred to the fish: "The horror began . . . of believing myself prisoner in the body of an axolotl, metamorphosed into him with my human mind intact, buried alive in an axolotl."[34] Even prior to the transformation, the man feels that the axolotl have a consciousness. They know. For this reason, what occurs is perfectly natural: "*So there was nothing strange in what happened*" (my italics).[35] Careful to negate the strange at this point, assuring us in fact that this transformation from man to fish is not only perfectly normal but also inevitable, "que eso tenía que ocurrir" ("that [that] had to occur"), he moves from his former position—outside the fishbowl looking in—to the one he will assume for the remainder of the story—inside the fishbowl looking out:

> My face was pressed against the glass of the aquarium, my eyes were attempting once more to penetrate the mystery of those eyes of gold without iris, without pupil. I saw from very close up the face of an axolotl immobile next to the glass. No transition and no surprise, I saw my face against the glass, I saw it on the outside of the tank, I saw it on the other side of the glass. Then my face drew back and I understood.[36]

Ambiguity Resolved: Axolotl Speaks

The act of attributing the human consciousness to the fish cancels our first impression that the man is the text's speaker and crystallizes the impression that the axolotl tells the story. The need arises to replace our first naive reading with a more analytical one for the purpose of reorganizing all those apparently confusing details that emerged from our initial reading. As we do this, we recognize that our second reading can no longer be ambiguous.

The narrator who we thought was the man is really the axolotl in the present, thinking back to a past moment when he came to the museum. The axolotl, remembering when he was the man, is the one who *really* enunciates such sentences as "I got to them by chance one spring morning" and "obscurely I seemed to understand their secret will."[37] Conversely, the narrator whom we perceived at moments to be the fish

is the axolotl in the present: " . . . the most sensitive part of our body";
"It's that we don't enjoy moving a lot."[38] The speaker of the story is
not the deluded man claiming to have become the axolotl, but the axolotl himself who, once a man, tells us the story of how he became an
axolotl.

From the story's inception, Cortázar provides the clue that the axolotl speaks: "Ahora soy un axolotl." On our first reading we see this
sentence, but our tendency is to ignore the intrusion of the confusing
image of man as axolotl. For one thing, we do not know what this
sentence means, not having as yet witnessed the transformation. For
another, we approach the story locked into a certain frame of mind,
ready to accept the man as narrator. The effect of Cortázar's fantastic
depends on the reader's continuing to read as though the story's speaker
were the man, as though the story's actual past were its present moment.

By inverting these priorities, Cortázar's story helps to accustom us
to certain assumptions about narrative development in twentieth-century writing. Cortázar's fantastic system as presented in "Axolotl" ultimately severs the conventional covenant between reader and subject-
narrator implicit in the nineteenth-century narrative form, where this
contract is ultimately honored, despite various kinds of ironic play, carrying the reader step by step in a forward progressive movement cul-
minating in revelation. Cortázar's reader, accustomed to the conventions of realism, will identify with the I-narrator and think of events
described as subordinate to him. Consequently, our first reaction is to
assume that man "speaks" the axolotl: they are his subject matter and
objects. The real case, however, is that the axolotl "speaks" man. Our
traditional notion of "man is narrator" is undermined (this the effect of
the shifting pronouns which confuse our perceptions). Ultimately, we
find that what we read is not at all what we assumed we are reading,
the story of a man looking into a fishbowl, but something else—the
story of an axolotl with the mind of a man speaking from inside a
fishbowl.

If we admit the premise that the rules of the nineteenth-century
fantastic demand a linear reading, one from left to right, from beginning to end, then we can postulate that the rules of Cortázar's fantastic
require a nonlinear reading, one from right to left, from end to beginning.[39] For it is precisely at the story's "closure" that the reader finds
out that the conventional contract has been severed. We must reread
and rethink the story, a process that underscores the notion that integral

to Cortázar's text is a synchronic and reversible structure, that integral to Todorov's fantastic examples is a diachronic and irreversible organization.

If the axolotl has had all along the consciousness of the man, what then can be said about the man on the other side of the glass? Given the rules of this narrative, it is not farfetched to conclude that he has had all along the consciousness of the axolotl. What does it mean to say this? Some hint of its meaning is given in the story's last sentence: "I [the axolotl] console myself by thinking that perhaps he [the man] is going to write a story about us, that, *believing he's making up a story,* he's going to write all this about axolotls" (my italics).[40] From this can be inferred the notion that "man" is to be classified not only within the categories of "narrator" and "character," but also within that of "writer." The point is that as "writer" the man must be conscious of the axolotl to write about them. In this sense he has the consciousness of the axolotl.

But since man is no longer "narrator," no longer "character," and even no longer "writer" in the realist tradition of these terms, how then are we to conceive of his "new" function as writer? The words "believing he's making up a story" imply that the man-writer does not really know what he sets out to write. In another sense, then, the man-writer cannot be conscious that he has the consciousness of the axolotl. Believing he is creating a story, he writes about the axolotl, unable to write about anything else. It is as if Julio Cortázar were trying to tell us that the writer cannot but write what he writes, as if some outside power were controlling him.

So the subversion of the realist principle, "man is narrator," has ramifications for the writer himself. He is no longer an autonomous unit controlling his material. The realist conventions of "man is narrator," "man is character with whom the reader identifies," and "man is autonomous writer" are no longer formal priorities. They have become old-fashioned, to be seen now as mere motivation and pretext for the narrative's production. This attack on the old-fashioned narrator, character, and writer also includes the old-fashioned reader.

In denouncing the rules of realism, Cortázar's *cuento fantástico* calls for a "new," a more "active" reader. Cortázar himself has called this reader *el lector-cómplice,* whom he opposes to the "old," more "passive" reader, or el *lector-hembra.*[41] The reader-*cómplice,* upon finishing a story like "Axolotl," returns to the beginning and rereads the text in a new light. Under the illusion that we are "free," that we are

"active," we will decipher its meaning. "Axolotl," after all, is not a
story about a man who becomes a fish, but about an axolotl who speaks
of the very process that brought him into being: "This is how I, an
axolotl, once a man, became an axolotl."

ARLEN J. HANSEN

The Meeting of Parallel Lines: Science, Fiction, and Science Fiction

> Scientists can agree that a Newton, Lavoisier, Maxwell, or Einstein has produced an apparently permanent solution to a group of outstanding problems and still disagree . . . about the particular abstract characteristics that make those solutions permanent. They can, that is, agree in their idenitification of a paradigm without agreeing on, or even attempting to produce, a full interpretation or rationalization of it.
>
> Thomas S. Kuhn, *The Structure of Scientific Revolutions*

> As individuals, scientists can be as pigheaded about their ideas as anyone else. . . .
>
> Nigel Calder, *Einstein's Universe*

In 1855 a twenty-four-year-old physicist stepped before the prestigious Cambridge Philosophical Society and delivered a paper, "On Faraday's Lines of Force." The young man opened his remarks with a discussion of the importance of models in scientific thought. Then James Clerk Maxwell proceeded to lay out his own mathematically stated model of the structural features of Faraday's theories. Maxwell acknowledged that his version of Faraday was "mere speculation," but he hoped that it might prove of use to experimenters in the laboratory. Launching into his text, Maxwell asked his audience to consider "a purely geometrical idea of the motion of an imaginary fluid."[1] "The substance here treated of," he said,

> must not be assumed to possess any of the properties of ordinary fluids except those of freedom of motion and resistance to compression. It is not even a hypothetical fluid. . . . It is merely a collection of imaginary properties. . . . The use of the word "fluid" will not lead us into error, if we remember that it denotes a purely imaginary substance. . . .[2]

51

In effect, Maxwell was creating a fantasy. He was drawing upon unnatural, unreal phenomena.

The scientist's need for and use of fantasy is not often noted by
those of us outside the fields of science. We tend to think of scientists
as the ultimate realists—we call them "physicists" and "naturalists."
Surely, we think, they have no truck with fiction or fantasy. Yet, like
Maxwell in his allusion to an "imaginary substance," many theoretical
scientists themselves freely acknowledge their indebtedness to fantasy.
Their laboratories are fantasy worlds where electrons look like billiard
balls and where black holes are as common as side pockets.

Werner Heisenberg has suggested one reason modern physicists
require the assistance of fantasy. "To the nineteenth century," Heisenberg notes, "nature appeared as a lawful process in space and time, in
whose description it was possible to ignore . . . both man and his in-
terference. . . ."[3] Nature, that is, was simply "out there"—a panoply
of things and activities for the typical nineteenth-century naturalist to
study objectively. Heisenberg himself helped revise this view of the
relationship between man and nature when he showed that the measure-
ment of a physical system alters its behavior.

Let me illustrate. Suppose we want to measure the temperature of
a glass of water. We stick a thermometer in the glass. And that is close
enough for most purposes. We can ignore the fact that the thermometer
itself has a temperature and that when we shove the warm thermometer
into the cold water we will raise the water's temperature ever so slightly.
In most instances, then, we overlook the fact that our acts of measuring
alter what is being measured. But the physicist cannot ignore such gross
distortions when he is dealing with tiny, say, subatomic, particles or is
seeking infinitesimally precise accuracy.

So what is to be done? How is today's nuclear physicist to observe
or measure phenomena without, in fact, altering them? He does it the
way scientists have been doing it for centuries. By pretending. Through
fantasy.

When Galileo theorized that two bodies of unequal mass will hit
the ground simultaneously, if dropped at the same time from the same
height, he was *not* suggesting that a goose feather and a cannonball
would strike the street beneath the tower of Pisa at the same time. Not
the *real* street, anyway. Galileo was speaking of objects falling in a
friction-free atmosphere. And where, in those days before the Saturn
rocket, was he to find a friction-free atmosphere? In the same place
Maxwell found his "imaginary fluid" and Roger Penrose today finds his

"twistors"—in the world that is accessible only to man's imagination, a make-believe world, a fantasy world.

Ernst Nagel, in his work *The Structure of Science*, distinguishes between "experimental laws" and "theories." The former, Nagel says, are observable, empirically verifiable. But "theoretical notions," Nagel observes, "may either not be associated with any experimental ideas whatever, or may be associated with experimental ideas that vary from context to context."[4] A theory, in other words, is a model that may have no consistent application to actual phenomena; indeed, it may have no correlative in our physical laws at all.

Such a condition, however, does not minimize the value of theoretical models, however fantastic or "unrealizable" they may be. The fantasy-model of one physical system, for example, may shed light on another physical system. That's what Maxwell was attempting: to create a model of Faraday's observations that would help him understand and conceptualize electromagnetic forces. Or take another example. Two centuries ago, Joseph Black arrived at certain discoveries about heat by thinking of it as a fluid. Thus the existing theories of fluids gave him a model for his conception of heat. Similarly, Christian Huygens appealed to the wavelike nature of sound as a model when he developed his wave theory of light.

Before Maxwell, scientists tended to prefer physical analogies. Heat resembles fluid; light resembles sound. Maxwell, however, translated Faraday's notions of force into a mathematical model and applied this abstract version to his own area of interest, electromagnetic fields. And Lord Kelvin, for one, objected. Maxwell's version of Faraday, we might say, was too remote, too unnatural, too fantastic for Lord Kelvin. To put the matter in Todorov's terms, the "hesitation," which is necessary to the sensation of the fantastic, was for Lord Kelvin not a hesitation at all, but a distinct and unbridgeable break. Maxwell's mathematical fantasy-model, to Kelvin's way of thinking, remained "marvelous" and inapplicable. Thus Kelvin reacted to Maxwell's version of Faraday as readers raised on Willa Cather or Hamlin Garland often react to Asimov's narratives: the fantasy is too "unreal" for their tastes.

The popular notion of the scientist's job of work is based on our image of the nineteenth-century naturalist. The scientist, we commonly assume, works inductively. He "does research" and "collects data," and then his experimental discoveries are marshaled into an overriding theory that accounts for his fieldwork or laboratory experiments. This popular notion, however, has been widely disputed by the scientists themselves. We learn from Einstein's letters and journals, for example, that his general theory of relativity was inspired by the image of a man falling off the roof of a house. The genesis involved no fieldwork or research of any sort. Moreover, Einstein's remarkable but uncelebrated theory that accounts for riverbank erosion came to him one morning at breakfast while he was dreamily staring at the tea leaves swirling in his cup. Again, there were no laboratory experiments.

Einstein and Leopold Infeld stress this very point in their book, *The Evolution of Physics*. Maintaining that modern scientific theories do not begin with comprehensive or random experiments, they note that "fundamental ideas play the most essential role in forming the physical theory. . . . Thought and ideas," they add, "are the beginning of every physical theory."[5] Amplifying this point, Einstein and Infeld claim that scientific theory begins with a "principal guess." Thus they observe that "science is not just a collection of laws, a catalogue of unrelated facts. It is a creation of the human mind, with its freely invented ideas and concepts."[6] And they repeat this critical idea: "Physics really began with the invention of mass, force, and an inertial system. These concepts are all free inventions."[7]

I would agree that scientific theories are creations of the human imagination. But whether or not they are "*free* inventions" is another matter. Nagel speaks to this point:

> It is a matter of historical record that there are fashions in the preferences scientists exhibit for various kinds of models. . . . Theories based on unfamiliar models frequently encounter strong resistance until the novel ideas have lost their strangeness. . . . What is nevertheless beyond doubt is that models of some sort . . . have played and continue to play a capital role in the development of scientific theory.[8]

Scientists, in short, are not "free" any more than the rest of us to invent their fantasies. They have preferences and inclinations, some of which they may not even be aware of. And their unconscious preferences have often dictated the kinds of theories they have formulated or invented.

In looking back over the past century, one can see three basic structures that have dominated scientific theorizing: the closed structure, the open-ended structure, and the looped structure. The late-nineteenth-century physicist and naturalist tended to prefer the closed model. In the 1920s some radical young physicists cast their theories in open-ended fantasy-models. And in the 1950s computer scientists and mathematicians embraced the loop model.

By "closed structure," I refer to the kind of model that yields up distinct, finite conclusions. It is the fantasy that gives way, in the end, to complete and thorough explanation. In Todorov's terms, a fantasy cast in a closed model would produce the "uncanny," for all of the hesitation or mystery will be eventually resolved in a demonstration that "the laws of reality remain intact."[9]

As I have indicated elsewhere, Einstein's argument with his close friend, Niels Bohr, at the Fifth Solvay Conference in Brussels in 1927 showed his instinctive preference for theories whose structures closed off in definitive resolution.[10] Einstein, the inventor of "relativity," did not like uncertainty. Even though his special theory in 1905 and his general theory in 1915 referred to relativity, he was not proposing—as some cocktail-party scientists infer—that everything is relative. Indeed, Einstein at one point considered calling his view the *invariance* theory. He had always searched for order, trying to establish what could be considered in fact absolute and attempting to smooth out the contradictions between Newton's views of gravity and Maxwell's views of electromagnetism.

At the Solvay Conference, Bohr and his associates proposed a conception of things that ran counter to Einstein's. They described some aspects of the physical world in a fantasy-model that incorporated indeterminancy and probability. Einstein did not like Bohr's open-ended model, just as Kelvin did not like Maxwell's. To his dying day, Einstein spent his energies searching for a unified field theory which would harmoniously accommodate and resolve the contradictions between quantum and field theories. But no satisfactory unified field theory was ever formulated. Thus Einstein died looking for a fantasy-model that would generate scientific certitude and closure.

Even though some of Einstein's early work, including the photon theory that brought him the Nobel Prize in 1922, contributed to quantum theory, he could not accept the conclusions Bohr, Heisenberg, and others reached. For one thing, they were proposing that probability, however firm the laws of chance might be, governed much of our physical world. Consequently, their theories required a conceptual model that could tolerate ambiguity, indeterminancy, probability, and uncertainty. To this view of things, Einstein said, "God does not play dice with the universe."

The concept known as Maxwell's Demon indicates just the kind of model Bohr's views required. When we measured the temperature of that glass of water, we were in fact measuring an average. The molecules inside the glass were colliding and bouncing around at various rates and in various directions. The temperature reflected the average rate of their activity, since those which were moving faster than others would read "hotter." Now, imagine a fantastic coincidence—one so improbable that it has likely never happened in the billions of years of the earth's existence. Suppose that the fastest moving molecules all happen to bounce up to the top of the glass. In such an instance, the water at the top would boil. However improbable this fantasy is, it *could* happen. Theoretically, at least. If it did happen, the phenomenon would be attritubed to Maxwell's Demon. Only an open-ended fantasy-model can describe such a universe where Maxwell's Demon ever lurks about, ready to capitalize on that one-in-a-billion-billion chance.

Bohr's notion of complementarity also requires an open-ended model. In addressing the question "Are electrons particles or waves?" Bohr discovered that they are either, depending on what we are looking for. An electron is both an orbiting bit of matter and a smear that appears to be all places at once. That is, we can measure electrons either as discontinuous quanta or, if we like, as continuous wavefields. To accept this view of an electron is to display perhaps what Scott Fitzgerald called a "first-rate intelligence," for quanta and waves are contradictory, if complementary, notions. Thus Bohr's fantasy-model of the electron had to be open-ended in order for him to conceptualize it as both a thing and a field.

In the 1950s and '60s, while physicists continued to theorize in open-ended terms about gravitinos that may or may not exist, about black holes that cannot be seen, and about foamy space that has no geometry, a new fantasy-model gained popularity among mathematicians and computer scientists. I am referring to the loop, a fantasy-structure that has made possible amazing developments in computer technology and artificial intelligence systems. A simplified picture of the programmer's work might be conceptualized like this: the programmer sends a heroic little impulse off in search of data. He loops the little guy around and around until he finds what he is looking for. "Try this," the programmer tells his electric impulse, "and if that doesn't work, loop on back and try this other." Thus the impulse races off, heuristically searching down a tree of options and returning to search down yet another and yet another until it reaches a satisfactory result— or runs up an enormous electric bill. The loop is a model essential to this kind of work.

The power and richness that the loop model can generate is to be found in a variety of places: in the music of Bach (indeed, perhaps in all Western notions of harmony)[11], in Zeno's paradoxes, in Escher's drawings, in Lewis Carroll's fables—not to mention the narratives of Barth, Borges, Burgess, Beckett, or that most famous of all looped novels, *Finnegans Wake*. The loop, it seems, is everywhere. The one-sided loop known as the Moebius strip has been amusing school children for nearly two centuries. The rock musician and his roadie dread the sound loop, whereby amplified sound is endlessly fed back from speaker to microphone in an ear-splitting squeal. Time warps are actually space-time loops. The business executive's flow chart incorporates loops of work units. When we recycle our aluminum cans, we accelerate the ecological loop, by means of which nature sooner or later claims its own. And story makers employ the loop when they recount stories-within-stories, making the reader push down into an embedded story and then pop back up to resume the containing story.

But it was Kurt Gödel, the mathematician, who gave special scientific endorsement to the loop model in his 1931 attack on Russell and Whitehead's *Principia Mathematica*. Gödel demonstrated, in effect, that our logical systems, including mathematics, are loops whose power derives ultimately from some larger, external construction that contains the looped system. Gödel's proof opened the door to a new appreciation of set theory, to new ways of conceptualizing systems of logic and games, and to a new understanding of intelligence. Rather than attempt here to indicate the manifold and complex ways in which the loop model has revitalized mathematics and computer science, I direct you to a thorough and stimulating discussion of mathematical loops and their nonscientific isomorphs: Douglas R. Hofstadter's brilliant book, *Gödel, Escher, Bach: An Eternal Golden Braid*.[12]

Whatever fantasy-structure a scientist uses to contain his theoretical notions, Nagel's words of caution must not be forgotten. Scientists have preferences as have the rest of us. Ages have preferences. And our preferences can limit or blind us, as Einstein's preference for the closed model blinded him to Bohr's open-ended theories or as Kelvin was blind to Maxwell's contributions. When light was first conceptualized as a wave, the results were so impressive that scientists did not abandon the wave model for nearly a century, and thus certain explanations or possibilities did not even occur to them until Einstein drafted a new model, the light-bundle. Black's treatment of heat as a fluid made for great discoveries in thermodynamics, but that model also closed off further progress for over a century until a new way of modeling heat was dreamed up. Rudolf Clausius' misleading conception of entropy produces a false and limited understanding of energy still today, even though Ludwig Boltzmann's far more accurate and useful version of entropy has been around for three-quarters of a century. And someday, perhaps soon, our currently beloved loop model will have taken us as far as it can, and a new model, say, the sine curve or the helix (two models currently gaining favor), will have to be adopted. Whatever happens, we must remember that the loop is just one way of structuring our fantasies, whether they are logical, musical, literary, or scientific.

Scientific theories, that is, are temporary expedients. They are functional fantasies, not absolute truths. As products of human inventiveness and creativity, they are as rich a subject for the critic and analyst as is science fiction or any other form of verbal art. In the final analysis, then, we might do well to focus on the similarities rather than the differences between scientific and artistic propositions. And that is where the field of science fiction becomes so important. For more than any other literary form, perhaps, it is science fiction that compels us to recognize that fantasy serves the ends of both science and art. This recognition may lead to new understanding of the function of science fiction as literary form. For where Isaac Asimov, in a clearly positivistic fashion, sees it as "concerned with the impact of scientific advance on human beings,"[13] it should now be evident that this "advance," to the degree that it rests on a series of theories and hypotheses, may itself be seen as the sum of a set of fantasy constructs. What science fiction does—and, it is hoped, will do more of—is to confront scientific models, clearly recognized as such, with those other models, associated traditionally with our humanist past, which are the accepted narrational structures of Western literature. By studying, then, in science fiction, the various interactions between these two-model building processes— and the ways in which one inflects or alters the other—we can tap a process of creation that may, it is hoped, lead to new forms.

DAVID CLAYTON

On Realistic and Fantastic Discourse

In Memory of Robert C. Elliott

I

By a perverse twist of fate, attempts at defining the role of the fantastic in literature seem destined to partake of the insubstantiality of their subject. How large is the scope of the fantastic? Is it a genre? In reading books devoted to these questions, such as those of Tzvetan Todorov or Eric S. Rabkin, one has the impression that the critic has no sooner supplied an answer than he must qualify it—as if it were the essence of the fantastic to escape, wraithlike, from one's hands just at the moment one thought one had a firm grasp on it. Rabkin, in *The Fantastic in Literature*, after having rather schematically defined the fantastic throughout the book as a 180 degree reversal of the "ground rules of a narrative world."[1] announces toward the end that "all art, all mental wholes, are, to some extent at least, fantastic."[2] Although most readers would be inclined to agree with Rabkin's earlier assertion that, "in varying measure, every narrative that uses the fantastic is marked by Fantasy, and offers us a fantastic world,"[3] the subsequent generalization implies a concept of the fantastic that is everywhere in general—and thus nowhere in particular. But if Rabkin's definition, which seems initially too stiff, ends by claiming for itself the whole domain of artistic production, that of Todorov, who sharply distinguishes the fantastic from the "marvelous" and the "uncanny," is far too restrictive: "The fantastic is the hesitation experienced by a being who knows only natural laws, faced with an apparently supernatural event."[4] Despite his repeated appeals to structuralist methodology, I do not see how Todorov's definition could serve to establish a genre, much less a structure.

Confronted with two mutually exclusive alternatives such as these,

59

one must, I think, give the advantage to Rabkin. The concept of genre, by its very nature, seems not to provide a solid basis for dealing with this question. As Yuri Tynyanov argued, the system of genres, far from providing a fixed background against which one can observe the vicissitudes of literary history, itself undergoes a constant process of internal metamorphosis: marginal genres become major ones, and once dominant genres become peripheral ones.[5] One must agree with Rabkin that it is possible to discern fantastic elements in works that would not otherwise be considered fantastic; at the same time, it should also be possible to make the definition of the fantastic conceptually precise—to limit it in such a way as to guarantee its effectiveness as a descriptive tool.

There are a number of different ways of defining the fantastic, but most fail to provide us with a very high degree of conceptual rigor. If, for example, we try to extract the essence of the fantastic by means of a comparative analysis of various works of fantastic literature, then we run the risk that our definition will be biased by the peculiarities of the works in question. The procedure which seems to me to satisfy best the requirement of stringency and which I have adopted in this essay involves two stages: first, that of defining the fantastic in a purely formal way, as a component of literary discourse; second, that of interpreting the fantastic discourse thus defined as an investment of literary discourse by unconscious desire. Evidently, one cannot achieve the ideal of a combinatorial method in which the term "fantastic" would signify no more than x or y in an equation; nevertheless, by momentarily setting aside the question "What is the fantastic?" and concentrating upon the elaboration of a syntax which situates the fantastic within the global context of literary discourse, one secures a logically consistent foundation for any further speculation. We start with a fundamental assumption: that of the existence of a specific literary discourse which announces its presence through a repertory of linguistic signals—lexical, syntactic, stylistic, etc.—and thus constitutes itself as an autonomous region within the amorphous mass of ordinary language while differentiating itself from other possible discourses. The most striking property of this discourse, however, which radically demarcates it from other modes of discourse, is its suspension of the judgment of existence. In our everyday communication, and even more acutely in scientific discourse, our primary concern is with the truth or falsity of a statement. We want to know: does what the statement refer to exist or not? But literary discourse, to the horror of philosophers from Plato's time down to our own, violates the law of the excluded middle and neither affirms nor denies. It is just as misleading to characterize literary discourse as fictional in nature as it is to try to anchor it in some supposedly more real world.

Although literary discourse presents itself as a coherent totality in relation to the discourses exterior to it, viewed from within it decomposes into a multiplicity of subdiscourses. One of these discourses we shall designate as "fantastic" and assume to be an intrinsic constituent of literary discourse as such; according to our hypothesis, every work of literature will contain some quantity of fantastic discourse, no matter how attenuated its proportion. As yet, we know nothing of the content of this discourse, and at this stage our axiomatic method forbids us from going outside the model to find an answer. However, this restriction has an important function: it reminds us that if all literature were purely fantastic, the concept of fantastic literature would no longer have any meaning; literary discourse and fantastic discourse would then be synonymous and the term "fantastic" could only be defined by comparing literary discourse with some standard of the "nonfantastic" external to it. In that case, the theoretician would find himself in the undesirable position of saving literature at its own expense: he would have a literary discourse whose purity was certified by its inferiority to a locus of reality transcendent to it. Fantastic discourse can be defined only by its differential relation—of conjunction and opposition—to another discourse and not to some extralinguistic reality; only language considered as a global entity has this relation, which we may well assert but cannot imagine.

We must exercise some diffidence in labeling the discourse complementary to the fantastic; the evident semantic ambiguity of the term "realistic," for example, as well as the tacit affirmation of a "real," make it unusable for our purposes. Another, possibly less problematic candidate would be "cognitive"; Robert Scholes and Darko Suvin both have emphasized the function of such a cognitive aspect of literary discourse in counterbalancing the fantastic.[6] Yet I find it difficult to see how one can have cognition without simultaneously admitting the dubious Cartesian legacy of the *cogito*;[7] and I propose to use the term "noematic," which I have taken from Husserl without attempting to remain true to his conception of it.[8] This term seems valuable to me for the following reasons: first, the suffix directs our attention to the effect of the discourse as an act of noesis and eliminates any reference to a transcendental reality or creator that the text is deemed to represent; second, unlike "realistic," "noematic" does not lend itself to a confusion of conceptual with material reality. (For the sake of terminological parallelism, I shall also add this suffix to the name of the other discourse and henceforth speak of noematic and fantasmatic discourse.)

Our axiomatic procedure has led us from the assumption of a uniquely defined field of literary discourse to its subdivision into a pair of component discourses; although we intuitively anticipate the contents of the two, they still remain a blank for us. For the time being, I wish to postpone a more specific conceptualization of these discourses and instead to focus upon their interrelation. Since we have defined the two in terms of their difference, each necessarily implies the existence of the other; moreover, neither can exist independently of the other without exploding the only framework which meaningfully includes them both, that of literary discourse. Pushed to their respective logical extremes, the noematic would become indistinguishable from scientific discourse while the fantasmatic would dissolve into the foggy abyss of preverbal unconscious fantasy. Nevertheless, we must imagine the boundary which separates the two as being fluid, subject to an ongoing, external process of historical revision. In the first place, the zone of interest shifts, so that what was neomatically relevant in one era only possesses archaeological significance in another—the novels of Jane Austen, for example, in their own time undoubtedly served as guidebooks for young ladies on the lookout for a suitable mate; today, they have forfeited this value, and their noematic interest resides in their sharp perception of social behavior in Regency England. Or an even more far-reaching shift can occur: what was formerly noematic—for example, the existence of supernatural beings capable of intervening in human affairs—may be subsequently perceived as purely fantasmatic; and, though it is the less common case, in science fiction we have the example of a shift in the opposite direction. Still, our model requires us to impose essential limits upon these fluctuations in order to maintain the structural interdependency of the two discourses; we cannot foresee that one of them would be vanquished by the other or disappear completely. In practice the exact balance of noematic and fantasmatic in a specific text can be determined only by the subjective appreciation of the reader in a given epoch, but our model assures us of their necessary copresence.

An example, that of the "myth of reference" from Lévi-Strauss's *The Cooked and the Raw,* will perhaps give a greater degree of concreteness to the preceding remarks. I have no intention of attempting to demonstrate the subsistence of a noematic component in the text, since that was the goal that Lévi-Strauss set for himself and which he already announced at the end of his essay on the structural study of myth: "Perhaps we will discover one day that the same logic is at work in mythic and scientific thought. . . ."[9] But what about the fantasmatic? It is not the occurrence of such apparently fantastic elements as the hero's ability to transform himself into an animal or to sustain the loss of his posterior anatomy to ravenous vultures—elements fantastic from our point of view, but not necessarily from that of an indigenous audience—which testifies to the presence of the fantasmatic in the narrative: it is the act of incest which initiates the sequence of events that the myth recounts. A future society which no longer punished incestuous relations would hardly be likely to encourage them; the commission of such a deed, under almost any foreseeable circumstances, would continue to be a prototypic example of a prohibited desire. And the text itself verifies our hypothesis in a striking fashion when it tells us, marking the peripeteia of the hero's successful descent from the heights on which his father had abandoned him to perish, that "he returned to himself 'as if he had awakened from a dream.'"[10] The tabooed desire, although realized in fact, has to be rejected into the realm of dreams in order for the story to progress. Even then the fantasmatic does not wholly relinquish the field to its adversary in the remainder of the narrative, but leaves its traces at the conclusion in the form of aquatic plants—the metamorphosed remains of the vengeful father.

If we allow each discourse its autonomy in relation to the other, we still cannot envision either existing isolated from the other; unlike matter and antimatter, which are supposed to annihilate one another upon contact, the noematic and the fantasmatic have no choice but to interact with one another, and, in doing so, they enter into a symbiotic relation. One might best approximate the nature of this symbiosis by applying to it the formula which Jacques Lacan has employed to describe the relation between the real and the fantastic in psychoanalytic theory: "The real supports the fantasy, the fantasy protects the real."[11] The term "interaction" expresses this relation in its most general and unspecific form; in practice, we will have a series of possible interactions which in turn map out a set of generic categories whose content will depend on the connotative value of the labels we use in classifying them. Let us take an example: if we refer to one of these interactions as a "violation" of the noematic by the fantasmatic, the corresponding generic category will be that of the traditional horror story, in which this violation is indicated by a typical narrative element—the unwanted return of the dead to life.

The latter interaction, one with which we are all familiar, does not exhibit a high degree of complexity; an interaction of a more subtle and intriguing kind takes place when the fantasmatic transforms itself into a simulacrum of the noematic. The result of this transformation will be allegory, a genre with a manifestly fantasmatic content but a highly organized formal structure that seems indebted to the noematic; this structure, rather than conflicting with the content, performs an important function which complements the role of the latter: it points to an implicit level of signification which enables the reader to decipher the meaning of the fantastic events that make up the narrative. Of allegory, one could say what Marx said of the "misty region of the religious world": "Here the products of the human mind seem endowed with a life of their own, independent figures that stand in a relation with one another and with human beings."[12] It is no accident, I think, that the great allegories of modern literature, *The Faerie Queene*, *Pilgrim's Progress*, and the "mental epics" of Blake, all appeared during periods of tumult, religious, civil, or otherwise, in which the conflicts that had broken loose in the writer's world provided a strong motive for taking refuge in a highly structured ideal world that was strategically affirmed as the real one. (The more complacent and more realistically oriented age of the Enlightenment, by contrast, viewed allegory as a barbaric vestige of an era of superstition; one need only remember Dr. Johnson's contemptuous dismissal of *The Hind and the Panther*.) In this sense it is allegory that most accurately corresponds to Rabkin's definition of the fantastic as a wholesale reversal of the real; the literary fairy tale, some examples of which he analyzes in detail, is a kind of degenerate allegory—the fabulous superstructure minus the ideal signified.

Of equal interest, but frequently neglected, is the complementary transformation, in which the noematic approaches the fantasmatic without becoming flagrantly unreal, giving us the grotesque. Unlike allegory, the grotesque insists upon the substantiality of the everyday world, but does so with such vehemence that the quotidian takes on the appearance of a nightmare. The grotesque supplants the transcendent reality of allegory with the opacity of a material one. William Van O'Connor is certainly right when he argues in his essay "The Grotesque: An American Genre" that, in the works of Stephen Crane, Sherwood Anderson, Erskine Caldwell, Nathanael West, or Nelson Algren, "undoubtedly the more significant sources of the grotesque in most of their stories are well below the level of social and political injustice."[13] Nevertheless, I do not find very convincing his attempt to explain the grotesque as a symptom of the collapse of humanistic values: "For the modern creator of the grotesque, man is an inextricable tangle of rationality, irrationality, love and hatred, self-improvement and self-destruction. He appears caught in his own biological nature."[14] O'Connor's thesis fails to recognize that the grotesque is as historically specific as allegory: if the latter belongs to periods of gestation and parturition, in which a new social formation comes into being amid the ruins of its predecessor, the grotesque seems typical of periods of stagnation which experience an intensely felt discrepancy between the proclaimed ideals of a society and their lack of realization in practice—for example, the period of industrialization that followed the Civil War in this country and saw the rise of big cities afflicted by poverty, ethnic conflict, and overpopulation, compensated only by tinsel pleasures. Given the contemporary preference for the grotesque over allegory, one would not be wrong, I think, in drawing a parallel between the role allotted to this genre in the economy of literature and that allotted to dissonance—that "insignia of all modernity," in the words of Theodor Adorno—in music.[15]

The musical allusion points up an important peculiarity of the genre which distinguishes it from allegory: the extent to which the success of the grotesque depends on a delicate economy of effect. The more arbitrary the treatment of the material becomes, the more the work in question turns into low farce and loses the power of the grotesque. A novel such as Thomas Pynchon's *Crying of Lot 49*, whose characters bear such names as Oedipa Maas and Stanley Kotex, does not present us a mask that is alternately one of comedy and of tragedy, but the twisted grimace of a stand-up comic at his wits' end. Yet, as Jay Martin remarks in his excellent biography of Nathanael West, "Not one of the characters in *The Day of the Locust* is imaginatively distorted: the distortion has already taken place in reality."[16] Successful grotesque requires aesthetic distance, not outrage, and its spectacular triumphs in American literature—*The Confidence Man*, various episodes in *Huckleberry Finn*, *As I Lay Dying*, the novels of West and of Carson McCullers—differ from straightforward realism only in their inclusion of an element of fantasmatic dissonance. In particular, the most gifted creators of the grotesque have possessed an inverted sensibility which allowed them to see in the horrors of a fallen world reminders of the absence of beauty and to record this lack as the aesthetic equivalent of pain. No one has articulated this feeling better than West himself in the concluding paragraph of the first section of *The Day of the Locust*: "It is hard to laugh at the need for beauty and romance, no matter how tasteless, even horrible the results of that need are. But it is easy to sigh. Few things are sadder than the truly monstrous."[17]

One can perhaps now better understand why I characterized Rabkin's definition of fantasy as a 180-degree reversal as overly schematic, since we must anticipate the existence of different types of interaction for each well-defined genre. Not the least of the advantages of a structural model lies in its flexibility: the range of possible interactions, on the one hand, and their generality, on the other, keep the system open to the advent of new, unforeseen genres. We could also reverse the procedure we used before and start with a genre—for example, science fiction—and ask what type of interaction corresponds to it. A tentative analysis would show us that most examples of classical science fiction, from Verne down to Heinlein, assume, if they do not explicitly present, a familiar context as their point of departure; we thus commence with the dominance of the noematic, but the latter quickly gives way to the fantasmatic—a transition often symbolized in the text by means of a journey via rocket ship, time machine, or whatever—only to subsequently disavow it by positing the attainment of a new, hitherto unsuspected level of scientific and technological knowledge. More importantly, Rabkin's unmediated juxtaposition of "fantasy" and "reality" overlooks the subtle composition of forces which must obtain for a text successfully to achieve its effect: when either discourse strives to assert its mastery over the field of literary discourse, a necessary ingredient, that of the tension between the two, disappears. The most compelling examples of fantastic literature—Le Fanu's "Carmilla," the short stories of Poe or of Kafka, the ghostly tales of James—are all works which build up a convincing realistic facade in contrast with which the unforeseen intrusion of the fantastic seems far more disturbing than it would in a world governed entirely by fantasy.

2

But we cannot remain satisfied with an abstract formulation of these discourses which simply defines one in terms of the other; we want to know more about their content, and to do so we have to go outside the limits of our model. One possibility comes to mind almost automatically: whoever thinks of fantasy at the present time can hardly do so without connecting it with the psychoanalytic concept of unconscious desire. Yet we must proceed with caution at this point, since to place our model wholly under the auspices of Freudian theory would establish psychoanalytic discourse as a transcendental signified underlying literary discourse—a step which would compromise the free play of the latter and have the further effect of privileging the fantasmatic at the expense of the noematic. In terms of Freudian theory, as J.-F. Lyotard states, " . . . reality is constituted on the basis of the imaginary. It is the fantasmatic object which comes first. . . . Reality is never anything but a sector of the imaginary field that we have consented to abandon, from which we have consented to withdraw our fantasies of desire."[18]

In fact, Lyotard's book, *Discours, Figure*—in my own opinion, one of the most significant attempts to date to work out a theory of art based on Freudian concepts—illustrates the two major drawbacks of any such aesthetic: its difficulty in reconciling the claims of fantasy with those of reality and its reduction of the conflict between the two to an intrasubjective event. While Lyotard has no intention of confronting the Dionysian irrationality of the unconscious with the Apollonian discipline of the ego, he still can only conceive of the emergence of the fantasmatic as an act of violence: " . . . the work of desire results from the application of a force to a text. Desire does not speak: it violates the order of speech."[19] On this basis, however, I find it hard to see how unconscious fantasy could enter into any kind of relation with language—which Lyotard, moreover, defines in the most rigid structuralist terms as a "neutral, empty space, plane of pure oppositions."[20] No doubt Lyotard has reason for criticizing Lacan's equation of the unconscious operations of condensation and displacement with the rhetorical figures of metaphor and metonymy, but he does so by opposing the concept of the unconscious to that of a normative concept of language in which " . . . the normal word . . . is transparent: its signification is immediate and that is what one receives—the phonic or graphic vehicle is not perceived, so to speak. . . ."[21] The unique example of a discourse in which the transparency of the sign occurs with the degree of regularity which Lyotard ascribes to the "linguistic order" is that of the scientific; even the description of language cited above seems more applicable to the translation of natural languages into the descriptive metalanguage of linguistics than to ordinary language, which is characterized, as Viktor Shklovsky observed, by its half-spoken words and unfinished sentences. The difficulty one has in seeing how to mediate these two aspects of the literary work of art, the fantasmatic and the noematic, derives in no small part from Lyotard's notion of language, but equally so from the central role he assigns to the dream: " . . . at first glance the 'language' of the dream appears to be neither more nor less than that of art. [The 'language' of the dream] is its principle, it is perhaps its model."[22]

At this point, we need to recall that we are dealing with a fantasmatic *discourse*. The dream text, whether verbalized by the analysand on the couch or recounted by Freud himself in *The Interpretation of Dreams*, has already had to pass through the "defiles of the signifier,"[23] and, if the fantasmatic had no place within language, how could it play a part there, even a mute one? Our task is to explain the mode of functioning of a linguistic event, not an oneiric one, and for this purpose we require a more appropriate model than that of the dream, a model that will not force us to leave the medium of the text. We have such a model in the joke, a species of microtext whose mechanism Freud brilliantly analyzed in *Jokes and Their Relation to the Unconscious*. The joke, like the work of literature, is both a linguistic and a social event; as Freud himself emphasizes in comparing the joke with the dream, the principal difference between the two phenomena "lies in their social behavior. A dream is a completely asocial mental product; it has nothing to communicate to anyone else; it arises within the subject as a compromise between the mental forces struggling in him, it remains unintelligible to the subject himself and is for that reason totally uninteresting to other people."[24] "A dream," he adds, "still remains a wish, even though one that has been made unrecognizable; a joke is a developed play."[25] Lyotard has erred in choosing the dream—which has a close affinity with psychotic states, according to Freud—as a model; but even the dream, as I have indicated above, has to manifest itself textually in order to be analyzed, and in the joke we have an example of a purely linguistic phenomenon which reproduces the operations of the primary process—condensation and displacement—by means of the resources of language.

What are these resources? Can we, in other words, find a specifically linguistic process that will permit us to account for the liaison between unconscious desire and fantasmatic discourse and that does not also "violate the order of speech"? There is such a process: that of the interchangeability of semantic units of unequal magnitude. "Expressed in a naive fashion," writes A. J. Greimas in *Sémantique structurale*, "this principle means that a thing can be presented in either a simple or a complicated fashion, that a word can be explained by a longer sequence, and that inversely, a single word can often be found to designate what was initially conceived in the form of a development."[26] The two complementary aspects of this process Greimas calls expansion and condensation; the first of these "assumes its full signification only if a sequence in expansion is recognized as equivalent to a unit of communication syntactically more simple than itself."[27] The second, "*condensation* . . . must be understood as a sort of compressed decoding of messages in expansion."[28] Although part of the ordinary functioning of language, these two processes represent a transgression of the structure which constitutes it: " . . . discourse, conceived as a hierarchy of units of communication embedded in one another, contains in itself the negation of this hierarchy, owing to the fact that the units of communication with different dimensions can be simultaneously recognized as equivalent."[29]

The first of the examples that Freud presents in *Jokes and Their Relation to the Unconscious* provides an almost perfect illustration of these two processes. In an anecdote taken from Heine's *Reisebilder*, the narrator tells how the itinerant lottery agent Hirsch-Hyacinth boasted of his reception by Baron Salomon Rothschild; Hyacinth says of the rich man that "he treated me quite as his equal—quite famillionairely."[30] As Freud realized, this portmanteau word is an example of linguistic condensation, and he classifies the joke as an instance of "condensation with substitution formation,"[31] for which he supplies the corresponding expansion in the form of a paraphrase designed to show that the effect of the joke depends on the condensation. Yet the neologism "famillionairely," which is no slip of the tongue or spontaneous bon mot, but the invention of a gifted writer, does not seem very appropriate to exemplify the usual functioning of condensation; one would be more inclined to see in it a specimen of that "deviating technique" which Viktor Shklovsky claimed to be the essence of literary discourse. Superficially, it would appear impossible to combine the two approaches: the joke, in Freudian terms, produces a kind of verbal short circuit, typified by a more than usual economy of expression, while deviation, for Shklovsky, aims at making the ordinary process of communication more complicated: it is a technique "which increases the difficulty and duration of perception, since in art the process of perception is its own end and must be extended. . . ."[32] But this discrepancy quickly vanishes if we take into account Freud's own admission that the economy of the joke is a false one. "What does a joke save by its technique?" he asks. "The putting together of a few new words, which would mostly have emerged without any trouble. Instead of that, it has to take the trouble to search out the one word which covers the two thoughts."[33]

A more fundamental obstacle to combining these concepts—the Freudian one of the intervention of unconscious desire in language by means of condensation and Shklovsky's of literary discourse as the result of a technique of deviation—lies in Shklovsky's insistence upon deviation as a conscious act—in fact, Shklovsky explicitly states that it is ordinary language which is governed by an unconscious automatism. (Shklovsky did not, of course, use the term "unconscious" in a Freudian sense). Nevertheless, Shklovsky's thesis seems to me debatable for psychoanalytic as well as linguistic reasons, and I am going to revise the concept of deviation for the sake of the present discussion. Instead of accepting Shklovsky's definition of it as a deliberate artistic strategy, we will interpret deviation as the sign of the fantasmatic. Our model informs us, however, that what the fantasmatic deviates must be the noematic, and not ordinary language, as Shklovsky thought. Why should it do so? Such an assertion can mean only that the noematic strongly resists any encroachment upon its domain—and there are good reasons for making this inference.

The noematic discourse, like the scientific, with which it has close affinities, does not represent a passive gathering of empirical data: it strives to impose conceptual order on the environment and in doing so furthers that "demythologization of the world" which Max Weber perceived as the driving force behind the rise of modern science. At the same time, it would be false to see in this activity the sign of some divinely implanted rational faculty; as Max Horkheimer and Theodor Adorno argue in *Dialectic of Enlightenment*, demythologization has its origins in fear: it grows out of the need for survival in an originally hostile world and confronts the violence of natural forces with a violence of its own—not of strength, but cunning—which aims at bringing them under control. Even in its most developed form, that of scientific research, demythologization manifests an aggressive compulsion to subject everything to its law, the law of identity; in the lapidary formulation of Horkheimer and Adorno, "Enlightenment is totalitarian."[34] Although I can hardly do justice to the intricacy of Horkheimer and Adorno's argument—which draws upon Hegel, Marx, Freud, and Weber, among others—one might rightly object that I cannot rest such a broad generalization on the narrow foundation of a single work. However, one can find a remarkable psychoanalytic complement to the material thesis of *Dialectic of Enlightenment* in Jacques Lacan's assumption of a paranoid component inherent to the human personality which he has thematized as the "mirror stage" in the genesis of the individual. As a result of passing through the mirror stage, the subject constitutes itself as an ego, but only at the cost of permanent alienation in a narcissistically invested reflection of itself—the core of the imaginary in all its future experiences.[35] Starting from almost antipodal points of view, the two theories, the historical-materialist and the structuralist, dovetail and agree on the point which concerns us: that our "love of knowledge" has its roots deep in the irrational. Whichever explanation one prefers, one thing is clear: the effect of a sense of coherency lacking in our daily life that literary discourse often gives us—and which Rabkin attributes to the fantastic[36]—is rather the goal as well as the illusion of the noematic.

Seen from this perspective, our model takes on a more dynamic appearance: the fantasmatic does not meet the noematic on neutral ground, but limits its continuing expansion, and by means of deviation momentarily crosses its frontiers. Proust, in one of the incidents in *Swann's Way*, offers a prototypic illustration of the way in which the fantasmatic carries out its work. The narrator tells how he sent his mother a note designed to trick her into coming up to his bedroom: "Now I was no longer separated from her; the barriers were down; an exquisite thread reunited us," he writes.[37] Is not this note itself, the textual vehicle of Marcel's interdicted desire, the concrete realization of the fantasmatic, which transgresses the barriers erected by the noematic and sets them at naught just as the note eradicates the distance dividing Marcel from his mother?

3

To return to our model, one could provisionally describe the fantasmatic as an investment of unconscious desire and the noematic as one of "instrumental reason"[38]—investments which occur at a premordial level of linguistic articulation and therefore cannot be identified with the manifestly fantasmatic or noematic elements of a given text. If I have avoided defining the two discourses more rigorously, it is for the sake of not restricting their freedom in advance: each has to function as a variable that can assume a wide range of values, from the tacit affirmation of things as they are through the analysis of complex social relationships in the case of the noematic, and from the "once upon a time" of a fairy tale through an inquiry into the ways of desire in that of the fantasmatic. Keeping in mind the constitutive variability of the two, we can avoid making a false, if common assumption: that which equates the fantasmatic with the "unreal." As the foregoing discussion should have made sufficiently clear, the fantasmatic can only contract a relation with the noematic—which conceptually organizes the real—and not with unmediated reality.

Even in a traditional novel such as *The Ambassadors*, which lacks any apparent element of fantasy, it would certainly be wrong to infer the absence of the fantasmatic. When Strether comes upon Madame Vionnet and Chad at the country inn, it is not the explicit recognition of the sexual nature of their relation which affects him as much as the implicit recognition of his own desire, which has been lurking all the time behind the idealized tableau he has fabricated for himself. (James's use of pictorial language in this episode brings out clearly, in a kind of brilliant intuition, the predominance of the imaginary in Strether's relation to his environment.) We cannot mechanically apply the model to separate one discourse from the other: for every text that we read, we will have to supply the relevant axiological context of other discourses—economic, political, sociological, etc.—which will enable us to accurately determine the content of the noematic and fantasmatic in that case. The model can provide us with an effective point of departure for undertaking this task; in particular, we see here how the model performs a regulative function as well as a descriptive one: it admonishes us that we must look for these two discourses nowhere but in the text itself.

It would go beyond the limits of this paper to attempt to demonstrate in detail how the concepts of noematic and fantasmatic could be applied in analyzing a specific text, but I would like to conclude with a brief account of the role of the fantasmatic in "The Fall of the House of Usher." Yet although this story is one of the oft-cited examples of fantastic literature, one might experience some difficulty in pointing to the features which make it so: apart from the denouement, there is neither an eruption of irrational violence nor the presence of blatantly fantastic elements—supernatural beings or occurrences—in the story; were it not for Madeline's return from the crypt and the final disappearance of the Usher mansion, one would be inclined to classify the story as "atmospheric" rather than "fantastic." Is it only these climactic events which make up the fantasmatic dimension of Poe's story? One might also point to the heightened sense of spatiotemporal displacement—where does the story take place if not "outside of space and time"?—as well as to Poe's idiosyncratic style, the deliberate, evocative choice of words which imparts a dreamlike quality to the narrative. Although the fantasmatic operates on all these levels, one can detect it already at a more fundamental level, that of the relation between the story and its title. The action dramatizes the title, but does so in a way that probably diverges from the reader's expectations: where he would have anticipated a purely figurative use of the phrase "fall of a house," he finds it complemented by the literal one of the collapse of a building. In many stories the relation between the title and the action resembles that between a rebus and its solution; in this case one has to ask: which is the rebus and which the solution?

Poe thus commences his tale with a powerful gesture of deviation, one which alerts the reader to be on the lookout for textual phenomena of a similar, if less evident kind. The two meanings of "house," the literal and the figurative, which Poe emphasizes by means of the title-story relation, sets up the first terms of a progression; once we have determined the relation between the first terms, we can go on to infer the existence of a third, implicit term. The initial relation is one of synonymy: "edifice" and "race" are both synonyms for "house," and we need not search far to discover a third, less common if not irrelevant, synonym: "erection." Using the terminology of Greimas, one could describe the title as an expansion with three possible senses: (1) collapse of a building; (2) decay of a race; (3) detumescence. Just as one would err in privileging the first two senses while ignoring the third, one would prejudice the effect of the story by interpreting it as the representation of a latent phallic signified—which presumably pops into the reader's mind like the light bulb which comic-book iconography of bygone days used to symbolize the dawning of an idea.

The new territory that Poe has opened up for exploration is a textual one, and the task of interpretation requires us to traverse the fragile semantic network which links the title to the body of the text. The narrative action explains the double meaning of "house"—this "quaint and equivocal appellation," as Poe calls it; the synonymy of "house" and "erection" illuminates the conclusion; as a whole, this system of relations produces the effect at which the epigraph hints: resonance. However, the third of these senses of "house" has a status which sets it apart from the other two: an instance of semantic condensation, it also corresponds to the operation in a psychoanalytic sense by fusing erotic and nonerotic significations within a single, apparently innocent word. (At the same time, this fusion is not unmotivated: the fall of an erection and the decline of the Usher family certainly have something to do with one another.) While the first two senses exhibit that transgression of the structural hierarchy of language which Greimas ascribes to the phenomena of condensation and expansion, in the third case this transgression stands directly in the service of desire. The third meaning does not complement the other two; it supplements them with an excess of signification.[39] "The Fall of the House of Usher" is not the representation of a sexual act manqué—it is a fulfilled act of desire which more closely resembles a shaggy-dog story than a dream. Poe's tale certainly produces a hallucinatory effect, but it uses only words to produce this result; Poe's text is a "developed play," and the techniques it employs—reversal of expectation and the double entendre—are homologous to those of the joke.

Moreover, "The Fall of the House of Usher" can itself furnish us with a paradigm for the interaction of the noematic and the fantasmatic discourses. As the price for having made a successful attack upon the domain of its antagonist, the fantasmatic must almost immediately relinquish the territory it has seized. Fantasmatic discourse participates in that "temporal pulsation" which, according to Lacan, accompanies all manifestations of unconscious desire: they seem to appear only for the sake of vanishing into thin air.[40] As long as these phenomena last, however, they provoke a disruption of the time scheme of the everyday world, its irreversible flow blocked by the unexpected emergence of an extratemporal maelstrom. The atemporality of desire can aid us better to understand the role of the sexual isotopy in the economy of "The Fall of the House of Usher": if the various sexual elements to which Poe more or less obliquely alludes—masturbation, narcissism, homosexuality, incest—have the function of signifying the presence of desire, the final detumescence graphically records its ebb. Sexuality provides a symbolic framework for the act of desire that Poe's text accomplishes; at the conclusion, as the narrator flees back to the "real world," the fantasmatic gives way to the noematic, and Roderick Usher's erection disappears—back into the "deep and dark tarn" of the inkwell from which Edgar Allen Poe had conjured it.

Considered in isolation, the story is a formidable demonstration of Poe's skill as a writer, but it possesses a far more important historical significance: it marks a new stage in the process which governs the development of fantastic literature in modern times, that of its secularization.[41] "The Fall of the House of Usher" dispenses once and for all with the supernatural props which previous writers had used to support their creations; for the supernatural Poe substitutes the unnatural—a less circumscribed, but more disturbing, region because of its greater proximity to our own experience. It is no higher nature which intervenes at the conclusion to punish the culpable Roderick Usher; nature itself cracks open in an act of self-immolation to swallow him in its abyss much as it does Schreber at the beginning of his psychotic delirium.[42] Such an argument, however, contradicts the thesis advanced by Todorov, who, in the final chapter of his book, asks, "Why does fantastic literature no longer exist?"[43]

In fact, Todorov offers two different, if not unrelated, answers to this question. The first, one of astounding naiveté in light of Todorov's pretensions, is that psychoanalysis has rendered unnecessary the use of supernatural motifs to disguise interdicted sexual themes such as incest or necrophilia: "We can go further: psychoanalysis has replaced (and thereby even rendered useless) fantastic literature."[44] To this assertion one can raise the same objection that Todorov himself raises in the preceding chapter to the abuse of psychoanalytic concepts by literary critics: that they treat the fantastic material as if it were an allegorical representation. As he rightly states, " . . . the very idea of looking for a direct translation must be rejected, because each image always signifies others, in an infinite game of relations. . . . We refuse this manner of reducing images to signifiers whose signifieds would be concepts."[45] If it is true that fantastic literature signifies something more than its psychoanalyzable content, why should the discovery of psychoanalysis suffice to eliminate the need for it? The second answer, if less disingenuous, seems to me no more tenable than the first; it states that fantastic literature depends for its effect on a sharply defined opposition between "fantasy" and "reality," an opposition to which the sophisticated twentieth century can no longer lend its credence: "The nineteenth century, it is true, lived in a metaphysic of the real and the imaginary, and fantastic literature is nothing other than the bad conscience of that positivist nineteenth century. But today we can no longer believe in an unchanging, external reality nor in a literature which would be the transcription of that reality."[46]

The flaw common to both these explanations as well as to the book as a whole is a lack of historical perspective; history, which the self-proclaimed structuralist has apparently excluded as a category, returns to wreak its vengeance by undercutting the validity of his premises. The sharp division between "fantasy" and "reality" which Todorov locates in the nineteenth century certainly belongs much more to the Age of Reason; already in a collection of aphorisms dating from the years 1797–1798, Novalis declared that "the dark road leads within. In ourselves or nowhere is eternity with its worlds—the past and future. The external world is one of shadows—it casts its shadows in the world of light."[47] The attack upon commonsense realism runs like a leitmotiv through the intellectual and artistic culture of the nineteenth century; fantastic literature, far from being the "bad conscience" of nineteenth-century positivism, was, for obvious reasons, a powerful weapon in the revolt against the values of the Enlightenment that commenced with the Romantics and the German idealist philosophers at the beginning of the period and that culminated with Nietzsche and Mallarmé at the end.

It is not in this point alone that Todorov's facile generalizations betray his argument: his definition of the fantastic itself makes more sense when viewed from a historical, rather than a structuralist, standpoint. As we have seen before, the boundary between the noematic and the fantasmatic constantly shifts; generally these changes represent slight readjustments of the frontier between the two, but in the eigh-

teenth century a shift of cataclysmic proportions occurred which rele-
gated those "wonders of the invisible world" that had been formerly
accepted as matters of fact to the netherworld of superstition. Nevertheless, this debris of medieval Christian culture which the Enlightenment
left in its wake could be salvaged by the Romantic artist and put to
quite another use: to serve as expressive equivalents for states of consciousness. The terrible corporal punishments to which the Christian
martyr had gladly submitted as evidence of his faith, once internalized,
provided the raw material for dramas of sexual passion, while the fascination which the discredited realm of demonic beings—ghosts, vam-
pires, witches, succubi, and all the rest—continued to exert upon the
Romantic artist attested to his suspicion that an infernal kingdom really
did exist: in his own heart. The quality of hesitation, which for Todorov
constitutes the hallmark of the fantastic, reflects the perplexity of the
nineteenth-century writer confronted with two mutually exclusive and
equally unattractive alternatives: to short circuit the eighteenth century
and return to an age that believed in the reality of supernatural phenomena or to assume the burden of discovering their reality within himself.

As principal evidence to support his claim that fantastic literature
no longer exists, Todorov adduces Kafka's story "Metamorphosis." Unlike examples of traditional fantastic literature, in which "the strange or
supernatural occurrence was perceived against the background of that
which is judged normal or natural," in the case of Kafka "the supernatural no longer provokes hesitation, because the world described is
completely bizarre, as abnormal as the event for which it supplies the
background."[48] In other words, if everything is fantastic, nothing is
fantastic. Yet is this what happens in "Metamorphosis"? Not at all.
Kafka evokes the oppressiveness of the Samsas' domestic life with a
power which makes similar descriptions of the horrors of petit bourgeois life in the pages of Dreiser or Dos Passos pale in comparison. To
revert to our own terminology, Kafka, instead of dissolving the noematic in the fantasmatic, pushes the antagonism between the two to a
point of almost unbearable intensity—and he does so without any reliance upon the supernatural. The concept of the supernatural implies a
higher causality from whose point of view the meaning of fantastic
events would become apparent, and I do not see any evidence for such
a point of view in "Metamorphosis": Gregor is neither the sacrifice of
a benevolent deity who punishes those he loves nor the innocent victim
of maleficent forces. Kafka completes the shift from the supernatural to
the unnatural that we have already seen in Poe—with the important

difference that the transformation of Gregor Samsa takes place in an ordinary Prague household and not at a remote estate which still has evident affinities with the haunted castle of the Gothic novel.

Todorov may be correct in his assertion that the supernatural furnished the writer with a convenient device for dealing with otherwise forbidden themes; however, such a relation between the fantasmatic and the supernatural could only involve the subservience of the former: if this ruse permitted the writer to sneak his nominally censorable productions past the authorities, it also enabled him to keep their disagreeable implications at a comfortable distance from himself. In this way the writer perhaps gained a greater degree of control over his material, but at a high price: that of confirming the very repressive mechanism he seemingly aimed at circumventing. One might also recall that in the majority of nineteenth- and early-twentieth-century horror stories, supernatural motifs serve as a rationale for the continued repression of tabooed sexual desires, not for their emancipation; in *Dracula*, for example, the violence directed against the vampire clearly indicates the panic which any explosion of subterranean forces was capable of unleashing among the bourgeoisie of the period. (It can hardly be an accident that one of the novel's main characters is the director of a lunatic asylum.) I can only second Todorov when he states that the fantastic literature of the nineteenth century has given way to a new kind of literature; not, as he thinks, a literature in which everything is fantastic, but one in which the fantasmatic appears for the first time in its own right.

ROGER SALE

The Audience in Children's Literature

If we exclude a few minor derogatory disignations, then "children's literature" is the only literary category that defines an audience rather than a subject or an author. Not any book is a children's book, but just about any *kind* of book can be, and certainly any author can write one. Furthermore, since many people who are not children read children's literature, even the designation of its audience is not very clarifying or defining. Nonetheless, the term is used, and is usable, and even turns out to be of odd and powerful importance both for the makers of children's literature and for its readers. Here I should like to treat it as a kind of stick, and to pick it up first at one end and consider what kind of shaping, good and bad, the idea of children's literature does for its authors. Then I want to pick it up at the other end, and ask what kind of shaping, also good and bad, it may do for its readers. These may seem like separate subjects, and could easily be made into two distinct discourses, but here I want to try to relate them, if not exactly make them one.

When Hamlet says to Ophelia, "You jig, you amble, and you lisp, you nickname God's creatures," he is being what we can quickly see as a misogynist, a sexist. Women do these things, and, because Adam was chosen by God as the namer of God's creatures, women only nickname them. The nicknames, one presumes, are diminutives, pretty, cute terms: not "hen," "cock," "goose," but "henny-penny," "cocky-locky," "goosey-loosey." Though it need not have been the least part of Hamlet's, or Shakespeare's, intention to have created an implicit alliance between women and children at this moment, the fact remains that, long before and long after Shakespeare, women and children were allied by men. As part of that alliance they both became nicknamers of God's creatures, and women taught children to be this, to say what the cow and sheep say, "Moo" and "Baa," to create a special language suitable for children. Ophelia, we may presume, did not do this, but, in the three centuries after her, the identification of children as a special class of being led, not just to a good deal of nicknaming of God's creatures, but to a language, a tone, a rhetoric, a subject matter, even, for children.

We, coming at this matter, not as Ophelia looking down the coming centuries, but as would-be historians looking back from a late-twentieth-century perspective replete with the follies and victories of Queen Victoria's age, Freud, progressive education, and the creation of huge industries to deal expertly with the matter of children, might be surprised at how the history of a langauge and a set of subject matters created for children evolved. It is within recent memory, say, that primers we associate with the names of Dick and Jane have been assaulted, in part as a nicknaming of God's creatures, to be replaced by the work of that masterful and very different nicknamer, Dr. Seuss, whose *Cat in the Hat* seemed to begin a new and freer era. Dick-and-Jane books are a product of this century, but it might be allowed that standard fare for beginning readers had been at a low and nicknaming level for a long time, if it was not simply the Bible or *Pilgrim's Progress* that was used. There was a long period, though, in England and America, when what was suitable for children was what we might think of as pretty stiff stuff, not Henny Penny or Dick and Jane, but, for instance, *Filial Piety*, a work of the late eighteenth century. In *Filial Piety* a woman is incarcerated in a prison and is punished by being denied food. Her daughter, herself grown, comes to visit every day, and, miraculously, the mother continues to live and thrive. One day the jailor discovers how, when he oversees the daughter nursing the mother as though she were her child.

We were not raised on such a tale, and, indeed, many of us perhaps would have been sheltered from it, though it certainly delineates filial piety, on which at least some of us were raised. Though my brother was born when I was five, I think I was never encouraged to know that mothers could and often did nurse their children, and I am quite sure, judging by my shocked and sentimental reaction to the final scene of *The Grapes of Wrath* when I first read it at age seventeen, that I had no way to imagine taking the nursing mother out of the madonna situation. To say this, though, is to say only that, between the 1790s and the 1930s, changes, often great, had taken place, concerning what subjects and what language were appropriate for the young. At the end of the eighteenth century, and maybe fifty years on either side, the items to be screened out were the fairy tales, the magical or fanciful, while the morally uplifting was to be screened in. I was, if not raised on fairy tales, raised including them and other works of wonder and magic as part of what was clearly proper fare for me. Offering and witholding were being done all the time after children were invented as a class of human being and after children's literature was invented. The rhetoric changed, but the intention and the fact of the rhetoric have been there all along.

I want now to make a generalization that probably is too sweeping, but that is remarkably accurate at least in general outline: no great work of children's literature was written in clear obedience to this apparently essential idea of a suitable rhetoric or suitable subject. It is only fear of being exposed as ignorant of some body of literature that at the moment does not concern me that keeps me from expanding the generalization to say thus: No great work of literature of any kind has ever been written according to the dictates of what the audience was and what was or was not appropriate for it; rhetoric, considered as an adaptation of language to and for an audience, is simply a net to catch the wind of great literature. A Romantic notion this, surely, but I would suggest before returning to the particulars of our particular subject that the upper reaches of literature conceived of as being written for a particular group, and limited by that conception, is something like Ben Jonson's masques, or the Declaration of Independence, neither of which is the best writing of its author.

This assertion, whatever its shortcomings or cues for tedious argument, does, I am quite sure, bear strongly on the mere facts of the creation of the great children's books. In order to clear some ground, let me offer a list of particulars to show the kind of assertion I am trying to make. Lewis Carroll's *Alice in Wonderland*, explicitly written for a particular child somewhat under age ten, is not once governed by the fact, but is clearly, and on every page, more a book by Charles L. Dodgson than it is a work for Alice Liddell. *Through the Looking Glass* begins with a poem that frankly acknowledges that, whatever the relation was between Dodgson and Alice, the relation is now tenuous, close to lost, and the book itself then proceeds to go its own way. Beatrix Potter began the finest set of all children's books with a letter to the son of her former governess: "Dear Noel, I do not know what to say to you so I will tell you a story: Once upon a time there were four rabbits," and so on. That great triumph of a minor talent, Kenneth Grahame's *Wind in the Willows* was originally conceived as tales for his son, Alistair, but reveals on every page, and usually in every sentence, Grahame's interests, languages, and compulsions, not any desire to create an idiom, a rhetoric, or a set of subjects particularly to please his son, from whom, incidentally, Grahame lived apart mostly and who had to exist for Grahame mainly as a creation of his own imagination. E. B. White's *Stuart Little* was written explicitly for White's nephew, and, I would suggest, that is precisely what goes wrong with it; White finds a sort of piquant beginning, something that might please many children or some adults, then gradually loses interest, and the story has to be picked up and carried along after the first few chapters. Conversely, *Charlotte's Web* is White's "hymn to the barn," and is a book that emanates from deep feelings White himself had about our relations with the seasons and with other animals; it is only perchance a work for children, and is infinitely better. Tolkien's *Hobbit* was a book he cut for his son from his long musings about Middle Earth, begun long before Christopher was born and continued long after he grew up. My sense is that the opening, all about how we just are too clumsy to see hobbits these days, is indeed created for the son, and is indeed awful writing, and that after that Tolkien is better, though always a little under wraps, so that *The Hobbit* is decent stuff but not a patch on *The Lord of the Rings*, explicitly not written for children (though many children have enjoyed it tremendously) and obviously written for himself.

This is not a definitive rundown by any means, and I offer it first to suggest that the tie of writers of children's books to their audience is seldom clear, especially when a very good or great book is being written. Many good books, and thousands of mediocre books, have been written with some kind of formula about the audience "children" in mind to guide the language and tone, to shape the characterization and narrative. Without insisting on the point theoretically or absolutely, I would suggest that rhetoric, thought of as the shaping of language with an audience in mind, is usually the enemy of the imagination, thought of as what a writer would write if free from all but the most obvious limitations of language and audience. And, having made the assertion, I need to offer an example. It comes from the first of C. S. Lewis's Narnia series. Lewis as a critic is almost always someone worth reading because he was a reader of great erudition and interesting sympathies. Lewis as a Christian apologist I find slacker, more given simply to setting up straw people called skeptics or athiests and knocking them over. Lewis as an adult novelist I happen to find repulsive a good deal of the time, but I think I know why in a way that shows me why others might like him. But Lewis as a writer of books explicitly written for children is a writer of self-imposed manacles, false rhetoric.

The passage at hand is the announcement to the group of children come to Narnia by the herald, the Beaver, about the Christ figure of the series, Aslan: "They say Aslan is on the move—perhaps has already landed." Lewis then explicates:

> And now a very curious thing happened. None of the children knew who Aslan was any more than you do; but the moment the Beaver had spoken these words everyone felt quite different. Perhaps it has sometimes happened to you in a dream that someone says something which you don't understand but in the dream it feels as if it had some enormous meaning—either a terrifying one which turns the whole dream into a nightmare or else a lovely meaning too lovely to put into words, which makes the dream so beautiful you remember it all your life and are always wishing you could get into that dream again. It was like that now. At the name of Aslan each one of the children felt something jump in his inside. Edmund felt a sensation of mysterious horror. Peter suddenly felt brave and adventurous. Susan felt as if some delicious smell or some delightful strain of music had just floated by her. And Lucy got the feeling you have when you wake up in the morning and realize that it is the beginning of holidays or the beginning of summer.[1]

Lewis was never stupid, and that is a very cleverly written passage, but it is false as well. "The moment the Beaver had spoken" the words announcing Aslan on the move, "everyone felt quite different." Why can only be a matter of Beaver's tone and the word "Aslan," but Lewis wants to make sure that no one associates Aslan simply with things that go bump in the night, so he insists that the tone and the word should make you feel certain ways, and, furthermore, will make you feel in ways that reveal the truth about you. Aslan is like "a nightmare or else a meaning too lovely to put into words," depending on who you are, so Edmund, the innocent lover of the witch, is horrified, Peter is in an adventure, Susan is thoughtfully sensitive, and Lucy is a real good kid.

One way of spotting the falsity here is to say that any adult reading this passage knows that what Lewis is doing is wheeling his big gun into place without describing it. It is set-up language, designed for those children who want to be set up, who enjoy Lewis's cue-card writing: Aslan, Aslan Now Hear This. Lewis is fond of such setting up in all his writing, but he would never write as he does here if the subject were Chaucer or the King James Bible and if his audience were presumably adult. This is religion for children, calculated to give just as much awe and wonder as Lewis thinks a child can stand. Lewis insists on a reader or listener's feeling anticipative without giving us anything more to anticipate, though no one, reading this, should be surprised that Aslan dies in a sacrificial way and is later reborn, and into a world not altogether ready to accept him.

Now another example, this time from *The Wind in the Willows*, a book that is full of rhetoric, but very little of it false. After Mr. Toad's first misfortunes with motor cars, Badger decides that Toad must learn his lesson once and for all. Rat is skeptical that Badger can do this by fiat, and, when Badger takes Toad into the smoking room to lecture him, Rat says, *"That's* no good. . . . *Talking* to Toad'll never cure him. He'll *say* anything." Badger returns, convinced that, because he has taught Toad the right lesson, Toad has learned it: "First," Badger says, "you are sorry for what you've done, and you see the folly of it all?" Then:

> There was a long pause. Toad looked desperately this way and that, while the other animals waited in grave silence. At least he spoke.
> "No!" he said a little sullenly, but stoutly; "I'm *not* sorry. And it wasn't folly at all! It was simply glorious!"[2]

Now, Grahame knows about all the impulses involved here. He knows, with Badger, the desire to make someone wrongheaded see the error of his ways, so that he can have Badger say, after Toad has had further misadventures and after his house has been taken over by weasels and stoats and after *Rat* wants to say they all should be taught the error of their ways: "But we don't *want* to teach 'em, we want to *learn* 'em— learn 'em, learn 'em! And what's more, we're going to *do* it, too!"[3] There's the perfect schoolmaster. Grahame knows also, with Rat, that *"talking* will never cure" Toad. And of course he knows, with Toad, that "it wasn't folly at all! It was simply glorious!" He even knows that, after all, after the stoats and weasels have been driven from Toad Hall, after Toad has been humiliated in countless ways, Toad's next impulse is to give a banquet at which he gives all the speeches.

The point I need to make is not that Grahame is secular and decent and honorable to all points of view while C. S. Lewis is sneakily religious, though I do think that is true. Rather, it is that Grahame is writing here to please himself, to satisfy contradictory feelings that he felt and knew he felt. His language and tone, therefore, are not designed to satisfy his son, but himself. There are messages aplenty in *The Wind in the Willows*, about passions and their controls and cures and satisfactions, and the passion for home is indeed better than the passion for motor cars, because home makes us able to love the world whereas cars only make us exclude the world; still, to drive a car very fast is "glorious," and of course Toad is not sorry, not yet and perhaps not ever. Grahame may be saying all this to his son, but he is saying it for himself, and the difference turns out to be crucial.

The great trap for a writer of children's books, then, is to have an idea of children, of what children like, or of what children either should be taught or should learn. If children's literature were a genre, it would be hopelessly wrong, all dead, but fortunately it is not. It is, rather, a collection of books with no clearly defined boundaries, no set of rules or occasions, no fixities. Most of the classics of children's literature in the last century or so were written by people who wanted to write something and for whom the obvious dominant modes, the novel and the extended lyric, were no good. The major traditions were, for them, the wrong traditions. Perhaps, feeling that wrongness, and perhaps even feeling lesser or odd, or wrong, they made or had made for them an alliance with children, who also have a difficult time with novels and extended lyrics. The alliance was never secure, born as it often was of the sharing of an absence, or of a shared lack. Others who felt the need to write out of the major traditions did not make this alliance—writers such as William Morris E. R. Eddison, or David Lindsay wrote fantasies and romances that bear little relation to novels or to children's literature. Others, such as George Macdonald and Tolkien and, in a different way, Stevenson and Kipling, wrote a whole series of books that were never quite straight novels and that some of which were, or have come to be seen as being, children's books. Alexandre Dumas was a popular fiction factory, and a few of his works became children's classics, though he never himself conceived of children as his audience. It was as though a huge amount of wine were being made, but only some of it fell into bottles that could be conveniently and clearly labeled "Drink Me," with clear specifications as to who should and should not drink. Isolated individuals, often writing in clear ignorance of each other, obeying dictates that originate from within and that are only slightly tempered or altered by dictates from without, not availing themselves even of what tradition might be said to be available a good deal of the time—that, I think, is how most great children's books have come to be written. It may well be that the first important writer of children's books who was also a real expert on the literature was and is Maurice Sendak.

If it is true that it is almost requisite for a writer of children's books to ignore children, child psychology, pedagogy, and the like, it is nonetheless true that children do read these stories. Here I am come to the other end of my stick, and I must pick it up somewhat more tentatively than I did the first. Having said to get rid of children, I must now get them back in here, and I can do this legitimately only if I do not try to speak of children in the mass, but in the individual, not to have an idea of the child reader, but a knowledge of individual readers. The individual readers we know most about are ourselves, of course, but we are not at all totally locked into our own experiences, important though they may be.

In the years since I have begun teaching and writing about children's books, I have met many people who have told me about their experiences, as children or older persons, with various books of children's literature, and the overwhelming fact is that the way we read as children, what we liked and responded to most deeply, differs from person to person. What we developed allegiances to as children is often simply impossible to give up, no matter what our later experience may tell us. I once alleged that the *Alice* books seemed better fare for adults than for children, and many have confirmed my experience to the extent of saying they cannot read the books now because they disliked them years ago, whereas other say the opposite. I had a long conversation with a man about Kipling's *Just-So Stories*, and I think I managed to convince him that these often betray a good deal of snobbery toward animals and racism toward other people. At the end he began telling me about the gray-green greasy limpopo river and the satiable curiosity of the Elephant Child, and smiled and said he was not about to give all that up. C. S. Lewis makes what seems to me, and indeed to most, a grave critical error in loving *Squirrel Nutkin* best among the Beatrix Potter books, but *Squirrel Nutkin* gave him an idea of autumn that was an access to joy, and who can possibly quarrel with that, or want to?

Of course, this does not mean that we go on being loyal to everything we read and loved as children. Sometimes people return to something well loved when young, perhaps even to the same tattered and torn copies they once knew, and are shocked to find that they can locate absolutely nothing of whatever it was they first felt; others discover that their present experiences are so much at odds with their first ones that they feel they barely understand themselves as they were. Many say they are pleased they were not made to finish something they did not like as children because that freed them to enjoy it freshly later, as adolescents or adults. The variables here are not infinite, but they are indeed many. I have, elsewhere, written about rereading L. Frank Baum, Dr. Seuss, Jean de Brunhoff, and A. A. Milne in order to recreate and then to compare my experience as a child reader with my later one as an adult.[4] As is not surprising, some of my allegiances were as present as ever, as strong as ever, and I was pleased that I could say I still loved what I had loved, whereas in other cases this was not so at all. In later rereading of other books I read when young, I found that, although the works of Munro Leaf or Lucy Fitch Perkins were well known to me as a child, they must have entered nothing more than the surface of my consciousness. I could add this: my experience as a child reader is now about forty years old, whereas my experience as a reader to my children is now about twenty years old, and, in going back to books I enjoyed reading for the first time to my children, I find roughly the same is true: some seem fresh, bright, and to bring forth a flood of memories of that time, whereas others are dead as doornails. Of course, when one turns to books read and loved as a child, then read aloud to one's children and also loved, one has a mini-autobiography staring one in the face, if one could only see how to write it rightly.

My subject here, however, is not autobiography as such, though I do not see how it can be shunned entirely at any point in this consideration. The subject is children as readers, and what clues we can gather about the child reader as parent to the adult reader. Let me create an imaginative field by turning to Wordsworth, who can lay claim to having had the first important childhood, felt and known to be parent to adult experience:

> O Heavens! how awful is the might of souls,
> And what they do within themselves while yet
> The yoke of earth is new to them, the world
> Nothing but a wide field in which they were sown.[5]

Wordsworth's difference from many is that he sees as might and power what others see as innocent victimage, so that we can easily be tempted while reading about his childhood to see it as extraordinary, strange, lonely, magnificent, but, therefore, unlike ours. Yet he goes on:

> Points have we all of us within our souls
> Where all stand single; this I feel, and make
> Breathings for incommunicable powers;
> But is now each a memory to himself?—[6]

This is a grand way of saying what I have just suggested, namely, that our lives as children, as child readers too, are single, and that each of us has separate memories, and that these memories and the experiences they recall shape experiences often radically different from someone else's. Wordsworth glories in that fact, sees in it a source of strength, "for there's not a man that lives," he insists, "who hath not known his godlike hours."[7] This may seem overstated, heady, true for Wordsworth but not for all. But to the extent that we can feel something like the power of our experiences as child readers to shape our experiences as adult readers—in a way analogous to saying our experiences as children were parent to our experiences as adults—we can locate something not easily ignored or cast aside, and, if what we attended to and loved at age six or eight is still the least bit alive for us in later years, we are admitting that the might of souls when first the yoke of earth is new is great and awful.

The child reader is not much of a literary critic, usually, and feels no need to be. Most people speak of their memories of books read when young in a fairly restricted vocabulary: "I loved," "I hated," "I was frightened," "I knew." The very primitiveness of the language conveys, however, a sense of power, of an imprinting, that is quite willing to leave the questions of how and why behind, as mysterious or secondary or, indeed, unimportant. I would suggest, though, that the very openness of the child reader to such primitive power must have its effects on the child. These will, almost certainly, help shape the adult, and since the shaping is often in ways not easy to recognize, they can all too easily be summarily acknowledged and dismissed as of no great importance. But suppose I posit a few of my stronger, adult feelings as a reader, suppose I say that I quite prefer reading *The Faerie Queene* to reading any Shakespeare play, that to the extent I revere very highly parts of *The Lord of the Rings* I dislike other parts and all the Narnia books of Tolkien's friend Lewis, that, although a great many works we would now call either sexist or racist I truly shun because they are so, George Macdonald's *Lilith* continues to haunt me, tied up though it is with some of the worst and most violent sexist fantasies. Does anyone imagine that these facts about myself are not entwined with my experiences as a child, indeed as a child reader? Points have we all of us within our souls where all stand single, and I can only say that these are some of my points, that these are breathings for incommunicable powers, that these are in part passports back into my childhood, and to my childhood reading, just as they are not quite my safe-conduct passages out of those years and into the light of common day.

To go back via these passports into my childhood reading would be, indeed, to move directly over into autobiography even further, and what I want to do is to suggest something about the possibilities of literary criticism that I think many more people believe than would admit to doing so. When it comes to reading, it seems to me, most of us admit to having points within our souls where all stand single; that is especially true of our testimony concerning our childhood reading, but is still true with our adult reading, of children's literature, fantasy, or any other kind. As readers we know we find ourselves picking up some books and not others, finishing some books and not others, and enjoying the prospect of talking and writing about some books and not others, and we know this is not always or entirely describable as a matter of value. Is not children's literature or fantasy literature in general only the most obvious place where this is true, where our responses, our receptivity or our shutness, are most clearly and obdurately what they are, not something to be shunned or ignored?

What little I have read of reader-oriented criticism and theory seems so abstruse or so insistently psychoanalytic in the bad sense that I am helpless to say what connection my questions and assertions make with anything someone else has written. When I read about constructing, deconstructing, and reconstructing literary texts, I feel what is being described is much closer to the act of unmaking and making jigsaw puzzles than it is to the act of reading. It is as though the very place where the strange separateness of our experiences ought to lead us into the candid admission of a mystery has led instead to the false rigors of a false objectivity, when neither the rigors nor the objectivity is wanted or required. Children's literature or children as the audience for this literature is merely the most obvious place where these falsenesses can be found, or most easily shown to be false.

My first image was of a writer who writes best when writing out of some individually felt need. Such a writer often must make some adjustments, after the original imaginative effort has been made, to an audience, in this case an audience that may not know an elaborate vocabulary or instantly respond to a complex tone, and so the audience must be acknowledged in a late or last revision. My second image is of a reader, reading out of some individually felt need, reading as a child, but reading later in a fashion that articulates long-ago needs as well. If the message that the experience of writers of children's books holds true, then readers have their own obligations when they start to talk, discuss, become literary critics. They are people, sharing with others, and in the act of sharing discovering not only whatever communality they find, but also their individuality. What excites one depresses another. What one feels tepidly, another feels strongly and tenaciously.

In another time and place, such facts might be so many other coals being carried to Newcastle. But in this country, in this latter part of this century, that is hardly likely to be the case. If we are in danger, it is the danger of making totems cut of the false god of objectivity, when the name of that god is flexibility and generosity, of making a false god of professionalism, of standards, or of criteria (totally specious) of accurate demonstration in our literary commentary, when in fact the name of that god is responsibility and common sense. No one now imagines that the mere statement of a feeling or a preference is the beginning or the end of any matter concerning literature. No one in anyone's memory has made a speech or written an article that merely articulates an individual's taste. No one except college students encouraged to do so imagines that sympathizing with the plights of one's grandfather is a necessary or sufficient guide for the understanding of *King Lear*.

No, our collective sins lie on the other side, in repressing our experiences as individual readers when we come to address others whose experiences are clearly not our own, in imagining that literature is susceptible to the rigors of method, that scholarship consists of saying what no one else has said and, in most cases, no one would say. If reading is individual, so must criticism be, just as any writing must be.

Children's literature is, in this respect, a Pandora's box. We can, as people first coming to the criticism of that literature, say that here is a new chance to begin criticism anew, here because we know that with this literature we are more apt to respond in personal, individual ways and so must write in obedience to that response, just as writers of that literature have obviously done before us. Or we can treat it as just another part of the establishment, the Library of Congress classification system and the MLA panels and the proliferations of journals devoted to "the field." We can acknowledge a mystery or subsume it, and, if we do the latter, we may let loose a whole host of demons from the box without knowing that that is what is being done.

G. R. THOMPSON

The Apparition of This World: Transcendentalism and the American "Ghost" Story

Where do we find ourselves? In a series of which we do not know the extremes, and believe that it has none. We wake and find ourselves on a stair; there are stairs below us, which we seem to have ascended; there are stairs above us, many a one, which go upward and out of sight. . . . Sleep lingers all our lifetime about our eyes, as night hovers all day in the boughs of the fir-tree. All things swim and glitter. Our life is not so much threatened as our perception. Ghostlike we glide through nature.

Emerson, "Experience"

This living world, where we sit by our firesides, or go forth to meet beings like ourselves, seemed rather the creation of wizard power, with so much . . . resemblance to known objects that a man might shudder at the ghostly shape of his old beloved dwelling, and the shadow of a ghostly tree before his door. One looked to behold inhabitants suited to such a town, glittering in icy garments, with motionless features, cold, sparkling eyes, and just sensation enough in their frozen hearts to shiver at each other's presence.

. . . such was the apparition . . . too shadowy for language to portray. . . .

Hawthorne, "Alice Doane's Appeal"

The ghost story we have been taught to regard as a minor popular form of later nineteenth-century literature, relatively unimportant in the mainstream of literary history, and standing to one side of the central intellectual and artistic concerns of the age. Yet in a broader sense, the tale of the "supernatural" was a major concern, not only of the nineteenth century as a whole, but also of the early twentieth century; most

90

of the major nineteenth-century writers in Britain and America tried their hands at some form of the "ghost" story. By sheer numbers of writers and tales, the British would seem to be preeminent in the genre. But, while I myself have thought of the later nineteenth century as indeed the "golden age" of the British ghost story, I had also always assumed that this high Victorian-Edwardian plateau was at least Anglo-American. Further, I had assumed that the ghost story derived in part from groundwork laid by the Gothic and Romantic writers of the first half of the century and before. Between Horace Walpole and Charles Dickens, important British ghost stories were written by Matthew G. Lewis, Sir Walter Scott, Thomas De Quincey, James Hogg, Elizabeth Gaskell, and others. And yet these ghost stories are noticeably different from those of their major American contemporaries, Charles Brockden Brown, Washington Irving, Nathaniel Hawthorne, and Edgar Allan Poe, acknowledged masters of early American fiction.

How are the American tales different? For one thing, Poe's ghostly tales contain no real ghosts. Hawthorne's ghosts are wrapped in moral as well as psychological ambiguity. Irving's ghosts are treated with a polyphony of tone from portentous to ironic and comic. Brown's ghost-like illusions are clearly illusions. The diachronic pattern seems to move from explained ghosts, to playfully entertained ghosts, to ambiguous ghosts—though that is an oversimplification. But one thing is clear: despite heavy reliance on the Gothic tradition, the earlier nineteenth-century American writers—unlike their British contemporaries—have left us few outright ghost stories. Such an omission seems surprising in view of their exploration of various supernatural "phenomena" as emblematic of some demonic agency at large in the world, or in the mind of man. After all, among the motifs from the Gothic tradition that we find over and over again in their writings are such things as witchcraft, alchemy, reincarnation, transmigration of souls, visionary dream states, family curses, doubles, magical mirrors, prophetic pictures, and the like—all, however, like their ghosts, treated ambiguously.

This essay explores one central question of American literary history, for which there is doubtless no conclusive answer. How is it that, in an age of Gothic fantasy that saw the rise of the ghost story, the major American fiction writers of the Romantic period wrote so few out-and-out *ghost* stories? Although, with a little searching, we can find ghost stories by writers for the popular magazines of the time, recourse to a realm of the unambiguous supernatural by major American writers is minimal. Instead, they raise the possibility of supernatural agency in tension with various kinds of misperception. When seemingly supernatural events are not rationally explained away, as in Charles Brockden Brown's *Wieland* (1798), presumption of an actual realm of the occult is qualified by a prevailing skepticism woven into the text or implied through narrative frames. Patterns of discontinuities in the text imply that out-of-the-ordinary happenings in the main narrative result from psychological imperception, but only inconclusively so.

This predilection of course is not so much a matter of an author's belief as it is a matter of his artistic encounters with a mind set or world view and of his artistic conception of the norms of the fictive world he creates in the text as governed by concepts of genre. The fictive world presented in the text is governed both by literary tradition and by historical philosophical context. What I want to argue here is that the "ghost" story in America is a subgenre of the Gothic tale, focused on the illusion of the ghostly appearance as an icon for the apparitional nature of all existence. The American "ghost" story embodies ontological, epistemological, and axiological concerns central to the Romantic dilemma of subject and object. This dilemma is reflected dramatically in the early development in America of the intricate techniques of the supernatural tale and the inconclusive ghost story. The relative lack of straight ghosts in American fiction of the Romantic period, I contend, reflects the philosophical uncertainties of the dominant intellectual movement of the time—Transcendentalism. I offer here speculation in very broad terms on the interaction of literary tradition and historical philosophical context as a matter of (1) the relation of the ghost story to the Gothic, (2) the relation of the Gothic to Transcendentalism and Romanticism, and (3) the problem these matters pose for the early nineteenth-century writer of fantastic fiction. A basic assumption is that, however the forms of the ghost story are defined, historically they issue from a Gothic matrix. The Gothic is the major countermovement of the Romantic age in America, defined by and itself defining historical Romanticism.[1]

I

Most critics and historians of the ghost story as a genre attempt to dissociate it from the Gothic. One recent critic, Jack Sullivan, writes that Gothic ghosts were largely "decorative," lacking the more "menacing quality of modern ghosts."[2] Like most critics of the genre, he is careful to point out that the term "ghost story" is a loosely defined "catchall" term. The texts he is interested in, he says, deal with the "apparitional in one sense or another."[3] But his concept of the "modern" ghost depends on an imprecise distinction between ghostly tales of the Romantic period and those after 1869, when, he claims, Sheridan Le Fanu's "Green Tea" established the paradigm for the modern tale: in the modern ghost story, the ghosts seem simultaneously "to emerge from within as well as invade from without."[4] Other critics as well, such as Julia Briggs and Pamela Search, point to the ambiguous or inconclusive nature of the "modern" ghost story, where *possible* supernatural agency is balanced off against *possible* psychological explanation with indeterminate results.[5] Search writes that this kind of tale is more effective than the "old-fashioned" ghost story because "when the horror is left undefined it becomes all the more real to us in our imagination, and the inconclusive ending of the tale leaves us with our doubts and fears unresolved and therefore more terrible."[6] She associates the form principally with Walter De La Mare in the earlier twentieth century, with faint antecedents in Henry James's *Turn of the Screw* (1898), and even fainter ones in Le Fanu's "Green Tea."

How all this is different from the tales of Hawthorne, Poe, and Irving in the early years of the nineteenth century is unclear. Ghost story critics seem to assume that the various apparitions of these earlier tales either (somehow) do not qualify as ghosts or (contradictorily) are to be taken in the text as actual spirits from an "other" world of the occult and therefore are simply "old-fashioned." Sullivan, for example, excludes Poe's "Fall of the House of Usher" from the genre by calling it an "exercise in cosmic paranoia rather than a ghost story."[7] But the same might be said of the so-called archetypal ghost story that Sullivan identifies, namely, Le Fanu's "Green Tea," where the "apparition" seems to come simultaneously from within and without. Other critics tend to read tales such as Poe's "Morella," "Ligeia," and "Usher" as old-fashioned tales of ghosts without any ambiguity.[8]

But, as mentioned, the ghostly tales of the major American Romantic writers of fantastic fiction show little, if any, presumption of an actual realm of the supernatural as traditionally conceived. Even Hawthorne's ghostly series, "The Legends of the Province House" (1838–1842), presents a remarkable metafictional sequence that calls into question both the legends and their manner of presentation. The famous ghostly tale "Alice Doane's Appeal" (1835) is even more overtly metafictional than "Legends of the Province House." Toward the end of this story, Hawthorne's narrator writes that ghostly forms of "this living world" seem to him "the creation of wizard power"; there is just "so much resemblance to known objects" that one might "shudder at the ghostly shape" of his own dwelling and the "ghostly tree before his door." Here "beings like ourselves" with "cold sparkling eyes" and "frozen hearts" and "motionless features" might "shiver at each other's presence." These beings are like "souls accursed" or "fiends counterfeiting" saints. "Such was the apparition . . . too shadowy for language to portray. . . ."[9]

The ghostliness of the tale is not of an occult, other world, but of *this* world, as shaped by the narrator's imagination playing over the everyday natural world, connecting the present with past human history, and manipulating the conventions of the genre for a more profoundly horrifying effect than the conventional ghost story. Having in fact told a conventional ghost story and been disappointed in the response of his audience, the narrator raises ghosts of the historical past as an elaborate narrative metaphor in response to his own question of how most effectively to affect his listeners (two young ladies) and the potential readers of his previously abandoned tale. He makes of both the past fictive world and the present "actual" one in which he is telling his tale a ghostland, a shadowy apparition. He comments, metafictionally interrupting himself: "By this fantastic piece of description, and more in the same style, I intended to throw a ghostly glimmer round the reader, so that his imagination might view the town through a medium that should take off its every-day aspect, and make a proper theatre for so wild a scene as the final one."[10] The wild final scene of the tale merges history with fiction and past with present. The narrator conjures up a vision of Gallows Hill with Cotton Mather and the victims of the Witchcraft Trials and other executed felons as temporal and yet atemporal apparitions of the physical spot, as *though* risen from ghostly graves. Thereby he chills his listeners through the power of subjective imagination more deeply than the central story of Alice and her lovers. Not only do all the ghosts have ambiguous ontological status within the texts of "Alice Doane" and "Legends of the Province House," but also the multiple frames and repetitions emphasize a basic epistemological question regarding the characters' perceptions within the fictional worlds *and* the narrator's perceptions *and* his symbolic relation to an implied author. These matters are central to other of Hawthorne's more or less apparitional works such as "The Hollow of the Three Hills" (1830), "Wives of the Dead" (1832), and "Young Goodman Brown" (1835), where the world of dreams and the world of ordinary cognition blur eerily together.

Such blurring of the subjective and the objective, of supernatural and natural, is a recurrent feature of Poe's tales as well. Poe advances philosophical doubt about the real and the unreal as a major source of horror or terror. The major feature of his stories is the dramatization of existential thirst for self-torture; and this self-torture often takes the form, as in "The Pit and the Pendulum" (1842), of entertaining the *possibility* that the external, objective world does not really exist. This horror is more terrible than any threat from a supernatural, other realm, and the solipsistic question is much more pronounced in Poe than in Hawthorne. In Poe it is always as if the natural world of objects (including other human beings) were merely an apparition or projected image of one's own tortured consciousness. Of Poe's tales involving the supernatural or apparent supernatural, only a very few can be considered ghost stories. Those in which an apparitional element is pronounced include "MS. Found in a Bottle," "Morella," possibly "Metzengerstein," "Ligeia," "Usher," and "The Black Cat." Like Poe's other tales, they exhibit the theme of the mutual destruction of the murderer and the murdered and the collapse of the objective world into an apparitional subjective one—all without *necessarily* implying a supernatural world other than the purely objective physical world or the purely subjective mental world.

There *are* a few ghosts in Irving, however. In his rendering of the folk legend of "Dolph Heyliger" (1822), a ghost leads Dolph to treasure, and he sees a ghost ship unambiguously there and not suspect as a mental aberration, as in Poe's "MS. Found in a Bottle." (Or is it?) There are apparitional figures in *Tales of the Alhambra* (1832); and there is an explained ghost in "The Spectre Bride-groom" (1820) and a fake ghost in "The Legend of Sleepy Hollow" (1820). In *Tales of a Traveller* (1824), Irving experiments with various forms of the ghost story and methods of telling the ghost story. The opening section is an interconnected sequence called "Strange Stories By A Nervous Gentleman." At the center is the most ghostly of the tales, "Adventure of the German Student," which is ambiguous at best. The possibility that the mad German student has hallucinated making love to a guillotined young woman emerges not only in the main narrative, but also in the dialogue between the narrators and their listeners, who keep questioning the veracity (and effective telling) of all the stories. The series concludes with several linked stories of the "Mysterious Italian," whose portrait unnerves the various guests, but we find out at the end that they have not seen his real portrait at all; the host has told them the story and then shown them a different painting, which their imaginations have made into an enchanted portrait emanating sinister feelings, much as in Hawthorne's "Prophetic Pictures" (1837). Irving makes each succeeding tale in the sequence call into question the preceding tales and thus itself—the whole surrounded by an overall semicomic narrative frame. These "ghost" stories are not about occult ghosts at all, but about psychological misperception, moral ambiguity, and the aesthetics of tale telling itself, features also characteristic of the broader Gothic mode.

Although literary historians used to divide the Gothic romance into two types—the supernatural and the explained supernatural—modern criticism sees at least four modes.[11] Historical Gothic is ontologically undifferentiated with regard to the supernatural; the presence of an occasional demon or ghost is not necessarily significant for either the ontology or the epistemology of a text. Examples might include Clara Reeve's *Old English Baron* (1778) or Sophia Lee's *Recess* (1783–1786). In supernatural Gothic the occult is in fact an assumption of central interest, as in Horace Walpole's *Castle of Otranto* (1764–1765) or M. G. Lewis's *Monk* (1796). In explained Gothic the final assumption is that the supernatural does not, at last, penetrate into the everyday world. All seemingly occult phenomena are the result of misinformation or misperception, as in Mrs. Radcliffe's *Mysteries of Udolpho* (1794) and other of her novels. But in ambiguous Gothic it is the unresolved tension between the supernatural and the natural that generates dread—a limbo of uncertainty for characters and readers that Tzvetan Todorov has too broadly labeled the "fantastic"[12] and that ghost story critics have labeled the "inconclusive" ghost story of the later nineteenth century. This technique is not a development of the second half of the century, but is central to Ludwig Tieck's "Fair-haired Eckbert" (1797) and other of his tales, to the tales of E. T. A. Hoffmann such as "The Sand-Man" (1817), to the elder Richard Henry Dana's *Paul Felton* (1821), and, as indicated, to the tales of Irving, Hawthorne, and Poe. All of these modes share, though in varying degrees, the impulse to generate or to portray dread, supernatural or otherwise.

2

Whereas the Gothic, in its impulse to create a sense of apprehension and dread, would seem to be the obverse of optative Trancendentalism, it is a distortion to assert that the Gothic alone subverts the optimistic Romanticism of the age. The reverse is true as well, so that there is a double inversion. The straight supernatural tale is almost, as it were, co-opted by the uncertain materialism of the spiritual doctrines of Transcendentalism. In America, Transcendentalism and Gothicism exert a reciprocal shaping force that produces a binary paradigm of literary and philosophical concerns: an unresolved dialectic of faith and doubt about spirit and nature. While, like Hawthorne, some of the fictionists seriously entertain the idealist or even the occultist ideas of Transcendentalism, they also manipulate the conventions of Gothic fiction for fictional ends, while yet in these fictions qualifying and even undercutting any serious belief in a Gothic occult realm. Thus neither a positive Transcendentalist vision of nature and spirit nor a negative Gothicist view of a sinister supernaturalism is fully embraced by American writers of fiction.

Among the possible contextual explanations for the paradox of American fiction writers' apparent rejection of the outright ghost and their immersion in the Gothic tradition, the most striking is the unresolved conflict in Romantic attempts (on both sides of the Atlantic) to fuse the natural with the supernatural, to negate the matter-spirit schism. In America this activity, curiously, is heightened by the Transcendentalist movement to which the major fiction writers directly respond. It is clear that for them American Transcendentalism offers a sometimes contradictory program of seeing the material world as the ultimate apparition, which yet *cannot* be an apparition merely.

The import of this relation can be illustrated in the intimate connection between the "minor" form of the ghost story and Romantic philosophy in America as represented by Transcendentalism. American Transcendentalism begins with the Kantian formulation of transcendent ideas—ideas which transcend finite, physically based existence and which are inaccessible to cognition. It then transforms this concept into transcendental *knowledge*—knowledge based on the empirical, the experiential in the physical world, but extending to another, "higher" realm comprehending both. German philosophy mutates into an American literary world view that emphasizes holistic reintegration of the dissociated fragments of man's existence. The new, higher Reason as Emerson and Whitman understood it is an integration of body-spirit, head-heart. The Romantic attempt to achieve a grand synthesis of these things has been described as "natural supernaturalism" by Meyer Abrams, who takes the phrase from Carlyle. The first of the two great climaxes of *Sartor Resartus* (1833–1834), as Charles Frederick Harrold observes, occurs after the three chapters "The Everlasting No," "The Center of Indifference," and "The Everlasting Yea."[13] Teufelsdröck progresses from doubt to indifferent skepticism to affirmation of the spirit symbolized in the apparition of nature. The second climax occurs several chapters later in the lyric, pantheistic affirmation of the conclusion of the "Natural Supernaturalism" chapter. As developed by Americans from Carlyle and from German *Naturphilosophie*, the concept of the "natural supernatural" has at its heart the "redemption" of physical

existence by the infusion of the spiritual into it. And it becomes a reciprocal process. The result is a harmonious monism of some sort that
also collapses time into the eternal present. Monistic natural supernaturalism in America receives its best-known statements in Emerson's
Nature (1836), in Thoreau's *Walden* (1851), and in such poems of
Whitman's as "Song of Myself" (1855), "There Was A Child Went
Forth" (1855), "Crossing Brooklyn Ferry" (1856, 1860). The Romantic
imagination as exemplified in Whitman and Thoreau searches concrete
physical nature for supernatural clues supplied beforehand by the mind
in a pattern of harmonious reciprocity of subject and object. The physical and the spiritual fuse in the mind. In *Walden* it is the "intellect" that
is presented as a cleaver through falsehood, a burrower after physical
and spiritual reality.

The Transcendentalists at different times assert that everything exists within the mind of God, or in the spiritual realm of the Oversoul.
And yet the spiritual realm is fused with the apparition of the natural
world—a world of appearances that are still somehow real. Emerson's
early writings, greatly indebted to Carlyle, again and again come up
against the Transcendentalist paradox of valuing and believing in the
external world while seeing it as the apparitional symbol of a higher
world. The 1836 *Nature* wavers back and forth over the question, as
Emerson turns to the higher prospects of nature in the philosophical
constructs of idealism and his personal sense of an all-encompassing
higher spirit. The struggle that it is to be fair to both tendencies in
himself—to worship physical nature and to worship the truer reality
behind or within it—becomes especially evident as Emerson attempts
to conclude his treatise.

In the beginning, however, Emerson's tone is confident: "let us
interrogate the great apparition, that shines so peacefully around us.
Let us inquire, to what end is nature?"[14] And in the penultimate chapter
(chapter seven, "Spirit"), he concludes that the "noblest ministry of
nature is to stand as the apparition of God."[15] Yet he is careful to insist
that he is not devaluing physical nature. In chapter six, he writes that
religion and ethics "both put nature under foot. The first and last lesson
of religion is, 'The things that are seen, are temporal; the things that
are unseen, are eternal.' It puts an affront upon nature. . . ." (Cf. II
Corinthians 4:18.) In the next paragraph, he writes:

> I own there is something ungrateful in expanding too curiously the par-
> ticulars of the general proposition, that all culture tends to imbue us with
> idealism. I have no hostility to nature, but a child's love to it. . . . Let us

speak her fair. I do not wish to fling stones at my beautiful mother, nor soil my gentle nest.[16]

In chapter seven again, Emerson addresses what he sees as the major problems of the idealist view:

Idealism acquaints us with the total disparity between the evidence of our own being and the evidence of the world's being. . . . Yet, if it only deny the existence of matter, it does not satisfy the demands of the spirit. It leaves God out of me. It leaves me in the splendid labyrinth of my own perceptions, to wander without end.[17]

The answer is to go beyond Idealism, to a pervasive sense of the spirit as simultaneously emerging from within and pervading from without. "The world proceeds from the same spirit as the body of man," Emerson declares. "It is a remoter and inferior incarnation of God, a projection of God in the unconscious." Objective nature does differ somehow from the incarnate self, however, because it is not subjected to the human will: "Its serene order is inviolable by us."[18]

In the final chapter (chapter eight, "Prospects"), Emerson addresses the prospect of an unredeemed or ruined world:

The problem of restoring to the world original and eternal beauty is solved by the redemption of the soul. The ruin or blank that we see when we look at nature, is in our own eye. . . . The reason why the world lacks unity, and lies broken and in heaps, is because man is disunited with himself . . . until he satisfies all the demands of the spirit.[19]

Thus he ends with an appeal to innately human divinity, to reciprocity between nature and mentally perceived spirit (object and subject). The world is still capable, apparently, of showing us a blank if we are not sufficiently transcendental in our outlook. But if the "beautiful mother," nature, presents us with a serene and inviolable order that is the basis of beauty, language, and intellect—the structural basis of the first two-thirds of the book—then the precise relation of nature-mind-spirit is left somewhat problematic if not opaque.

As Americans, Hawthorne and Poe responded, like Melville, in their own ways to Emerson and the group generally allied with him, as Irving did directly to the German Romanticism that gave rise to American Transcendentalism. Although for writers on the other side of the Atlantic the process toward natural supernaturalism was also ultimately inconclusive, the formation of the Transcendentalist school in America seems to have exaggerated the schism between optimistic monists and pessimistic doubters, whether monist, dualist, or pluralist. F. O. Matthiessen's caveat not withstanding,[20] the major American Romantic writers do split into two opposing groups: Emerson, Thoreau, and Whitman are aggressive proponents of benign monism; Hawthorne, Poe, and Melville are finally skeptics of both traditional dualism and the new monism.

But the matter is not so simple. In each opposing camp, there is a doubled and redoubled dialectic of affirmation and skepticism about natural supernaturalism and about the spiritual world distinct from the world of appearances if natural supernaturalism is rejected. Even *Walden* builds toward an epistemological crisis in the "Brute Neighbors" chapter, juxtaposed toward the center of the book with "Higher Laws." Having confronted the brute level of existence, however, the narrator of *Walden* proceeds by the power of the will to reassert the harmonious oneness of physical nature and the spirit, for those who will see it. Although, in Emerson's later essays (most notably "Experience," 1844, 1850, and "Montaigne; or, the Skeptic," 1850), doubt about the benign oneness of nature and spirit is confronted, both essays are capable of being read as the triumph of the Transcendental vision over skepticism. But whether one accepts the thesis that the later Emerson backed away from the confident optimism of his earlier essays or whether one accepts the idea of a "cosmic scare" in Thoreau, it is clear that both confronted severe doubts, as did Whitman in such poems as "Of the Terrible Doubt of Appearances" (1860, 1867) and "As I Ebb'd With the Ocean of Life" (1860, 1881).

Like Emerson, Whitman begins confidently in "Song of Myself."[21] He immediately addresses the Emersonian dilemma of nature and spirit as separate yet fused:

> *I believe in you my soul, the other I am must not abase itself*
> > *to you,*
> *And you must not be abased to the other.*

It is clear from the start that this "other" of the self's soul is the body, physical existence, and these lines are directly followed by the famous (or infamous) scene in section five where the soul and the body erotically caress each other. The point receives graceful embodiment in "There Was A Child Went Forth," where the opening lines set forth clearly a philosophy of reciprocity between nature and soul, with increased emphasis on mental perception of relatedness:

> *And the first object he look'd upon, that object he became,*
> *And that object became part of him. . . .*

Mere external nature and the body are infused with the mental-spiritual apprehension of conscious human beings, and the widening experience of nature by the child encompasses also

> . . . *the sense of what is real, the thought if after all it should*
> *prove unreal,*
> *The doubts of day-time and the doubts of night-time, the cu-*
> *rious whether and how,*
> *Whether that which appears so is so, or is it all flashes and*
> *specks?*

The theme of reciprocal definition of spirit and body is reannounced in section five of "Crossing Brooklyn Ferry":

> *I too had receiv'd identity by my body,*
> *That I was I knew was of my body, and what I should be I*
> *knew I should be of my body.*

Here the body and all physical nature become a symbol of the interrelatedness of all things, objective and subjective, natural and spiritual; and the poem becomes a spiritual epiphany derived from the concrete sense of the physical.

Yet at times nature for Whitman threatens to become a ruin or blank, as in "As I Ebb'd With the Ocean of Life":

> *O baffled, balk'd, bent to the very earth. . . .*
> *I perceive I have not really understood any thing, not a single*
> *object, and that no man ever can,*
> *Nature here in sight of the sea taking advantage of me to dart*
> *upon me and sting me,*
> *Because I have dared to open my mouth to sing at all.*

Although the second half of the poem develops the idea that the "flow" of emotional and spiritual affirmation and certainty "will return" eventually from this ebbing, it is a desperate appeal couched in a parenthetical aside. The poem concludes with images of chaff and waste on the seashore, of "dead lips" exuding ooze, of broken torn blossoms, of

> *Tufts of straw, sands, fragments,*
> *Buoy'd hither from many moods, one contradicting another*

—all drifting at random under the impetus of the "sobbing dirge of Nature" as much as by any "blare of the cloud-trumpets."

> *We, capricious, brought hither we know not whence, spread*
> *out before you,*

You up there walking or sitting,
Whoever you are, we too lie in drifts at your feet.

While the burden of Whitman's "Of the Terrible Doubt of Appearances" is celebration of the idea that only human friendship and love confirm reality, the initial statement of the poem throws into high relief the philosophical irresolution and anxiety we have been discussing:

Of the uncertainty after all, that we may be deluded. . . .
May-be the things I perceive, the animals, plants, men, hills,
  shining and flowing waters,
The skies of day and night, colors, densities, forms, may-be
  these are (as doubtless they are) only apparitions. . . .

The redoubled light-dark schism (whether between camps of opposing writers or within each) results in a similar obsessive concern with the mind, with perception. This obsession parallels the fascination with the conscious-unconscious and cognitive-intuitive aspects of mind in the worldwide Romantic movement emanating from Germany. Whether the Romantic writer in America is optimistic or pessimistic in disposition, whether he searches physical nature for correspondences between this world and a Platonic other world or projects spiritual or ideal constructs from himself onto or into nature, the mind becomes all encompassing. The drama of perception is played out in the mind, with its polar co-terminants: higher Reason, understanding, imagination—and misperception, hallucination, insanity. Once the mind is made the theater of action, axiological and ontological crises resolve into a larger epistemological crisis. Emerson recognized as much in "Experience" when he designated illusion, temperament, succession, surface, the surprises of chance and flux as the self-consciously subjective "lords of life."

The binary tension of American Gothic and American Transcendentalism is in large part focused on the epistemological drama of the mind. The Romantic era's obsession with the uncertain relationship of conscious and unconscious activity and perception is central to all this tangled speculation on the meaning of nature and the place of the spiritual. Between the realm of the spirit and the realm of physical nature lies the province of the mind, as the Transcendentalists emphasize. And Hawthorne and Poe write tale after tale dramatizing the perplexities of mental apprehension, so that the "occult" element of their fiction seems always to have a psychological dimension, if not an explanation. But, as mentioned, such implied rationalized psychological explanations are normally tentative and ambiguous, or inconclusive. At the end of "Young Goodman Brown" (1835), which is not a ghost story but a tale of witchcraft (although there are apparitions), Hawthorne raises the question of possible hallucination. But he leaves the question unanswered and concentrates on the psychological results of Brown's experience, whatever its ontological status. In this tale the psychological element is overt; more frequently, the psychological dimension of apparent supernatural occurrences is covert, insinuated inconclusively under or around the surface narrative. In Poe's more ghostly tale "Ligeia" (1838), the reader is very gradually led to wonder whether Ligeia actually returns from the dead or whether her return is the invention of the narrator's sick imagination. For throughout the tale we bit by bit become aware of his intensely disturbed mental condition and his reliance on drugs; at the end we may even question whether Ligeia ever existed in reality at all. Such ambiguous subjectivity is frequently suggested so subtly that the stories become, through tensions in narrative strategies, tales of the preternatural rather than of the supernatural. But even if interpreted in this way, the ontological status of the occult as opposed to the "real" world is unclear. In fact, the uncertain reality of the fictive world presented is pushed to the foreground by redoubling the uncertainty through calling into question not only the perceptions of the characters, but also the reliability of the tale tellers. Thereby such works become ultimately epistemological texts, and ontological uncertainty is magnified. In this concern they are centrally Romantic.

Just as for European writers, for American writers the human mind becomes the key element in the matter-spirit dilemma. Their world view is marked by a recurrent apprehension that all matter may be a mental construct, just as all dreams of the spiritual world may be a delusion. The subject-object dialectic is magnified for Americans by their intense interest in the progress of German philosophy and literature. Frederic Henry Hedge and great numbers of other translators and explicators were presenting German philosophy to Americans.[22] Kant as interpreted by such German writers as Fichte is interpreted again by Coleridge, and reinterpreted by Carlyle. Early in *Sartor Resartus*, Carlyle, deceptively casual, introduces the great theme. Teufelsdröck remarks of all perceptible existence, "These are Apparitions: what else?"[23]

The epistemological question is directly addressed in an early work by Hawthorne published immediately after *Sartor Resartus* during the same year as "Alice Doane's Appeal." This is his sketch "The Haunted Mind" (1835). The narrator pictures himself, or the reader, as having suddenly awakened from a midnight slumber to see a fantastic procession of allegorical figures who exhibit various aspects of the demonic for the guilty heart that "holds its hell within itself." Even without such a burden of guilt, this midnight time is "the nightmare of the soul." But this "heavy, heavy sinking of the spirits; this wintry gloom about the heart; this indistinct horror of the mind, blend[s] itself with the darkness of the chamber." Hawthorne underscores the ambiguous relationship of the inner darkness of the mind "blending" with the outer darkness of the "real" world, revealed "on the borders of sleep and wakefulness." Eventually, the sleeper has "an involuntary start" and finds himself "running a doubtful parallel" between "human life and the hour which has now elapsed." The didactic allegory that seems the initial impulse of the sketch dissolves. In such a midnight hour, Hawthorne writes, "you emerge from mystery, pass through a vicissitude that you can but imperfectly control, and are borne onward to another mystery."[24] Romantic desire for clear reciprocity between the subjective and objective here becomes a guilt-laden "doubtful parallel" between the "subconscious" realm of the "other" and the conscious world. In story after story by Hawthorne, this "doubtful parallel" of subjective and objective is embedded in ambiguous Gothic narrative.

For all the obsessive concern for the reciprocity of subject and object, once doubt establishes itself in the negative Romantic mind, it really does not matter whether one assumes the world to be objective or subjective—for the doubt perpetuates itself in a pessimistic dialectic. What if one contemplates the world as object—that is, as having an objective, firm, exterior reality separate from human perception? Then the world may seem to be a structure infused with spirit and supplying Neoplatonic symbols of a dynamic life beyond this one—or it may seem to be mere physical material with no objects beyond the immediate fact of existence. Being is still opposed by the possibility of Nothingness. On the other hand, what if one contemplates the world as subject? The same dialectic of belief and disbelief obtains: the world may seem to be a dynamic projection of the indwelling spirit of man himself—or a deceptive arbitrary imposition of idiosyncratic order upon Void. In either case, the doubt remains a perpetual possibility in the mind.

3

The philosophies of mind from Germany and Britain in the air of the times create both helixes and vortices in American thought and have reciprocal influence on both American Gothic fiction and Transcendental philosophy. The fiction writers grapple with these unresolved philosophical issues of Romantic speculation and respond in their own ways to Emersonianism, or Transcendentalism. Sometimes they write outright satire, as in Hawthorne's "Celestial Railroad," or Poe's"Mellonta Tauta," "Never Bet the Devil Your Head" and his reviews, or Melville's *Confidence-Man*. But their dominant response is within the framework of the Gothic. Whatever these writers inherited from the purely literary tradition of the Gothic, the negative or skeptical element is underscored by the irresolution manifest in many Transcendentalist statements. Perhaps the supreme example of the age is found in the epistemological intertwining of Gothic and Transcendentalist themes in *Moby-Dick*. For demonic Ahab (as interpreted by the sometimes Transcendentalist Ishmael), the world is inscrutable, a blank, all-color, no-color atheism, from which, Ishmael adds, we shrink. All visible objects are but pasteboard masks, Ahab thinks. If man *could* but strike through the unreasoning mask to some reasoning thing beyond, perhaps there could be some solace. His surrogate for peace is hatred. "That inscrutable thing is chiefly what I hate," Ahab declares; and it does not matter to him whether the natural object of the white whale is agent or principal. All he can do is wreak his hate, even knowing that there may be nothing behind the apparition of the world.[25]

The easy conclusion that the American Gothic tale subverts the world view of American optimistic Romanticism is, though hardly wrong, incomplete. For Transcendentalism not only feeds the fires of Gothic doubt by its own self-conscious doubts, but also actually subverts at least one traditional Gothic form, the ghost story. The greatest parodox of all is that the emphasis in the Emerson-Whitman world on a benign cosmos (in which distinctions between material and spiritual are ultimately dissolved) proceeds not by denial of the material world, but by a reinterpretation of the spiritual world that suggests that the supernatural realm of the wholly "other" does not finally exist. If the only ontologic reality is a mysterious dynamic interaction between two fictional constructs—the physical phenomenal world of sensations and the spiritual noumenal world of ideas—what happens to the apparitional? Which is the apparition? The concept of a natural world? Or the concept of a supernatural world? In the dialectic the natural and the supernatural fuse with each other—yielding what? Void? If they do not cancel each other out in a negative dialectic leading to subjective solipsism, they yet threaten all traditional values.

Whereas the traditional dualism of Christianity makes possible the supernatural ghost story, American Transcendentalism denies Christian

concepts that give coherence to moral retribution from a ghostly presence or a spiritual sphere. At the very least, American Transcendentalism, when it does not outright reject basic Christian assumptions, secu-
larizes them. Transcendentalism denies the sovereign authority of
anthropomorphic God. The Godhead becomes a "force" of some kind,
an impersonal oversoul. A "mystery" remains, but it resides in the divinity of living men and living nature—a Christian heresy. Not only is
the divinity of God the Father and of Jesus the Son denied, but also the
doctrine of original sin is rejected. Emerson puts evil in purely relative
secular terms in "Divinity School Address" (1838), declaring that
"evil" does not exist; seeming evil is merely "privative," a lesser form
of the larger good, as cold is merely a lesser degree of heat.[26] To reject
evil is not only to diminish the sphere of the supernatural for the writer
of Gothic fiction, but also to deprive the writer of the main rationale for
ghosts.

This is not, of course, to say that the American Romantic Gothic
is thereby deprived of the horrific. Quite the contrary. By one of those
frequent ironies of intellectual history, Carlyle's attempt to see the divine supernatural permeating nature also implies its negative, as in his
playful discussion of the traditional concept of the "ghost" in the "Natural Supernaturalism" chapter of *Sartor Resartus*:

> . . . could anything be more miraculous than an actual, authentic Ghost?
> The English Johnson longed, all his life, to see one. . . . Foolish Doctor!
> Did he never, with the mind's eye as well as with the body's, look round
> him into that full tide of human Life he so loved; did he never so much
> as look into Himself? The good Doctor was a Ghost, as actual and au-
> thentic as heart could wish; well-nigh a million of Ghosts were travelling
> the streets by his side.[27]

For the Gothic writer, the fantastic transformation of all existence—the
phenomena of the whole shining-dark world—into an ultimately unknowable apparition is in fact to universalize horror and thus to shape
the eighteenth-century Gothic concept of supernatural terror into new
form of pervasive dread. Just as the question of universal evil is simultaneously subjective and objective in such works as Hawthorne's
"Young Goodman Brown," so the uncertain *apparition* of *this* world in
American Romantic Gothic fiction intensifies universal dread. The living world is one where despite the fireside a man might indeed shudder
at the ghostly shape of his own dwelling, or at the shadow of a ghostly
tree beside his own familiar door, or at the ghostly inhabitants of his
own town, glittering in icy garments, with motionless features, cold

sparkling eyes, and just sensation enough in their frozen hearts to shiver at each other's presence. Or to paraphrase Hawthorne's great contemporary, it is the elusive quality of the apparitional world of nature that causes the thought of whiteness, when coupled with any object terrible in itself, to heighten the terror to the furthest bounds. The palsied universe lies before us a leper, and we gaze ourselves blind at the monumental white shroud that wraps all the prospect around us.[28] Ghosts come not so much from a spiritual realm of the "other," or even finally from the depths of the mind, as from the solipsistic self's perceiving finally that the whole perceived world is itself a vision of an all-encompassing, luminously opaque *ghost*.

ROBERT A. COLLINS

Fantasy and "Forestructures": The Effect of Philosophical Climate Upon Perceptions of the Fantastic

> Metaphysics lays the foundation of an age by giving it the basis of its essential form, through a particular analysis of the existent and a particular conception of truth. This basis dominates all the phenomena which distinguish the age. Conversely, it must be possible to recognize the metaphysical basis in these phenomena through sufficient reflection on them.
>
> Martin Heidegger, "The Age of the World View"

A comparative study of today's two major theorists of fantastic literature might well result in confusion as to whether the genre is "alive and well" or entombed in Paris. "Why does the literature of the fantastic no longer exist?" asks Tzvetan Todorov in his *Introduction à la littérature fantastique*.[1] Because "psychology has replaced it (and thereby made it useless)" is the ready response. Yet six years later, in a parallel study, Eric S. Rabkin reports a "worldwide movement toward an increase in the fantastic in 'high art.'"[2] How can one account for this discrepancy? Each critic, given the premises of his approach, might seem correct in his assessment. Yet radically different perceptions of "the fantastic" itself are involved.

The more obvious and superficial differences in these contrasting studies are easy to spot: Todorov attempts a rigidly structuralist approach, Rabkin a more flexible one; Todorov's definition is impossibly narrow, Rabkin's so broad as to risk the inclusion of all art. Yet these observations do not account for the radical differences in each critic's perception of "the fantastic." Presumably, before any critic arrives upon the scene, there have been legions of naive readers whose notions of genre roughly indicate the field of investigation. How can Todorov perceive the essential quality of the fantastic to be its link with the supernatural? Why does Rabkin reach, by contrast, for paradigms in satire, utopias, detective fiction, science fiction?

The essential difference in the nature of these assessments, I think, may be traced to preconceptions, conditioned and to some extent generated by a "philosophical climate" which controls the world view of the critic-perceiver. Despite their apparent contemporaneity, Rabkin and Todorov are "worlds apart." In order to approach the nature of the preconceptions involved, I appeal for a model of perception to the phenomenologists, particularly to Martin Heidegger, whose concept of *Dasein*, Being-in-the-world, seems relevant. For Heidegger (and others, of course) no process of perception may be characterized as objective; the process itself is impossible without both subject and object (perception is always perception *of* something), and thus the ordering principles in the world-as-perceived are always the result of an interpretive interplay between subject and object. The process of perception, moreover, is always for Heidegger to some extent circular. The ready-to-hand, the familiar, is immediately perceived "*as* something." Interpretive structures preexist, precede the perception. "The mere seeing of things closest to us bears in itself the structure of interpretation," Heidegger says, "in so primordial a manner that to grasp something *free*, as it were, of the *as*, requires a certain readjustment."[3]

In every case, Heidegger says, perception is "perception *as*," and is grounded in "something we have in advance . . . in a fore-conception." "All interpretation," he concludes, "operates in the forestructure." Language itself is a complex of such forestructures. "When an assertion is made, some fore-conception is always implied; but it remains for the most part inconspicuous, because the language already hides in itself a developed way of conceiving." In a concrete investigation such as exact textual interpretation, Heidegger observes, "one likes to appeal to what 'stands there'; then one finds that what 'stands there' . . . is nothing other than the obvious undiscussed assumptions of the person who does the interpreting."[4]

It should be clear at this point that the phenomenological model of perception is an attempt to describe the *reflexive* relationship between perceiving Beings and the "world" they inhabit. This "world," as Howard Pearce has remarked, is not "the conditions we share with animals on this planet. . . . in building on that base we have as human beings qualified the natural conditions, and the 'world' is the totality of possible structures in which we engage one another and things on the earth."[5] If we accept the phenomenological model (as Todorov probably would not) the intimate relationship of "philosophical climate" to the process of perception may be easier to conceive. Forestructures, for *Dasein*, Being-in-the-world, are simply present—how, or even whether, they are acquired is moot. Yet obviously, in the aggregate, they control the character of perceptions. I wish to suggest that the term "philosophical climate" can be easily and fruitfully understood in terms of such interpretive forestructures, which necessarily include language. Thus the presence of certain patterns of interpretation, more or less unquestioned, more or less cohesive, but *shared* to a significant degree by a group of Beings-in-the world, constitutes for me a "philosophical climate." Some notion of what is real, of course, is necessarily one of the most salient features of such a "climate."

Rabkin and Todorov are no doubt right in locating the notion of the fantastic in opposition to the prevailing notion of the real.[6] But if we may trust the linguistic evidence of the past, philosophical climates, with their concomitant perceptions of the real-fantastic polarity, change significantly. The second-century author of the *Tetrabiblos*, for instance, apparently did not bring to the perception of a comet the forestructures of a twentieth-century astronomer: "Comets," Ptolemy tells us, "naturally produce the effects peculiar to Mars and Mercury—wars, hot weather, disturbed conditions . . . and they show . . . through the directions in which the shapes of their tales point, the regions upon which the misfortunes impend."[7] Where Ptolemy recognizes an ominous portent, modern astronomers (such as Fred Hoyle) perceive an orbiting mass of gases. Each perception of the object is heavily dependent on forestructures, on preconceptions which shape one's notion of the real; yet for either Ptolemy or Fred Hoyle, the other's perception of the comet would be fantastic. Assessment of the real-fantastic polarity, then, depends on *Dasein*, Being-in-the-world, in time, subject to the patterns of interpretation then in vogue.

A cultural moment in which "science" itself appeared as "fantastic" occurred during the period of transition between the Ptolemaic and Copernican cosmologies. This period roughly bracketed the turn of the seventeenth century, beginning in 1572 with the appearance of a "new star" in Cassiopeia which Tycho Brahe, on the basis of negative parallax, asserted to be *within* "the sphere of the fixed stars." A comet in 1577 was likewise shown to be *above* "the sphere of the moon" (for Ptolemy, comets were "occasional phenomena of the upper atmosphere").[8] In 1604 another "new star," in Serpentarius, gave Galileo the opportunity to confirm Tycho's conclusions. Galileo's observations of spots on the sun, of the satellites around Jupiter, and so on, soon followed (1612–1618), as did Kepler's studies of the "irregular" (noncircular) orbits of the planets.

However, as this experimental evidence gradually emerged, it was characteristically misinterpreted or rejected by an intellectual establishment accustomed to a medieval analysis of the nature of existence. The perfect immutability of the heavens was one essential element in the Christian anagogical concept of creation. For perceivers whose notion of the real was conditioned by the elaborately cohesive metaphysics of the previous age, this new evidence, even if accepted, implied only the imminent decay of the cosmos, both macrocosm and microcosm. Typical reactions wavered between despair and ridicule.

"The World is tossed in a blanket amongst them [the new astronomers]," Robert Burton complains, "they hoist the Earth up and down like a ball, make it stand and go at their pleasures."[9] In the same satiric vein, John Donne attacks the "new philosophy" which "calls all in doubt": "The element of fire is quite put out;/ The Sunne is lost, and th'earth, and no man's wit/ Can well direct him where to look for it."[10] Sir Walter Raleigh observes that "the heavens themselves . . . wax old as a garment. . . . "[11] And William Drummond, summarizing the "enormities" perpetrated by cosmic speculators, concludes: "Thus, Science by the diverse Motiones of this Globe of the Braine of Man, are become Opiniones, nay Errors, and leave the Imagination in a thousand Labyrinths."[12]

The collapse of a philosophical perspective as ancient and venerable as that of Ptolemaic cosmology was not likely, despite modern "hindsight," to inspire much contemporary confidence in the theories of "science." Milton, though he knew of it, chose to ignore "new philosophy" in constructing a universe for *Paradise Lost*. Hakewill, though he rejected the "decay of the cosmos," preferred to regard "new stars" (super novas) as miracles rather than concede the mutability of the heavens.[13] A general skepticism, accompanied by that "metaphysical shudder" so aptly described by George Williamson, was the dominant reaction. For Burton, Raleigh, Donne, even that famous physician Sir Thomas Browne, the "new science" was, temperamentally at least, a "bad dream," a fantastic development that led to the basic conviction that man's powers of reason had decayed, and thus that any new scheme was likely to be no more than "new kinds of error."[14] "It is this concept which illuminates the 'valley of dry bones' in seventeenth-century thought, and turns a feeling about the afternoon of time into the moral that it is too late to be ambitious," as Williamson observes.[15]

While the conservative philosophical climate of the Renaissance found the "new cosmology" fantastic, it failed utterly to see its own traditional literature in that light. Spenser's *Faerie Queene*, for example, was not perceived as fantastic, if that term denotes a reversal of expectations. Rather, it was recognized as traditional, its ambience perceived as that of a golden age of civil and moral values. It certainly was not regarded as "a medieval fantasy" of knights, dragons, magicians, and so on. What strikes a modern reader as fantastic wore then the cloak of easy familiarity. If a modern reader doubts this, he has only to compare the ambience of Spenser's fairyland to that of the hundreds of prose romances issued by the popular press, among them Sydney's *Arcadia*, Lodge's *Rosalind*, Greene's *Pandosto*, Lyly's *Euphues*. If such fictions failed to mirror common, "everyday" life, they nevertheless embodied the common notion of "proper subjects" for fiction. For the Renaissance reader, "realism" and "naturalism," had they existed, would have been perceived as alien literary stances; they are indeed products of a different "philosophical climate," one dominated by an "exactitude in representation" suggested or demanded by the model of the natural sciences.[16]

The difference in literary stances can be quickly illustrated by a comparison of two representative allegorical "dream visions," Bunyan's *Pilgrim's Progress* and Henry James's "Great Good Place." The first may represent the last important work securely based on a "late medieval" perspective. Like Spenser, Bunyan proceeds from the assumption that God himself is an allegorist and that creation is a "dark conceit" for the trial of man's wit and the edification of his soul. Bunyan's dreamer needs no veneer of realism, beyond the commonplace features of an earthly landscape, to compel belief. In each episode the recognition of *religious truth* is the compelling force—the narrative surface is the thinnest, most perfunctory pastiche of literary conventions. Thus, despite the appearance of devils, giants, dragons, and so on, the ambience of the narrative is sober, dry, didactic. One can hardly mistake the author's conviction that this "dream" reflects the highest nature of reality.

James, on the other hand, wrote during the most triumphant era of scientific pragmatism, and consequently his dream vision is masked in realistic detail—even the fact that the narrative represents a dream is hidden until the denouement. James's elaborate and lengthy exposition of the dreamer's circumstances is in sharp contract to Bunyan's perfunctory "I laid me down . . . and as I slept I dreamed a dream." The sources of images in the persona's dream are carefully indicated in

James's story, and they are all derived from the dreamer's real-world experience, whereas Bunyan's are plucked arbitrarily from Christian exegetical archetypes. Nevertheless, the net effect of James's story, despite the trappings of realism demanded by the "philosophical climate" of his age, verges on the fantastic. James's idyllic vision of a "spiritual perfection" is antithetical to the "realities" of his world, yet it is very nearly brought to a literal, rather than figurative, acceptance; in fact, the dream itself is so circumstantial that "hestitation" as to whether the episode is real or imagined may well occur. James's use of "realism" thus facilitates an approach to the fantastic, whereas Bunyan's perfunctory use of "fabulous" personae does not. The explanation of this anomaly lies in the change in "philosophical climate." James's "dream structure" opposes the norms of his time, whereas Bunyan's routinely reflects the most conventional expectations of his.

Of course, the "scientific" imperatives which led to the climate of "literary realism" characteristic of James's era had their roots in the Renaissance. There is no need, I hope, to trace the gradual undercutting of the old, established theological models of existence. The process began, in England at least, with Bacon's *Novum Organum*; Richard Hooker's *Laws of Ecclesiastical Polity* was probably the first of repeated efforts by theologians to accommodate an essentially antithetical world view. Yet what was gained in the victory of science seemed to be overbalanced, for many, by what was lost. Repeatedly and perhaps compulsively, particularly on the continent, the strictures of science concerning the nature of reality were in turn undercut, by authors who sought at least a momentary acceptance of the "supernatural," an element of the now vanquished world view. By contrast, the medieval churchman, whose celebration of the Mass was popularly conceived as holy magic and whose missal contained rites for the exorcism of devils and evil spirits, could hardly perceive the "supernatural" as fantastic. For the writer of the nineteenth century, however, the prevailing philosophical climate denied reality to these things. Their literary, and perhaps spiritual, significance still exerted an appeal, but open acceptance carried the risk of censure from a society which had (more or less) embraced "science." The result was a corpus of literature which exploited the sense of loss, the sense of something absent from the metaphysical model of reality. This corpus, for whatever reason, became almost the sole focus of Todorov's study. The naturalistic tale which leads the reader into an ambiguous encounter with ghosts, devils and so on—Kipling's "They" is a good, brief example which Todorov seems to have missed—provides him with a paradigm for that "hesita-

tion" between realistic and supernatural explanations which is for Todorov the hallmark of the fantastic.[17]

Todorov's own philosophical climate, however, is never ambiguous. The scientific model of research, which dominates his concept of
the sphere of literary analysis, shows most overtly in his refutation of
Northrop Frye. The untidiness of the latter's inductive, intuitive approach exasperates him. "If we seek structures on the level of the observable images, we thereby refuse all certain knowledge," he complains. Taxonomies "form the weakest possible hypothesis." Rather
than elegantly hypothetical, Frye's structures are *"reduced* to an ar-
rangement in space." Todorov's solid acclimation in the dominant
philosophical climate of the late nineteenth and early twentieth centuries leads him to see "the fantastic" as regressive, to seek its sources in
the pathologies of psychiatric medicine, and to explain "major themes"
of the genre in terms of infantilism, drug addiction, and schizophrenia.[18] In this procedure, he strikes a contemporary American critic as
somewhat anachronistic.[19]

Nevertheless, to the extent that scientific pragmatism still prevails
as a philosophical climate among writers and their readers in the twentieth century, it forms a continuing (though evolving) basis for assess-
ing either an assertion or a literary effect as fantastic. Unlike Todorov,
for whom the nineteenth century's preoccupation with the natural-su-
pernatural conflict dominated and subsumed the real-fantastic polarity,
Rabkin recognizes a wide variety of literary assaults upon what he calls
"the preconceptions of our armchair world." Partly through a wider
awareness of historical context, and less certainty regarding the parameters of the "natural" ("our preconceptions of the impossible are
assaulted every day"), Rabkin turns from the question of the reader's
belief or unbelief to investigate the "ground rules" of perception implied in a literary text (partly through a study of grapholect). When
prevailing perspectives in the narrative are directly contradicted, he
concludes, the fantastic is produced regardless of general belief or
unbelief in the possibility of the event at the time of the reading. Application of this principle, the reversal of perspective, allows him to
identify instances of the fantastic in satire, detective fiction, the horror
story, pornography, the utopia, science fiction, the folk tale, romance—
even in the structure of metaphor and of art itself. Rather than constituting a minor and defunct genre, as it did for Todorov, "the fantastic"
for Rabkin is a phenomenon which "has a place in any narrative genre,"
though it is "exhaustively central in the class of narratives we call fantasy." Rabkin's "philosophical climate" contains none of the apostolic

certainty in the validity of scientific models characteristic of Todorov's—
it is willing to entertain phenomenological relativism, Jungian psychology, gestalt theories and game theories, and the graphics of N. C.
Escher. Nevertheless, "we enter a narrative world with the preconceptions of our armchair world intact," and "one must . . . know the normative in order to properly locate the fantastic."[20] Rabkin's cosmos is,
in terms of innocent faith in the scientific model, post-Lapsarian and
thus strikingly modern compared with that of Todorov, yet its "normative" forestructures are still derived from the basic preconceptions of
scientific pragmatism.

What is missing in Rabkin's treatment of the real-fantastic polarity
is a clearly articulated basis for the assessment of the real. Metaphysical
assumptions are hardly discussed. In fact, the author obviously assumes, *a priori*, that his assessment of the nature of "the existent" is
essentially similar to that of others. And like most of those who share
his metaphysical stance, Rabkin sees the work of many existentialist or
absurdist authors as violating or inverting common rational expectations, and thus as fantastic. Eugène Ionesco's *Rhinoceros*, for instance,
a play in which "people become pachyderms," is one of Rabkin's examples of "the fantastic . . . in contemporary literature."[21] The testimony of these writers themselves, however, if taken at face value,
would indicate that this assessment is a misunderstanding, something
like that which might result from placing Ptolemy and Fred Hoyle in
the same observatory.

According to his own account (and that of many critics), Ionesco's
art is that of the primitive, that is, of the unschooled artist who attempts, without benefit of technique or influences from tradition and
genre, to represent his own world view. "I write to say how the world
appears to me," he tells us, "what it seems to me to be, as honestly as
I can. . . . Putting the characters I imagine on the stage—and for me
they are real . . . is something that happens naturally or not at all. . . .
It matters little to me whether the vision is or is not surrealist, naturalist,
expressionist, decadent, romantic, or socialist. It is enough for me to
think of it as perfectly realistic. . . ."[22] And yet these plays present
human beings who literally fall apart, corpses which grow to monstrous
size and burst, foot first, on stage, characters who fly, or metamor-
phose, or die giggling. Concerning his most often admired play, *The
Chairs*, Ionesco said:

> The subject of the play is not the message, nor the failures of life, nor
> the moral disaster of two old people, but the [empty] chairs themselves,

the absence of people, the absence of the emperor, the absence of God, the absence of matter, the unreality of the world, metaphysical emptiness. The theme of the play is nothingness. . . . Nothingness can be heard, is made concrete.[23]

Of course, these "concrete images" are in some sense metaphors—yet, if they are fantastic, it is only in the sense that all metaphor, as Rabkin suggests, may be fantastic. On the level of philosophical stance, these "metaphors" are an assessment of the real. If Ionesco's protestations are genuine, another shift in philosophical climate has occurred, undercutting the complacencies of the "scientific pragmatist"; for those who share Ionesco's pattern of interpretation, the stance of the "true perceiver" has radically altered: scientific pragmatism no longer functions; it has evolved into that image of meaningless physical materialism which has been so much discussed in mid-century literature and which has been generally characterized as devoid of relevance to, or meaningful connection with, human existence. For these perceivers, the "world" has no meaning at all—physical materialism neither suggests nor supports any system of values. Assertions of the absurdity of the human condition in such a universe are decidedly *not* fantastic to these perceivers. "I have never quite succeeded in getting used to existence," says Ionesco, "not a single thing ever seems to me stranger than another, for everything is evened out and blurred by the all-embracing strangeness and improbability of the universe. . . . The fact of existence is unthinkable."[24] For a second-generation existentialist, apparently, those forestructures which relate to the nature of reality are largely negative. Nevertheless, Ionesco's absurdist drama is meant to represent Being-in-the-world, a dramatic assessment of the way things are. Intentionally at least, it is realistic, not fantastic.

To the extent that the "alienation" of man from his cosmos represents the philosophical climate of this century, it in turn has been undercut, not merely as in the late nineteenth century, with a few concepts contrary to scientific pragmatism (as in Todorov's literature of "hesitation before the supernatural"), but also a deliberate reversal of polarities, by an attempt to recenter the world on human value patterns, moral as well as physical, even within a cosmos in which such concerns appear to be irrelevant. To redress "mainstream despair," many English and American fantasists have intuitively reached for an *organic* vision of coherence, for a fantasy world in which meaning and value are integral, demonstrable, implicit in the very fabric of things-as-perceived. Tolkien's Middle Earth and Ursula Le Guin's Earthsea are representative examples. In such fantasy worlds a recognition of the perceiver's part in ordering the world itself is at least implicit.

In Tolkien's cosmos, for instance, moral as well as physical laws have force and meaning—indeed, the two are roughly equivalent, as Randel Helms has shown.[25] The reader's recognition of this correspondence, however, is carefully manipulated in a phenomenological way, so that the coherence of Frodo's world is disclosed as any Being-in-such-a-world might perceive it, incrementally and implicitly. The basic "ground" of Tolkien's "world" is built up of familiar things (as he suggests it must be, in the essay on *Faerie*): "tree and bird, water and stone, wine and bread, and ourselves, mortal men."[26] The properties of the ring of power are revealed gradually, and revealed as negative: invisibility first denies the senses, then negates Being, coerces the will, attenuates vitality. The "force field" of terror which surrounds the depraved Nazgul may be experienced as a concrete instance of a moral-physical equation. In such an ethically responsive physical cosmos, the moral character of the individual is gradually perceived as crucial: a good intention coupled with a moral means produces a favorable result; an evil intention or a morally reprehensible means triggers the opposite: witness the destruction of Boromir. In Heidegger's terms, the physical cosmos, the "ground" on which these sentient creatures perceive, is charged with meaning, with personal significance. Thus the philosophical climate of the reader whose empathy is truly engaged in this narrative may be radically restructured. On the other hand, if the narrative is perceived as "pure fantasy," as a 180-degree turn away from "reality," according to Rabkin's rule, the basis for our assessment can be only the nihilistic existential philosophical climate which Ionesco represents.

Ironically, Ionesco's famous story, of how he first perceived "nothingness" while memorizing phrases from an English primer, is an unconscious parody of Heidegger's account of the *primacy of meaning* in perception. If all perception is "perception *as* something, " Heidegger says, to grasp something "free . . . of the *as*" is a deliberate act, "not more primordial, but derived" from the perception of meaning. "When we merely stare at something, our just-having-it-before-us lies before us as *a failure to understand it any more*."[27] A "ground" (the physical world which we interpret as perceivers) "becomes accessible *only as meaning*, even if it is itself the Abyss [*Abgrund*] of meaninglessness" (my italics).[28]

One who understands this perfectly is Ursula Le Guin. In the final volume of the Earthsea trilogy, *The Farthest Shore*, Heidegger's image

of the Abyss (*Abgrund*) becomes the central focus. The modern nihil-
ist's horrified fascination with "nothingness," the author implies, stems
emotionally from loss of that personal immortality promised by theological models of the world. Le Guin's world, Earthsea, itself a metaphor for the balance of nature, falls sick with despair; the will to life
and power of its denizens becomes paralyzed by a frustrated longing
for eternal life. Since names, on Earthsea, are the essence of knowledge
and since magic subsumes the functions of science and technology,
these arts are abandoned. The "Lord of the Shadows," who guards the
portal, demands a negation of worldly power as the price of entry into
immortality. "My power," cries Akaren, "kept me from life. So I lost
it. I lost all the things I knew, all the words and names."[29] Obsessed
with a desperate effort to elude death, the citizens of Earthsea abandon
life—industry collapses, crafts decay, famine and disease spread. *The
Farthest Shore* is in part a parodic attack upon the Christian "contemp-
tus mundi," a deliberate antithesis to Augustine's *City of God*, the one
book which, according to Gibbon, epitomized the greatest single de-
moralizing force upon the civic energies of the Roman world.

   Of course, the horror of death, the appeal of immortal life, are not
dismissed lightly; they are seen as compelling sources of frustration, of
paralysis of will. Arren, infected by Sopli, abandons Ged, spiritually
and physically; he can no longer see any point in action—either in
saving himself or the world. "I thought there was no use in doing anything," he confesses to Ged, "I was afraid of death. I was so afraid of
it I would not look at you, because you might be dying. I could think
of nothing, except that there was . . . a way of not dying for me, if I
could find it."[30] In a key episode, the pair are rescued by the Children
of the Open Sea, whose raft-city ("It was a town, and under its floors
was the abyss") becomes a metaphor for the human condition. Arren
finds the experience "like an after-life or a dream, unreal":

> It was because he knew in his heart that reality was empty: without life
> or warmth or color or sound: without meaning. . . . All this lovely play
> of form and color on the sea and in the eyes of men was no more than
> that: a playing of illusions on the shallow void.[31]

Arren's despair is like Ionesco's; Ged's perception of the vitality and
coherence of the same phenomena is undoubtedly Le Guin's. The difference is one of perspectives, determined by the forestructures applied
to the things perceived. "This *is*," Ged tells Arren, "and thou art. There
is no safety and there is no end. . . . The dance is always danced above
the hollow place, above the terrible abyss."[32]

Consider, Arren. To refuse death is to refuse life. . . . Nothing is immortal. But only to us is it given to know that we must die. And that is a great gift: The gift of selfhood. . . . Would you give up the craft of your hands, and the passion of your heart, and the light of sunrise and sunset, to buy safety for yourself? That is the message [you] have heard. . . . By denying life you may deny death and live forever! And this message I do not hear, for I will not hear it. I will not take the counsel of despair.[33]

Ged's final act is to "close the door" between life and death, to reassert the balance of opposites, to affirm the coherence of creation, of the joy and the power of the world-as-perceived. World and Abyss are equally perceivable, equally potent—yet neither perception necessarily denies the other.

The only genuine reason for the artist to accept an exclusively nihilistic philosophical climate, then, may well be temperamental. If perception of the simplest objects is impossible without those forestructures supplied in some sense by the perceiver, all observations are at least partly subjective. The phenomenological approach emphasized the element of truth in the old aphorism: "things are what you think they are." Even the most sacrosanct techniques of the scientific materialist cannot *eliminate* the essential complicity of the perceiver in defining, forming, characterizing the thing-as-perceived. The front ranks of modern physicists are close to accepting this view.

From the standpoint of the phenomenologist, then, the physical materialist might appear to be clinging, masochistically, to a series of outdated preconceptions, perpetuating a system of microjudgments which interpret reality in a form *alien* to his own humanity. The concern of *Dasein*, Being-in-the-world, toward perceiving a "world" essentially relevant to himself, may indeed be "unscientific," but how can it be proved wrong? How, indeed, can the humanist concerns of Tolkien's Middle Earth or Le Guin's Earthsea be dismissed as escapist, when the source of all meaning is rooted in man's perceptions? If all knowledge is thus rendered "relativistic," it is nevertheless centered in sentient Being. Perhaps it is only the *angst* of those philosophers who fear the loss of certainty worse than nineteenth-century churchmen feared the loss of God that accounts for the persistence of the scientific materialist point of view.

One man's "world," then, may be another man's fantasy. No doubt the difficulties of establishing a definition of fantasy-as-genre can be traced in large part to the problems of defining the real. I have tried here to suggest the relevance of philosophical climate in approaching such a definition. For the description of a "philosophical climate," I have used a phenomenological model, since that model emphasizes the intimate connection between perception and preexistent structures, forestructures, which condition our perception of the real. Since the perceiver's assessment of the fantastic apparently depends, inversely, on his perception of the real, no analysis which fails to allow for shifts in philosophical climates will endure. For many readers Todorov's narrow structuralist approach seemed dated even before it appeared. Meanwhile, if we remind ourselves of the vagaries of world views, remembering that Ptolemy's comets were ominous portents, that Luther's devils were "real" and threw inkpots, that miracles were the mainstay of respectable sainthood, that astrology was, for Renaissance schoolmen, more credible than Copernicus, that Milton chose Adam as epic hero because he was "more historical" than Arthur, and finally that the "scientific model" of the cosmos may one day seem as quaint as a medieval armillary, we will at least maintain a grasp of the problem.

JOHN GERLACH

The Logic of Wings: García Márquez, Todorov, and the Endless Resources of Fantasy

Is fantasy dependent on certain themes, and, if so, might these themes be exhausted? My own response to one story, Gabriel García Márquez's "Very Old Man with Enormous Wings," a story in which theme and the atmosphere of fantasy that emerges from the theme are, if anything, negatively correlated, leads me to suspect that fantasy is not closely tied to theme, so that fantasies may be created in any age, without reference to theme.

The story might best be described by starting at the end. At the conclusion, an old man flaps like a senile vulture away from the village where for years he has been held captive. The woman who has grudgingly taken care of him watches him open a furrow in the vegetable patch with his fingernails in his first attempt to rise. She sees him nearly knock down a shed with his "ungainly flapping." As he gains altitude and begins to disappear, she watches "until it was no longer possible for her to see him, because then he was no longer an annoyance in her life but an imaginary dot."[1] George McMurray, in his recent study of Gabriel García Márquez, focuses on this final image and concludes that for the reader (and the villagers) the story is a "cathartic destruction of antiquated myths."[2] My own reaction was quite different: I had the prescribed catharsis, but I came away with my taste for myth and the supernatural intact. I could see how McMurray arrived at his conclusion, because this particular Icarus, with his "few faded hairs left on his bald skull" and the air of a "drenched great-grandfather," would hardly seem to inspire wonder.[3] But I felt as if I had witnessed the beginning of a myth, not its end, and the story had evoked for me the sense of wonder and marvel that one associates with myth at its inception.

Whether the story is best designated as a myth or as a fantasy is another matter. Myths present "supernatural episodes as a means of interpreting natural events in an effort to make concrete and particular a special perception of man or a cosmic view," as *A Handbook to Literature* would have it.[4] The old man of García Márquez's story does not stimulate the villagers to interpret anything. He is dropped into their existence unexplained, and leaves unexplained, clarifying nothing. It would be more accurate to consider the work a fantasy on the grounds that the story deals, to use the handbook's terms again, with an "incredible and unreal character."[5] I will eventually apply a more contemporary definition of fantasy to the story, Todorov's definition, but for the moment I prefer to pursue further the consequences of McMurray's approach. His view implies that the subject of myth, or, as I will have it, fantasy, determines our reactions. If the text parodies a mythic subject, then the reader would appropriately respond, not with an elevated sense of wonder, but with amusement at the exposure of nonsense. Since the subject matter in García Márquez's story does not diminish my own appreciation of the marvelous, I am left to conclude either that McMurray has misread the text or that the effect of a fantasy is not dependent on the subject. I have concluded that both propositions are true. McMurray has misrepresented the text, and, even so, something other than theme or subject matter creates what the reader responds to in a fantasy. "A Very Old Man with Enormous Wings" can be used to show that, as Todorov has predicted, the manner of telling, not the matter, creates the fantasy.

McMurray's points should first be dealt with in more detail. His interpretation is brief, but his argument is easily extended. Part of García Márquez's strategy, as McMurray suggests, was undeniably to diminish the grandeur of this unearthly winged creature. Similes used to describe him do not even grant him human attributes: matched with the villagers who stood around his cage he looked "like a huge decrepit hen among fascinated chickens."[6] Later it is said that he tolerates a child's "ingenious infamies with the patience of a dog who had no illusions."[7] A complex simile, to be sure, for the narrator is saying not only that the old man is like a dog, but also that the dog with his patience and lack of illusions is like a human being. Nevertheless, the effect of the simile is to emphasize the analogy to an animal. The syntax of the sentence which reveals the old man's wings also diminishes rather than ennobles him. Pelayo, the man who found him, heard something moving and groaning in the courtyard that he had recently cleaned of crabs and the stench they left behind. Pelayo "had to go very close to see that it was an old man, a very old man, lying face down in the mud, who, in spite of his tremendous efforts, couldn't get up, impeded by his enormous wings."[8] The long sentence, with its hesitations that duplicate in the reader the efforts of the old man, relegates the marvel of his wings to the terminal subordinate clause. Rhetorical decisions such as these have just as much effect on us as the content. It would seem that both the language and the content are pushing the reader in the direction that McMurray has outlined. The supernatural is described as something ordinary or, even more precisely, foul and repellent.

McMurray's analysis can be extended further. The narrator's motive in telling the story would seem to be satiric rather than inspirational. The credulity of mankind and greed—Pelayo's wife begins to charge admission to see the old man—are apparently the narrator's targets. The church is too, for the attempts of ecclesiastical bureaucrats to discover through correspondence with the resident priest whether or not the winged creature is an angel are bogged down by their desire to find out "if the prisoner had a navel, if his dialect had any connection with Aramaic, how many times he could fit on the head of a pin, or whether he wasn't just a Norwegian with wings."[9] Furthermore, the narrator's exaggerated manner of description seems to undercut even further our response to the old man. When Pelayo and his wife Elisenda first speak to the old man, "he answered in an incomprehensible dialect with a strong sailor's voice."[10] What it is that makes the voice sound like that of a sailor is not questioned by the narrator, who simply mirrors what is presumably the illogic of Pelayo and Elisenda. The narrator's complicity in this fabrication extends beyond mirroring. He notes that Pelayo and Elisenda "skipped over the inconvenience of the wings and quite intelligently concluded that he was a lonely castaway."[11] Since wings are certainly more than an "inconvenience," and the logical processes of Pelayo and Elisenda are therefore something less than intelligent, we have a narrator who, instead of striving to establish the credibility of this supernatural creature, is emphasizing the credulity of the villagers.

Similes that demean, satire, playful logic—it would seem that García Márquez is not about to honor a myth. Yet none of these devices totally cancels out the mystery. The diminishing suggested by these devices does not represent all of the truth about the old man and his wings. However decrepit the old man is, he does renew himself. When he arrived he seemed close to death, and several years later a doctor listening to the old man's heart concludes that it is impossible for him to be alive; yet after his release from his cage and with the onset of sunny days, stiff feathers begin to grow on his wings. Although the narrator continues to denigrate, calling the new growth "scarecrow feathers" that look like "another misfortune of decrepitude,"[12] the feathers do allow the old man to fly away. Something about the old man is greater than the narrator's estimation of him.

Other devices that the narrator used to increase rather than decrease our respect for the old man also need to be considered. When compared to those around him the old man becomes the model of patience, trying the best he can to "get comfortable in his borrowed nest, befuddled by the hellish heat of the oil lamps and sacramental candles that had been placed along the wire."[13] He refuses to eat the mothballs that one of the villagers thinks is the "food prescribed for angels," and subsists on eggplant mush. If he is "befuddled," that term has ironic value, for it is those that regard him who are confused.

Contrast with what seems to be even the sanest of mortals is illustrative. Father Gonzaga is the figure presented by the narrator as the most sane. He is not, as his parishioners are, ready to make the old man the mayor of the world or a "five-star general in order to win all wars," nor does he want to put him out to stud to create "a race of winged wise men who could take charge of the universe."[14] Father Gonzaga "had been a robust woodcutter" and so by implication is more realistic. He soberly approaches the old man and says good morning in Latin. Father Gonzaga has "his first suspicion of an imposter" when he saw that the old man "did not understand the language of God or know how to greet His ministers," and it is at this point we realize that Father Gonzaga is the one who fails the test, not the old man. Father Gonzaga notices that "seen close up" the old man "was much too human," and so the priest warns his parishioners not to be taken in.[15] In the light of Father Gonzaga's response, the comment that the old man is "too human" is particularly telling. Gonzaga's rationalism obscures his realization that although the winged gentleman may not meet doctrinal specifications, he still is miraculous. What begins to emerge is an image of the old man as someone possibly more human and reasonable than members of the wingless species.

The winged man's humanity is underlined by a foil the narrator creates, a woman who has been changed into a spider. Her presence distracts the villagers, and they cease to pay attention to the old man. Her exhibit costs less, and unlike the old man, she talks about her affliction. Where the old man refused, she encourages responses, readily accepting meatballs tossed into her mouth. There is nothing ambiguous or submerged about our perception of her. The old man's wings were slowly revealed; we are told bluntly that this woman is "a frightful tarantula the size of a ram . . . with the head of a sad maiden."[16] Though the narrator does not exaggerate the catalogue of her strangeness, she is in fact more grotesque than the old man.

The narrator's description of the villagers' response to her is familiar: once again the logic of the villagers is suspect; the crowd regards her a spectacle full of "human truth," a "fearful lesson." The facts of the lesson, however, are these: a lightning bolt of brimstone changed her form because she had been dancing all night without her parents' permission. The narrator's indirect exposure of the triviality of what the crowd considers a basic truth alters our response to the old man. We begin to admire more his silence and even his diet.

The way the villagers treat him is ultimately the best clue to how we should regard him. They poke, they prod, and at one point they burn him with a branding iron. Up until this point pain itself has seemed unreal. Those with ailments who come to be cured have only the most fanciful of afflictions, such as that of an old man "who couldn't sleep because the noise of the stars disturbed him" and that of "a poor woman who since childhood had been counting her heartbeats and had run out of numbers." But the old man with wings responds with true pain, ranting in his "hermetic language," tears in his eyes, flapping his wings to create "a whirlwind of chicken dung and lunar dust."[17] The villagers take the old man as no more than a creature of fiction, hence not subject to pain. They may not see the old man's humanity, but the reader should.

What I hope is emerging is a more complete sense of the role of the narrator. His denigrations of the protagonist have been systematic but not exclusive. He distorts by alternately exaggerating and understating. What could be called the outer or secondary level of distortion is the product of the narrator's supposed sympathy with the viewpoint of the villagers. This level, whose function is basically satiric, leads the narrator to call wings "inconvenient" or to exaggerate the church's concern in terms of the medieval problem of calculating the number of angels on the head of a pin. The narrator takes the viewpoint of the villagers themselves, pretending to be alternately detached or supportive, but everywhere he exposes irrationality and superstition. Underneath this level, however, is another, an inner or primary level of distortion, which grows from one central fact—there is an old man with enormous wings. That conception embodies even in its grammatical form a paradox in the contrast between "old" and "enormous," for we would not expect anything so powerfully endowed to be so decrepit.

Beyond this paradox is a kind of simplicity and unarguable solidity. The nature of the wings themselves does not change; what changes is our perception of their naturalness. By the end of the story, a doctor examines the old man and is surprised by "the logic of his wings," and the reader is prepared for a similar realization. These wings, as the doctor puts it, seem "so natural on that completely human organism that he couldn't understand why other men didn't have them too."[18] This old man, with his muteness, his patience, is in some ways more human, more natural, and even more believable, than anyone else in the story. The secondary level of distortion playfully exposes human folly; the primary level by contrast defines more desirable human traits.

At this point it is appropriate to define the genre of the work more precisely. The definition will allow us to see how the two levels of distortion work together to create the effects we associate with fantasy. Within the last few years, several critics, in particular W. R. Irwin, Eric S. Rabkin, and Tzvetan Todorov, have attempted to describe fantasy as a genre.[19] Of the three, Todorov's analysis provides the most instructive standards to apply to García Márquez's story. The fit is not perfect; Todorov, I believe, concludes that "fantasy" narrowly defined is hardly being written anymore. But even the divergence between "A Very Old Man with Enormous Wings" and Todorov's principles is in itself enlightening.

Todorov assumes that, first, fantasies produce the effect of hesitation. The reader is never wholly sure whether he is confronting a supernatural event or something that can be rationally explained. If the reader is able to conclude the event is explicable solely on the supernatural level, the story belongs to another genre, the marvelous, and, if the reader chooses the rational explanation, the story falls into the genre of the "uncanny." Second, the reader usually participates in the story through the medium of a character who believes in reason and order, so that the reader experiences the hesitation through the character's eyes. Third, the reader must not be able to explain away the supernatural events by considering them allegorical or poetic. In this case the reader would conclude that the supernatural is merely a shorthand for an idea, hence not to be taken literally. One of the clues to allegory is that no one in the story takes an aberration to be unusual, and so there is no sense of hesitation.

In the case of the García Márquez story, it is simpler to deal with the second point first. There is no character recounting for us his experiences. There is an implied narrator, and this narrator is a direct inversion of the sort of character that Todorov has posited. This is no rational human, but a creator of exaggerations. The hesitation that To- dorov speaks of as his first point, then, derives in this story not from the doubts of a character, but from our doubts about what the narrator is saying. Todorov's analysis allows us to see the ingenuity of what García Márquez has done. García Márquez has taken what would nor- mally be the index of normality, the village folk, and made them the greatest of exaggerators. The unreal character, in contrast, begins to appear normal and harmless. García Márquez has managed to make his central contrary-to-fact situation, the old man with wings (what I have been calling the primary level of distortion), seems altogether more rational and ordinary than the villagers. Those who follow Rabkin's definition of fantasy should be pleased, for the effect that I have de- scribed is replete with what Rabkin calls 180-degree turns in perspec- tive, the undermining of established expectations. As for the matter of allegory, it is possible that the wings themselves might be taken as allegorical evidence of the true dignity of man. What prevents us from taking the wings as allegory is the very insistence on the decrepitude of the old man, and elaboration of the reality of the wings, the "stellar parasites" in them. In the same way, the characters both are and are not taking the old man as unusual, so that the wings both are and are not allegorical. It is not that García Márquez is making hash of Todorov's categories. What he is doing by his exaggerations is creating the max- imum doubt and hesitation about not only the supernatural but the natu- ral as well.

We should now be able to reconsider some of the questions origi- nally raised by McMurray's interpretation. Although it might be pos- sible to contend that McMurray's reading of the text failed to take into account the double role of the narrator and the two levels of distortion, and hence he did not see the extent to which García Márquez has shifted our sympathies toward the old man and located the antiquated, ex- hausted view in the perception of the villagers, such a view does not fully account for the energy of the story. Arriving at the truth of the story and feeling its impact do not automatically result from peeling off the secondary layer of distortion and getting at the primary. It is not possible to take either level as the ultimate truth. The positive values may seem to be vested in the primary level, for García Márquez has made muteness and patience seem truly supernatural virtues, and by implication exaggeration the expression of human fallibility. But the center of the story is still an exaggeration. Men do not have wings. The process of distortion itself is the vehicle of our approach to the story. The very act of reading and interpreting the story rests not on muteness

and patience, but on the appreciation of exaggeration. In reading the
story the reader does not respond only to the truth of a particular idea,
in the case of this story, for instance, the idea that there is an indestruc-
tible, winged aspect of man that can fly despite its own aging or the
lack of appreciation from ordinary men. The story is a whole, not a set
of levels, and what causes the reader to respond, in the terms that Todorov has established, is the reader's hesitation over what is real.

This hesitation is built up from the minutest details, as can be
shown in one isolated segment, the ending. Even slight distortions in
lauguage are significant. The concluding phrase states that the old man
"was no longer an annoyance in [Elisenda's] life but an imaginary dot
on the horizon of the sea."[20] The antithesis of "annoyance" and "dot,"
contrasting an abstraction with something at least barely visible, might
make us grammatically uncomfortable, but the mismatch reproduces
the quality of the story itself. It is as if there were a rather easy flow
between our feelings and the things we find about us, so that a thought
might suddenly take a substance as real as our own, or just as suddenly
disappear. The energy created by unusual phrases works in the same
way. The idea of modifying "dot" by the adjective "imaginary" is plausible in that the dot may be so small that it is nearly imaginary, but the
conjunction of the two terms is also implausible; it has something of
the force of an oxymoron, for Elisenda is simultaneously seeing and
merely imagining. "Imaginary" is also apt in that the old man is by our
standards rightly considered imaginary. Structurally the close is effective because it complements the opening—the character was visually
constructed piece by piece for us, and now visually recedes into nothingness. Viewed from one perspective, humankind is relieved of a burden. Viewed from another, a creature more perfect, more logical than
man has achieved his freedom. The fact that the old man has escaped
from the perspective of the characters means to the characters that he
does not exist, he may be ignored. But we have seen him endure over
a period of time and can imagine him perhaps going back to whatever
imaginary place it is that he lives in, one that has as much validity to it
as this imaginary town into which he has fallen.

The cluster of possibilities here matches the possibilities advanced
in the rest of the story. Clusters such as this give the story its power and
create the effects we identify with fantasy; the clusters work much the
same way as the hesitation over the natural and the supernatural. Because the effect of the story, the sense in which it is a fantasy, is created
by the treatment, not by the subject or theme, the number of fantasies
that can still be written should be endless. At one time myths may have

been man's way of imagining the unimaginable, but now, even though literal mythmaking is no longer used to explain the world around us, the sense of wonder that myth brings with it need not in consequence be abandoned. It does not matter that we cannot take the fanciful as literally as man might once have, nor does it matter that the subject of a myth is decrepit, toothless, and featherless. The sense of wonder that a myth or a fantasy evokes inheres not in the subject, but in the telling. Fantasy is more the how than the what.

Put in terms of Todorov's discussion, fantasy is created initially by something significantly contrary to the ordinary. The task of the reader is to naturalize, to recuperate, that is, to make intelligible, this break from the norms of the reader's experience. The most significant thing about the genre is that the break should not readily be bridged; the circuits must be kept open as long as possible. In Todorov's words, the hesitation must continue. What the reader ends up recuperating is ultimately the process, the broken circuit itself. It is not what the break is about, it is that there *is* a continuous break that makes a fantasy. Since fantasy is a process, not a result, its resources are endless, and it is in no way dependent on the fashion of the conventions it adapts.

The final matter to consider is the effect of parody in the genre. Does the parody of a myth or fantasy make the story a last gasp, as the Russian formalists have asserted in other cases, of a genre that is about to expire or assume a new form? I think not. Parody is not central to this story. The mention of stellar bugs and scratchings is only a way for the narrator to make the mystery of the old man more, not less, incredible. There are parodic elements, but this is not a parody as such. What one ultimately grasps in a fantasy is the potential of language to construct a world partly, but not wholly, like our own. Fantasy is the logical extension, the wings, of language itself. Literature in general and fantasy in particular are the magic which our customary language so dimly represents.

DAVID KETTERER

Power Fantasy in the "Science Fiction" of Mark Twain

I

There is a parallel world, or so Norman Spinrad affirms, where Adolf Hitler is an acclaimed Hugo–award-winning author of science fiction.[1] Actually, Hitler's work is closer to "sword and sorcery," a brand of "heroic fantasy," than to science fiction proper. The novel for which Hitler won his Hugo, *Lord of the Swastika*, presented in Spinrad's *Iron Dream*, tells of the struggle between a party of genetically pure humans, led by the mighty-thewed, blond-haired, blue-eyed Feric Jagger, and the mutant hordes. After an atomic war Jagger rules over a fascist state. The Hitler we know did not have to content himself with such power fantasies; thanks to a set of circumstances obtaining in Spinrad's world, but not in our parallel one, he was able to actualize them.

The question arises: if the historical events of our world can become the subject of a fantasy novel in another which in most respects is like our own, where does that leave the distinction between fantasy and reality? Or should one conclude that there are fantasies and there are fantasies, some realizable and therefore in a sense concordant with reality and some not? A person might, for example, fantasize about being a bird and soaring freely above the ground. Such a transformation might well be met with in a work generically identified as a fantasy. On the other hand, a person may entertain a variety of sexual fantasies and then go out and indulge them. Correspondingly, such realized fantasies may well figure in the plots of what many people would agree to call examples of realistic literature.

On this scale of psychological fantasies, most power fantasies would be closer to most sexual fantasies than to most fantasies of becoming a bird. Which is to say that, although Hitler's *Lord of the Swastika* is closer to what many people would generically identify as fantasy rather than science fiction, the psychological fantasy which gives rise to Hitler's career might equally determine the subject matter of a realistic novel, or indeed a work of science fiction.

In fact, the theme of power fantasy (and here I use the word "theme" for its convenience rather than for its precise appropriateness) is far more prevalent in science fiction, especially American science fiction, than in fantasy. I am thinking of all those stories in which one man saves the world, solar system, galaxy, or universe, or one man manipulates the events of a world, solar system, galaxy, or universe. In addition, of course, much science fiction is concerned with the power of technology whereby the power of an individual man is anthropomorphically magnified. Worlds are blown up, rockets thrust themselves into the void, thanks to the existence of nuclear and other forms of power. Thus, although power fantasies may be expressed in terms of the characteristic plot furniture of fantasy, they would appear to be more at home with the characteristic plot furniture of science fiction.

The forms of power fantasy that I have mentioned so far go a long way toward explaining why science fiction has, until relatively recently, been considered a predominantly male preserve. But not all manifestations of the power fantasy theme in science fiction—or in fantasy—are stereotypically masculine in character. Fantasies of physical power may overshadow the various fantasies of mental power, but stories featuring evolved intelligences, ESP, and such psychic powers as telepathy and telekinesis are certainly not uncommon. All told, then, science fiction is so permeated with power fantasies of one kind or another that we might almost be talking about a generic characteristic.

We are not, however, talking about an exclusive characteristic. Clearly, the knotty problem of distinguishing between science fiction and fantasy is further complicated by the evidence that the theme or appeal of power fantasy may be identified in both genres. This confusion is conveniently epitomized in some of the work of Mark Twain, work that I have chosen to identify as "science fiction" in quotation marks. There seems to be little agreement about Mark Twain's importance as a science fiction writer, if he is one at all. He does not merit a single reference in Brian Aldiss's history of the genre, *Billion Year Spree*; and he is also conspicuously absent from Neil Barron's bibliography, *Anatomy of Wonder*.[2] On the other hand, in the course of a ten-page appraisal, Darko Suvin affirms that, had certain "fragmentary sketches . . . been completed and published, he would have beyond a doubt stood instead of Wells as the major turning point in the tradition leading to modern SF and instead of Stapledon as the inventor of fictional historiography."[3]

There would seem, then, to be a complete spectrum of possibilities in rating Mark Twain as a science fiction writer. At one extreme he is not a science fiction writer at all; at the other he is comparable to Wells and Stapledon. It seems necessary to confront (yet again, it may be objected) the question, begged thus far, of definition: what is science fiction? The term "scientifiction" was coined by Hugo Gernsback in 1926 and, by way of explanation, applied retrospectively to the work of Verne, Wells, and, less convincingly, Poe.[4] Some years ago now, C S. Lewis pointed out that science fiction is not a "homogeneous genre." It is, therefore, as Robert M. Philmus claims, a "heterogeneous genre," or is a heterogeneous genre a contradiction in terms?[5] There is no question that an element of heterogeneity characterizes Mark Twain's "science fiction." A genre, it must be recognized, can never be a watertight compartment—all combinations are permissible. Any generic labeling must depend on matters of emphasis.

In terms of emphasis, distinctions can be theoretically drawn on the basis of the credibility quotient obtaining in the relationship between a fictional world (understood literally) and the world of consensus reality. The literary world will, in different respects, be either like or unlike the world of human experience. If it is radically unlike the known world, the reader is faced with the alternatives of viewing the imagined other world in a manner akin to either revelation or make-believe (often of a nostalgic "once upon a time" kind). What we are dealing with here is a reading convention signaled by the author. Details in a text or relating to a text will signal which of the three possible relationships is most appropriate to an appreciative reading. The mere appending of the label "science fiction" to the title of a novel directs a reader that he or she should take whatever events, beings, places, or states described therein as belonging to that vast area which, in relation to the world of consensus reality, is designated quite simply the unknown. In many respects we clearly do not know what the world will be like in five years' time, just as we do not know whether life exists on other planets. By and large (although this may be changing), science fiction restricts itself to the physically unknown. Another form of writing, often described as visionary, concerns itself with unknown spiritual or metaphysical realities.[6]

The label "fantasy" tells a reader that the literary world concerned is to be viewed as a self-contained universe, realistic on its own terms but discontinuous with the known universe. In relation to the known universe and on a literal level, it belongs not to the unknown but to the unreal (insofar as these terms are conventionally understood). The relationship that does exist between a fantasy and the known world often depends on an act of allegorical translation, and the "message" that results will characteristically have something to do with human psychology and morality. It might appear to follow from this that any attempt to combine the magical or fairy tale elements of fantasy with the scientific or logical elements of science fiction is misguided and can only lead to incoherence. But such is not always the case. The intrusion of the fantastic into what appears to be a science fiction text or a naturalistic text often simply alters the function of the fantastic material. Instead of being encouraged to think about questions of psychology and morality, the reader is being encouraged to consider matters of epistemology: how do we know what we think we know about the nature of reality and how do we know what we think we know is accurate? It is the function of epistemology to relate any debate about the "real" and the "unreal" to the relationship between the known and the unknown.

Mark Twain, as will become apparent, is very much concerned with questions of epistemology. Consequently, although elements of science fiction and fantasy mingle freely in much of the work discussed below, there is, I would argue, in each case a distinct science fictional feel. However, there is some room for doubt and argument. Thus my references, in qualifying quotation marks, to the "science fiction" of Mark Twain provide for a necessary fluidity, a saving imprecision.

2

The problem of distinguishing Mark Twain's "science fiction" is clearly at one with the problem of distinguishing science fiction from fantasy. And if the blurring between science fiction and fantasy is in part attributable to the presence of hypothetically realizable power fantasies in both genres, nowhere is the blurring more apparent than in the power-fantasy–oriented "science fiction" of Mark Twain. Indeed, Mark Twain should be credited with originating the "theme" of power fantasy in science fiction. This claim rests, of course, largely on *A Connecticut Yankee in King Arthur's Court* (1889). In the feudal context of Arthurian England, Hank Morgan is able, more or less single-handedly, to revolutionize society thanks to his knowledge of nineteenth-century technology. The species of power-fantasy science fiction to which *A Connecticut Yankee* has given rise is predominantly American, and thus it is appropriate that L. Sprague de Camp—the author of *Lest Darkness Fall* (1939), a work which derives quite directly from *A Connecticut Yankee*—is himself an American. De Camp's hero, a modern archaeologist, travels back in time to ancient Rome where, thanks to his twentieth-century knowledge, he is able to prevent the collapse of civilization.

Any figure who exercises extraordinary power is obviously akin to the concept of the superman in science fiction. Frequently, such supermen, whether aliens or the product of evolution, or both, display astounding psychic powers. Mark Twain's intense interest in such matters is well documented. Two essays, "Mental Telegraphy" (1891) and "Mental Telegraphy Again" (1895) describe cases, some arising out of Mark Twain's own experience, of what we would today call "telepathy." This concern with extrasensory phenomena extended to a fascination with spiritualism, and, indeed, Mark Twain was a member of the British Society for Psychical Research from 1884 to 1907.[7]

The psychic ability to overcome the physical barriers of time and space bespeaks, of course, a desire for transcendence and thus there is good reason to ally the superman concept in science fiction with what Paul Baender calls the "transcendent figure" in Mark Twain's work.[8] Baender's "transcendent figure," epitomized by the Mysterious Stranger of the Mysterious Stranger manuscripts, turns up out of the blue and blows the minds of those with whom he comes into contact. From Hank Morgan to the stranger who corrupted Hadleyburg, to the Mysterious Stranger, this character gains in power and mystery. A couple of earlier instances of the type, admittedly somewhat less transcendent and less powerful, take to arriving quite literally out of the blue by balloon.

A notebook entry for 1868 indicates that, like Edgar Allan Poe, Mark Twain was interested in the possibility of crossing the Atlantic by balloon. (Clemens himself had made a balloon ascension in the late 1870s).[9] It is the distance involved, rather than the business of balloon travel itself, that places speculations like Poe's "The Balloon Hoax" in the general area of science fiction. In his notebook Mark Twain began a story about a frenchman's balloon journey from Paris to a prairie in Illinois, but left it unfinished because of the American publication (1869) of Jules Verne's *Five Weeks in a Balloon*. Since one of Mark Twain's mysterious strangers is involved, the piece might well be entitled "The Mysterious Balloonist." Mark Twain returned to the topic of transatlantic balloon travel in an unpublished manuscript written in 1876 entitled "A Murder, a Mystery, and a Marriage." In this case a Frenchman named Jean Mercier, having tipped his employer Jules Verne out of a balloon, drifts from France to America, where he becomes involved in the small-minded affairs of the people of Deer Lick, a remote village in Missouri.

"A Murder, a Mystery, and a Marriage" was written as Mark

Twain's contribution to a plan concocted by himself and William Dean Howells. Twelve authors were independently to write stories based on the same plot. The overall plan was never realized, but Mark Twain submitted his contribution to the *Atlantic Monthly*, only to have it rejected.[10] Years after Mark Twain's death, the manuscript was sold in 1945 to Lew D. Feldman and Allan Hyman, who arranged to have sixteen copies privately printed by Manuscript House. When the slim volume appeared in the same year, the trustees for the Mark Twain estate took the publishers to court for breach of copyright and won. As a result, "A Murder, a Mystery, and a Marriage" remains essentially unread and unknown to this day and presumably will remain so until such time as it appears in a volume of the University of California edition of the Mark Twain Papers.

While it would be grossly inaccurate to classify "A Murder, a Mystery, and a Marriage" as science fiction, the piece does illustrate what may be understood as an ironic, or at least uncomfortable, relationship between the tall tale and science fiction. Verne's science fiction novels, it is claimed, are actually tall tales, grossly exaggerated accounts of the mundane exploits which Verne supposedly employed Mercier to undergo. But the marvelous balloon voyage in Mark Twain's story is presumably true, that is to say, a genuine science fiction element. Mark Twain is making extrapolated use of one of those marvels of communication ("railways, steamboats, telegraphs and newspapers") which the insular inhabitants of Deer Lick exclude from their awareness as equivalent to "the concerns of the moon."[11] For them it is part of science fictional world.

Their limited horizons find an analogue in the money-grubbing, mean-spiritedness of the Gray brothers. Clearly, this tale belongs in the enclosed-world tradition of Johnson's *Rasselas*, Poe's "The Devil in the Belfry" and Wells's "The Country of the Blind." Like the French devil in Poe's tale, the French outsider in Mark Twain's story serves to awaken the villagers to the extraordinary nature of the reality beyond their narrowly circumscribed environment. He is the bearer of a broader and truer reality which will destroy their village world—the realm of the imagination (which perhaps the lovers to some degree symbolize) will eclipse the dull, factual world. The murder of David Gray by the French balloonist may be understood as symbolically analogous to the destruction of a limited reality. The "apocalyptic" structure which may thus be symbolically teased out of "A Murder, a Mystery, and a Marriage" corresponds to what I have elsewhere argued is the structure of science fiction.[12] Furthermore, read in this admittedly oblique way, the rather incongruous events which constitute the story do make a logical kind of sense.

But, even at this early stage of his career, Mark Twain's faith in the possibility of expansive bright worlds was fainthearted. For one thing he fears being duped by a tall tale, as no doubt do the villagers. Yet at the same time he wants to put himself beyond the boundaries of Deer Lick, Missouri, because it is the inhabitants of such places who are most susceptible to being taken in by tall tales (for example, they accept Mercier's fictional identity and the amateurishly fabricated evidence incriminating the man wrongly arrested for David Gray's murder). Consequently, Jules Verne, one of the early masters of science fiction, is treated in a peculiarly ambiguous fashion. On the one hand, he is exposed and seemingly attacked as a charlatan; on the other hand, Mark Twain's story vindicates Verne's speculation about balloon travel. True, Mark Twain damns Verne to hell, but the revelation which it is projected Verne will publish as "Eighteen Months in a Furnace" might well correspond to the Satanic gospel espoused by Mark Twain in his Mysterious Stranger manuscripts. And, of course, Jean Mercier is a type of the Mysterious Stranger.

3

It will be observed that, in both "A Murder, a Mystery, and a Marriage" and the Mysterious Stranger manuscripts, the power of the transcendent superman brings about the destruction of a known reality. The same correlation is apparent in *A Connecticut Yankee*. Some critics have felt that the destructively apocalyptic Battle of the Sand-Belt, with which the novel concludes, is out of key with its opening chapters and testifies to a change of direction in Mark Twain's conception of the plot.[13] However, notebook evidence indicates that he projected something like the Battle of the Sand-Belt when first roughing out his ideas for the book.[14] This evidence in fact bears out the conclusion that may be intuited from the way his other power-fantasy figures operate: the kind of total control that the fulfillment of a power fantasy necessitates manifests itself in some kind of reality, world or universal destruction.

The attempt to undermine, if not destroy, reality is not, however, dependent on the presence of the Mysterious stranger figure. There are other strategies, including that of the hoax with which Mark Twain's "science fiction" career began. Apparently, Mark Twain intended "Petrified Man," a piece published in the *Territorial Enterprise* for 5 October 1962, to satirize a mania for cases of natural petrification. However, the piece was taken at face value and reproduced in newspapers across America, readers having failed to realize the fact, or the implications of the fact, that the complicated posture, maintained for almost a century, of the human statue, so minutely described, is that of a figure thumbing its nose. Mark Twain includes an incidental "scientific" reference to the role which a deposit of limestone sediment, caused by dripping water, has played in anchoring the petrified man to the spot.

The perpetration of a successful hoax must always have the side effect of casting doubt upon the parameters of an accepted reality. If something incredible can be taken as factual, perhaps the factual world is actually a lie—perhaps, as No. Forty-four, the final version of the Mysterious Stranger, claims, the world and the universe itself is a hoax, an illusion, a dream. In other words, reality is a fantasy, and once again we come up against the difficulty of clearly distinguishing between the terms "fantasy," "science fiction" and "realism." For the moment, however, it should simply be observed that there is a logical development in the progression from the "Petrified Man" hoax to the solipsistic power fantasy embodied by No. Forty-four. Here as elsewhere it should be observed that the notion of power fantasy frequently transforms itself into a sense of the power of fantasy.

A conventional understanding of reality and human freedom can also be radically undermined, if not destroyed, by a rigorous application of the kind of deterministic philosophy to which Mark Twain was clearly drawn. In this context and in any consideration of Mark Twain as a science fiction writer, some attention should be paid to the Mysterious Stranger manuscripts. This is not to say that these materials should be classified as science fiction. I should prefer to locate them in the broad category of "apocalyptic" literature. But science fictional elements abound in these writings. In the "Eseldorf" (Bernard DeVoto's suggested title) manuscript (written between 1897 and 1898)—which constitutes all but the last few pages of the fraudulent, composite text, produced by Albert Bigelow Paine and his editor Frederick A. Duneka—the disquisition on determinism includes material which Jan Pinkerton has related to the parallel-world–alternative-universe class of science fiction.[15] Representative titles would be Ward Moore's *Bring the Jubilee* (1953), in which the South wins the Civil War, and Philip K. Dick's *Man in the High Castle* (1962), in which the Nazis win World War II. Inspired perhaps by an episode in Voltaire's *Zadig* (1748), Young Satan demonstrates how the course of events can be altered by very small changes in the chain of causality. For example:

If at any time—say in boyhood—Columbus had skipped the triflingest little link in the chain of acts projected and made inevitable by his first childish act, it would have changed his whole subsequent life and he would have become a priest and died obscure in an Italian village, and America would not have been discovered for two centuries afterward. I know this. To skip any one of the billion acts in Columbus' chain would have wholly changed his life. I have examined his billion of possible careers, and in only one of them occurs the discovery of America.[16]

Philip José Farmer has recounted one of those billion-less-one careers in "Sail On, Sail On" (1952). The leap from *A Connecticut Yankee* to this kind of speculation is, of course, relatively obvious. What would have happened to the course of English history if Hank had won the Battle of the Sand-Belt?

However playful, the assertion that reality is a hoax and the contradictory conception of a deterministic set of parallel worlds are both means of destroying reality as commonly understood and, as such, are both expressions of a kind of power fantasy. The same point should be made concerning Mark Twain's exploration of the microscopic-world concept in two important but unfinished works of science fiction. "The Great Dark" (DeVoto's title), written in 1898 but not published until 1962, is about an apocalyptic voyage in a drop of water. In "Three Thousand Years among the Microbes," written in 1905 but not published until 1967, the narrator, reduced to microscopic size by a wizard, inhabits the world-body constituted by a diseased tramp. It is implied that the universe we inhabit is actually God's diseased body. The idea for this tale appears to go back to a notebook entry written on 12 August 1884: "I think we are only the microscopic trichina concealed in the blood of some vast creatures veins, & it is that vast creature whom God concerns himself about, & not us."[17]

In all four of the plot formulations that I have described, the notion of apocalyptic destruction is concordant with a conceptual breakthrough. In other words, it is the power fantasy of superior knowledge—the primary attribute exhibited by Mark Twain's transcendent supermen—that manifests itself in the ability to destroy worlds. However, the variety of differing and inconsistent conceptual breakthroughs that Mark Twain entertained suggests that he was much less interested in the truth content of his new realities than he was in simply destroying an old reality with which he was too familiar. This predisposition is, of course, most strongly expressed by the idea that reality is per se a hoax or an illusion. Such a conception, as the "No. 44" Mysterious Stranger manuscript demonstrates, has the advantage of replacing conventional reality with nothing at all except the wandering, vagrant thought of its creator. Ultimately, the theme of power fantasy manifests itself as solipsism. Interestingly enough, the route from power fantasy to solipsism, from Hank Morgan to No. Forty-four in Mark Twain's work, has been retrod by (among others) the man known as the dean of contemporary American science fiction, Robert Heinlein.[18]

4

The account that I have presented thus far is complicated by two additional factors. In the first place, there appears to be one exception to my assertion that Mark Twain was drawn more to the power fantasy of destroying reality than he was to establishing a new reality of his own. "The Secret History of Eddypus, the World-Empire" (written between 1901 and 1902) describes a future dystopian world under the control of Mary Baker Eddy's Christian Science. All documentation in support of, or providing evidence of, an alternative or previous state of affairs has been destroyed. However, some of the writings of someone known to a subversive group as the Father of History have escaped this purge. Two texts in particular—"Old Comrades" and "The Gospel of Self"— have enabled the dissident group to arrive at something approximating a true conception of history opposed to the official Christian Science version. The Father of History is, of course, Mark Twain. "Old Comrades" corresponds to Mark Twain's autobiography; "The Gospel of Self," to *What Is Man?* (which Mark Twain wrote between 1898 and 1905 and published anonymously in 1906). Clearly, in "Eddypus" Mark Twain is indirectly indulging the power fantasy that a new order founded on his autobiographical writings and deterministic gospel will displace and destroy that founded on Mary Baker Eddy's gospel.

Mark Twain was a widely known and widely read figure in his time (as now) and to that extent he was indeed a powerful figure. He did confer with presidents and kings. He was also, from time to time, a wealthy man. It seems reasonable to conclude that the power fantasy incorporated in the "Eddypus" manuscript, no less than the power fantasy embodied in Hitler's *Lord of the Swastika*, does not belong altogether to the realm of the impossible.

So far I have explained the transcendent figure-world destruction equation in Mark Twain's "science fiction" as an expression of the power fantasy of superior knowledge whereby the unknown is made known. This aspect of Mark Twain's work, however, may be explained in totally different, indeed contradictory, terms—hence my second complicating factor. Concordant with Mark Twain's sense of his own power in the world was an anxiously acute sense of his own responsibility. When things turned out badly—when he lost his fortune, when his favorite daughter, Susy, died, when his beloved wife Olivia became ill and died—Clemens, as the god of his own universe, could not help but feel responsible. In some sense he was ultimately to blame. If, however, he was not the powerful figure he sometimes took himself to be, if, on the other hand, he was totally powerless, then how could he possibly be held responsible for anything?

Bernard DeVoto has speculated that at least two instances of what I have discussed as examples of Mark Twain's conceptual breakthrough, world-destroying power fantasies, may in fact serve the contrary fantasy of powerlessness.[19] If reality is indeed a dream, then nothing matters, and if nothing matters there need be no sense of responsibility. Equally, if the contradictory hypothesis is true, if everything is in fact determined, again any sense of personal responsibility is quite redundant.

The fantasy of power, of total responsibility, may then go hand in hand with a fantasy of powerlessness, of total nonresponsibility. Correspondingly, the fact of power may go hand in hand with the fantasy of powerlessness. We have here the makings of an answer to the conundrum with which I began. Why is it that the theme of power fantasy finds expression in works of outright fantasy, in works of science fiction, and in works of realism?

The presence of the power-powerlessness fantasy theme in certain examples of Mark Twain's work goes some way toward explaining their generic indefiniteness: are they instances of science fiction or of fantasy? There is a similar problem with Heinlein's *Stranger in a Strange Land* (1961), which centers on the messianic, "transcendent" Martian superman, Valentine Smith. Power fantasy in science fiction is totally responsible, in a literal cognitive sense, to and for reality. Power fantasy in fantasy bears no such responsibility. It provides, indeed, a sublimative escape from responsibility. In the event that the reality described or implied is of a solipsistic nature, that reality may be viewed as factual or delusional. If it is viewed as delusional, the work concerned will tend toward fantasy rather than toward science fiction. We are dealing here, once again, with the epistemological emphasis of science fiction as against the moral-psychological emphasis of fantasy. Any talk of the distinction between the two genres should be couched in something approaching these alternative emphases. The theme of power fantasy is but one instance of the general fact that the attempt to distinguish between science fiction themes and fantasy themes simply will not serve.

GEORGE R. GUFFEY

The Unconscious, Fantasy, and Science Fiction: Transformations in Bradbury's *Martian Chronicles* and Lem's *Solaris*

[A writer] floats on the heavenly lake; he steeps himself in the nether spring. Thereupon, submerged words squirm up, as when a flashing fish, hook in its gills, leaps from water's depth.

Lu Ki, *Wen-fu*

A writer psychoanalyzes himself, not with a psychiatrist, but with tens of thousands, hundreds of thousands, or maybe millions of readers.

Larry Niven, *Science Fiction Voices #2*

Those of us who come to fantasy and science fiction after years of studying the poetry and prose of the earliest periods of English and American history do so with considerable delight. We are delighted, first, because a substantial amount of the fantasy and science fiction published since 1950 is quality literature. We are delighted, second, because of the rich research opportunities the field offers.

Shivering and squinting in dark, dank cubicles, we in the past studied the crabbed, ambiguous handwriting of minor church functionaries, hoping thereby to settle longstanding arguments about the birthplaces and birthtimes of literary figures of major and minor importance. Similarly, we laboriously collated faded manuscripts of doubtful authority against multiple copies of badly printed folios, quartos, and duodecimos, with the modest hope of learning something, no matter how little, about the creative imagination of Shakespeare, Dryden, or even Traherne. As we went about our scholarly tasks, we now and then pictured in our mind's eyes the relative affluence of colleagues who had chosen to specialize in more modern periods. Surrounded by holograph manuscripts, galley proofs, personal letters, and taped interviews, those happy devils, in our imaginations, clucked and chortled to themselves as their typewriters rattled away.

Although on the whole exaggerated, that picture of modern scholarly affluence does contain a significant amount of truth. Our age, unlike the Middle Ages or the Renaissance, not only places a high premium on the works of the individual writer, but also attempts in general to preserve as much of his personal history as possible. Many modern authors are, of course, uncomfortable about the dogged attention paid to their lives and therefore cover their tracks whenever and wherever possible. They destroy their juvenilia, refuse interviews, and go to great lengths to avoid personal contact with the reading public. To the delight of critics and scholars interested in the creative process, a few, and here fantasy and science fiction writers seem generally to fit, happily write autobiographical articles for magazines, mingle with their fans at conventions, and grant interviews of various sorts. It is with provocative comments made by some of these writers in recent interviews and articles that I wish to begin my essay.

I

One of the staples of fantasy and science fiction magazines, amateur and professional, is the interview with a successful writer in the field. Because many readers of these magazines are themselves would-be writers, the interviewers tend to focus on the practical problems of writing, especially the writing of novels. In other words, although they may or may not delve deeply into the educational backgrounds, political philosophies, or reading tastes of the writers they are interviewing, they almost always ask the two questions of most interest to beginning writers of fantasy and science fiction: Where do you get your ideas? and How carefully do you work your stories out before you begin to write?

The answers elicited by these and similar questions fall roughly into two categories. A few writers say that a considerable amount of conscious preparation is necessary before they actually begin to write. Here, for example, are the responses of Poul Anderson to questions about his writing habits:

> Writing a novel is a complicated task. Once I determine, in a general sense, what I'm going to do, I'll sit down and start planning it in great detail. I'll try to figure everything out I possibly can about the world I'm trying to build. After I've calculated the mathematic skeleton of the story, I'll work on several more arbitrary things, such as drawing maps, iden-

tifying place names, researching life on the planet. I'll usually end up with pages and pages of closely written notes, just on that one planet, getting down to elaborate descriptions of flora and fauna. Then I'll start developing individual characters.[1]

Anderson, a fabricator of "hard" science fiction, is well aware that some writers work in a less conscious, less systematic way. In an autobiographical article published in *Algol*, he has distinguished two extreme methods of composition:

> Some artists proceed in a kind of frenzy, unheeding of what they are about until the project is finished. This is not necessarily bad. A numbe[r] of our finest works have been created thus. No two makers have identical methods. Of course, if he's any good, the headlong artist has all the skill and understanding that he needs; they just operate less on the conscious level for him than they do for most people.
>
> At the opposite pole we find the completely cerebral person who plans everything out beforehand, takes careful note of what he is doing while he does it, and afterward goes back to ponder over each smallest detail and revise until he is satisfied. People of this kind also produce their share of greatness.[2]

Lester del Rey, although not given to extensive revision, seems in general to follow a procedure similar to Anderson's. In an interview which appeared in *Science Fiction Review*, he says of his writing practices: "I know what my story is going to be before I ever write it. This I work out in great detail. I'm never surprised by the development of a character because I've known that before I ever put it on paper, because I've planned that all out ahead of time. . . ."[3] And, interestingly enough, L. Sprague de Camp, generally a producer of fantasy and science fantasy, appears to be one of Anderson's "cerebral" writers, not one of his "frenzied" ones. "I'm one of these meticulous outliners," he says. "Some people sit down and the whole thing pours out. . . . I don't work very much that way. I have a general idea, and then gradually fill it out, add more detail, add more complications and the like."[4]

Although Poul Anderson, Lester del Rey, and L. Sprague de Camp evidently construct their stories with the rationality and efficiency of an aircraft engineer working out the design of a new jet engine, a great many of the fantasy and science fiction writers interviewed during the last four or five years have indicated that their own creative processes are neither very rational nor very efficient. Gregory Benford, for one, notes that, knowing he is a scientist, many of his readers suspect him to be a "very rationalist writer, like Fred Hoyle." Actually, he says, "it seems to me that I'm a little more of a subconscious sort of writer." He does not, he adds, know where the "stuff" of his stories "comes from," and he is only able to put large chunks of his material together over long periods of time. A good case in point is his novel *In the Ocean of Night*, which grew out of previously published pieces of short fiction. He describes the making of that novel:

> I knew I was going to write the book for a long time, but I had to work out the details. . . . In the summer of '75, I sat down and tried to start on page one and go through and modify everything . . . and try to pull it together. It was mostly a subconscious process because I actually didn't know how major things in the book connected up with other major things. It was a series of revelations. I was in the middle of the book and just going along thinking about the plotline that I had laid out, and about 300 words before it happened I discovered that Nigel Walmsley's wife, Alexandria, was going to rise from the dead. I didn't know that! I suddenly realized that all that had been planted before, was all set up, and I hadn't even realized that I was planting it. . . . It was that kind of assembly work in which you slowly understand what is going on. . . . This seems to be the way that I have to write books. It takes a long time to put together the ideas and figure out what it means.[5]

According to the Jungian school of psychology, a frequently appearing symbol for the unconscious is the ocean.[6] In light of the large part that Benford's unconscious seems to have played in the creation of *In the Ocean of Night*, the title he chose for his book is peculiarly fitting. Among the various words one might use to characterize the unconscious, "ocean" and "night" would have to be at the head of the list.

Writing in *Algol*, Joe Haldeman recently discussed at length the problem of "getting ideas" for science fiction stories. Before suggesting a solution for writer's block, he described R. A. Lafferty's theory of artistic inspiration:

> R. A. Lafferty, than whom there is no more original writer in science fiction, claims that there's no such thing as an original idea, and writers who think they sit down and go through some rational process to arrive at a story are kidding themselves. He claims that all ideas float around as a kind of psychic public property, and every now and then one settles on you. That sounds dangerously mystical to me, subversive, but I think it's true.[7]

Again, the image is Jungian: ideas "float around" in a psychic ocean, which is accessible to everyone. Surely we are here only a half-step away from Jung's theory of the archetypes and the collective unconscious.

At times a writer finds that his, in Haldeman's words, "imagination has frozen solid," that "no ideas come floating down" to him. Here is Haldeman's solution to that, for a writer, most vexing problem:

> Start typing. Type your name over and over. Type lists of animals, flowers, baseball players, Greek Methodists. Type out what you're going to say to that damned insolent repairman. Sooner or later, perhaps out of boredom, perhaps out of a desire to *stop* this silly exercise, you'll find you've started a story. It's never taken me so much as a page of nonsense. . . .[8]

The science fiction writer who seems to have thought most about the part the unconscious plays in the creative process is A. E. Van Vogt. His introduction to the subject came about, he tells us, as a result of his attempts to find a successful treatment for a chronic medical disorder:

> I fell out of a second-storey window when I was age two and a half, and I was unconscious for three days, near death. Later, using hypnosis, and then still later, dianetics, in an effort to reduce the trauma of those three days, I discovered that unconsciousness has "on it" (in it) endless hallucinations. The normal part of my brain has probably spent a lifetime trying to rationalize the consequent fantasies and images. This could explain a lot about my bent for science fiction.[9]

Over the years, Van Vogt, who like Haldeman and most other writers at times suffered from writer's block, developed a unique way of freeing his blocked unconscious and thereby initiating stories or resuming halted ones. Noting that when he went to bed after a period of unsuccessful labor he often later in the night awoke with a solution to the problem which had frustrated him, Van Vogt, in order to prime his creative imagination, embarked on a demanding regimen: "Thereafter, I used an alarm clock to awaken me every one and a half hours. Throughout my career as a writer, I awakened myself by an alarm clock—and later with an industrial timer—about 300 nights a year. Thus, I enlisted my subconscious . . . in my ceaseless search for ideas and story solutions."[10] Eventually, Van Vogt's ruminations on the workings of the unconscious led him to a full-blown theory of composition which included, in addition to aspects of aesthetics, elements of archetypal epistemology and metaphysics as well:

> I had the theory that every grain of sand, every rock, every living cell contains within it a record of its ancient origin. The theory postulated that if we could but "read" that record, we could know the beginning of

all things, and their subsequent history. Obviously, science has long attempted to use its methods to comprehend this record. My method, however, was more exotic. At a certain point in each science fiction story, I would let my subconscious mind freely associate within the frame of the ideas of that story. My hope was that, as time went on, as more stories were written, my subconscious would progressively spew forth ancient images; and that a picture of the truth of the universe would gradually emerge.[11]

I could quote numerous additional fantasy and science fiction writers on the subject of the role of the unconscious in the creative process, but time and space will allow for only two more. When an interviewer recently asked Stephen R. Donaldson where he got ideas for his stories, Donaldson replied, "Where? from the un- or sub-conscious recesses of my own mind. . . . When I'm receptive, they can be fished to the surface [that Jungian image, again] by almost any kind of external stimuli (one whole sequence in *The Power That Preserves* was triggered by a can of disinfectant in a restaurant washroom)."[12] A little later in the interview, he added, "The single most crippling obstacle to this process is self-consciousness: Self-consciousness blocks receptivity."[13]

Finally, in describing the origin and completion of *Sword of the Demon*, Richard Lupoff emphasized not only the contribution of his "personal" unconscious, but also the indirect contribution of the racial unconscious, through the materials he first absorbed from Japanese myths and then subsequently incorporated into his novel. The following is his description of the complete process:

> The very opening of the book, the first chapter of it, just occurred spontaneously. It had no particular source that I knew of. The famous wellsprings of the subconscious, or whatever. I had no awareness of it having come from any place in particular, it was just there. And I didn't know where to go with it. It sat in my desk untouched for a couple of years because of that. Finally, I was looking through *The Larousse Encyclopedia of Mythology* and spent about the next six months reading Japanese cultural mythology. Just *submerged* [my italics] myself in it. All the characters and most of the incidents in the book are taken from Japanese mythology, but the book itself is not a literal retelling of any one particular story. . . . This book was produced by turning my head into some sort of solvent and filling it up with Japanese mythology until I got a supersaturated solution, and this book is the precipitate.[14]

Most lovers of literature find such vivid, personal statements about the creative process intrinsically interesting. What makes these statements especially interesting, however, is the remarkable way they echo key passages in C. G. Jung's most influential book, *Symbols of Trans-formation*. In the second chapter of that book, Jung's primary goal is the distinction of two fundamentally different kinds of thinking. One kind he calls "directed thinking"; the other he calls "fantasy thinking."

Directed thinking is, above all, verbal: "If we . . . follow out an intensive train of thought—the solution of a difficult problem, for instance—we suddenly notice that we are *thinking in words*, that in very intensive thinking we begin talking to ourselves, or that we occasionally write down the problem or make a drawing of it, so as to be absolutely clear." Directed thinking, Jung adds, is logical thinking. It is difficult, even exhausting. It copies reality and produces adaptation to it. Certainly, the "clearest expression of modern directed thinking is science and the techniques fostered by it."[15]

On the other hand, "What happens," Jung asks, "when we do not think directly?" "Well," he answers, "our thinking then lacks all leading ideas and the sense of direction emanating from them. We no longer compel our thoughts along a definite track, but let them float, sink or rise according to their specific gravity." Unlike directed thinking, this kind of thinking (fantasy thinking) does not tire us, and it "leads away from reality into fantasies of the past or future."[16]

Although directed thinking is a conscious phenomenon, most fantasy thinking, according to Jung, goes on in the unconscious. For the clearest, most concise description of this fantasy activity and of the two parts of the unconscious psyche—the personal unconscious and the collective unconscious—we must resort to another of Jung's works, "The Psychology of the Child Archetype":

> Modern psychology treats the products of unconscious imagination as self-portraits of what is going on in the unconscious, or as statements of the unconscious psyche about itself. They fall into two categories. Firstly, fantasies (including dreams) of a personal character, which go back unquestionably to personal experiences, things forgotten or repressed, and can thus be completely explained by individual anamnesis. Secondly, fantasies (including dreams) of an impersonal character, which cannot be reduced to experiences in the individual's past, and thus cannot be explained as something individually acquired. These fantasy-pictures undoubtedly have their closest analogues in mythological types. We must therefore assume that they correspond to certain *collective* (and not personal) structural elements of the human psyche in general, and, like the morphological elements of the human body, are *inherited*. . . . the fantasy-products of the second category (as also those of the first) arise in a state of reduced intensity on the part of consciousness (in dreams, delirium, reveries, visions, etc.).[17]

Very clearly, then, the first group of writers I quoted—Anderson, del Rey, and de Camp—are, in the language of Jung, "directed thinkers." Highly conscious and highly logical artists, they perform mathematical calculations, do extensive research, draw detailed maps, and make elaborate outlines before they actually begin to write their stories. The second group of writers—Benford, Haldeman, Van Vogt, Donaldson, and Lupoff—are, to varying degrees, what Jung called "fantasy thinkers." Less conscious and less logical as artists, they depend greatly on the promptings of the unconscious.

2

At first glance, the two books I wish to examine in some detail in the remainder of this essay would appear to have little in common. Ray Bradbury's *Martian Chronicles* is notable chiefly for its masterful stylistic effects. It holds our attention with its sensuous diction, its hypnotic sentence rhythms, and its skillful onomatopoeic devices. The scientific and technological materials of the book are unfortunately not so impressive; they are not only frequently self-contradictory, but they are also often in conflict with those of the world we actually inhabit. Stanislaw Lem's *Solaris*, on the other hand, is a masterpiece of philosophical fiction. In dealing with matters scientific and technological, it is always informed and sophisticated. Its rigorous and detailed epistemological speculations are in the main successfully integrated with fascinating character portraits and suspenseful incidents.

Surprisingly enough, these very different books do have, as we shall see, some significant points of contact. Those points of contact, I shall argue, are largely the result of the strong influence of the unconscious of each writer during the creative process. To begin, I must turn to the public statements Bradbury has made about his own methods of composition.

If his public comments about his methods of composition are to be trusted, Bradbury is a determined practitioner of what Jung called "fantasy thinking." In a speech in 1975, he rejected the notion that the conscious part of the mind should play a significant role in the creative process: "I have had a sign by my typewriter for the better part of twenty years, now, which says, '*Don't think*.' I hate all those signs that say Think. That's the enemy of creativity." Melville, the author of the greatest American novel, did not intellectualize; he relied on emotion. "Emotion, emotion wins the day. Intellect can help correct. But emotion, first, surprises creativity out in the open where it can be pinned down! Learn from Melville!" Like Melville, and Plato's Ion, for that matter, Bradbury is, he says, at the mercy of his Muse when he writes. He is not in control. Having written, however, he is better balanced, better adjusted: "I've only been to a psychiatrist once in my life. I don't happen to believe in it. . . . I think good friends, or the act of creativity itself, sustains us and saves us more often than not."[18]

In an interview published only last year, Bradbury again emphasized that, for him, writing is essentially an undirected process: "I never plan ahead. Everything is always spontaneous and passionate. I never sit down and think things out. I also do a great deal of daydreaming. Oh, I do some thinking in-between, but it's a very loose thing. I'm not super-intellectual. If it feels right, then I'll do it." How does he get ideas for stories? "Basically, I just go [into my office] with the idea of writing something. I usually start off the day with poetry. I go through a process of free association. I do the same thing with short stories."[19]

Like many fantasy and science fiction writers, Bradbury admits, then, to a significant amount of daydreaming. To a psychoanalyst the daydreams of an individual are at least as significant as his nightdreams. When an individual daydreams, his psychic energy (or libido) manifests itself as a stream of images linked by association, a stream which flows freely in the direction of least resistance. Good writers such as Bradbury differ from ordinary daydreamers, of course, by possessing an ability to abstract ideas from their fantasies and objectify them in good literary form. Before analyzing Bradbury's finest achievement as a writer of fantasy, *The Martian Chronicles*, I must first place one of its dominant themes in a more general context.

One of the most common themes in nightdreams, daydreams, and myths is that of transformation, or metamorphosis. All of us have had nightdreams in the course of which inanimate objects, plants, animals, or people have changed into very different inanimate objects, plants, animals, or people. Among the materials collected and published by Freud and Jung, numerous examples of such transformations can be found. Here, for instance, is a short transformational nightdream collected by Jung and printed in his *Essays on a Science of Mythology*: "A white bird perches on a table. Suddenly it changes into a fair-haired seven-year-old girl and just as suddenly back into a bird, which now speaks with a human voice."[20] Another dreamer provides a longer, even more intriguing example:

> We go through a door into a tower-like room, where we climb a long flight of steps. . . . The steps end in a temple. . . . The temple is of red stone. Bloody sacrifices are offered there. Animals are standing about the altar. In order to enter the temple precincts one has to be transformed into

an animal—a beast of the forest. . . . On the altar in the middle of the open room there stands the moon-bowl, from which smoke or vapour continually rises. There is also a huge image of the goddess, but it cannot be seen clearly. The worshippers, who have been changed into animals and to whom I also belong, have to touch the goddess's foot. . . .[21]

As far as transformational daydreams are concerned, the ones most familiar to us are those involving wish fulfillments. In our reveries we are often temporarily transformed into powerful heads of state, heroic soldiers, world-class athletes, celebrated musicians, prize-winning authors, glamorous moviestars—the list of possibilities is virtually endless. Freud and Jung frequently touched on the subject of daydreams, and Jung even went so far as to publish a number of the most significant ones he had collected. Of those printed by Jung in *Essays on a Science of Mythology*, one, from a woman "in middle life," is especially relevant to the thrust of this essay. Richer, more bizarre than the transformational daydreams of most of us, it is especially interesting for its ending:

> A magician is demonstrating his tricks to an Indian prince. He produces a beautiful young girl from under a cloth. She is a dancer, who has the power to change her shape or at least hold her audience spell-bound by faultless illusion. During the dance she dissolves with the music into a swarm of bees. Then she changes into a leopard, then into a jet of water, then into a sea-polyp that has twined itself about a young pearl-fisher. Between times, she takes human form again at the dramatic moment. She appears as a she-ass bearing two baskets of wonderful fruits. Then she becomes a many-coloured peacock. The prince is beside himself with delight and calls her to him. But she dances on, now naked, and even tears the skin from her body, and finally falls down—a naked skeleton. This is buried, but at night a lily grows out of the grave, and from its cup there rises the *white lady*, who floats slowly up to the sky.[22]

This daydream is interesting not only because of the number and variety of transformations it contains, but also because of the mythlike transfiguration at the end of it. The death and burial of the beautiful young girl and her subsequent rebirth in the form of a flower are, of course, paralleled by similar events in numerous well-known myths. In his *Metamorphoses*, Ovid, in fact, organized much of the mythology of Greece, Rome, and Babylonia around the theme of transformation; and, among the many different kinds of transformation he described, those involving the death of an individual and the subsequent rebirth of that individual in the form of a flower were amply represented. Because of their popularity with Renaissance poets such as Shakespeare, Milton, and Marvell, the Ovidian stories involving such myths (those about Narcissus, Hyacinthus, and Adonis, for example) are the best-known today. Overall, the tranformations depicted in *Metamorphoses* are more numerous and more varied than some of us will remember them to be: Chaos is transformed into an ordered universe, the coral "plant" into a rock, Syrinx into a reed, Daphne into a tree, the Thracian women into oaks, Ascalaphus into an owl, the nephew of Daedalus into a partridge, Daedalion into a hawk, Cadmus into a snake, Lyncus into a lynx, Lycaon into a wolf, Callisto into a bear, Galanthis into a weasel, Atlas into a mountain, Cyane into a pool, Arethusa into a spring, a dog into a marble statue, a city into a heron; nymphs are transformed into islands, ships into nymphs, and on, and on.

Over a hundred years ago Nietzsche suggested a relationship between our dream thinking and what he called the "whole thought" of primitive man. On the basis of dream analysis, Freud came to a related conclusion; he held that myths are the "distorted vestiges of the wishful phantasies of whole nations, the [age-long] dreams" of primitive man. And, finally, Jung himself wrote, "The conclusion that the myth-makers thought in much the same way as we still think in dreams is almost self-evident."[23] With these ideas about the nature and functions of night-dreams, daydreams, and myths in mind, we are now ready to turn to Bradbury's *Martian Chronicles*.

Near the middle of "Usher II," one of the stories in *The Martian Chronicles*, Mr. Stendahl, lover of fantasy and re-creator of the House of Usher, says of his architectural accomplishments, "I nurtured a medieval atmosphere in a modern, incredulous world."[24] Apt though they are for describing the house and grounds Stendahl created on Mars, Stendahl's words would have made an even more appropriate epigraph for *The Martian Chronicles* itself. Although superficially a book about a technologically superior world of the future, *The Martian Chronicles* is in reality a collection of atavistic daydreams, daydreams which derive much of their power from mythlike transformations.

One of the most mythlike stories in the book is "The Martian," a haunting tale of a Martian "boy" capable of changing his shape to accommodate the desires of the settlers from Earth. In what seemed like, in the words of the narrator, a "repeated dream,"[25] he moved among the settlers, assuming the shapes of their dead relatives and acquaintances. Always fearful of being "trapped" by the settlers, he eventually met his end beside a Martian canal, as members of a hysterical crowd struggled to hold him: "Before their eyes he changed. . . . He was melting wax shaping to their minds. They shouted, they pressed forward, pleading. He screamed, threw out his hands, his face dissolving to each demand. . . . They snatched his wrists, whirled him about, until with one last shriek of horror he fell."[26] This story, of course, reminds us of the myth of Proteus. A shape changer who also had to be constantly on guard against being caught and forced to satisfy the desires of his captors, Proteus, a god of the sea, sometimes assumed "the shape of a young man, at another transformed into a lion; sometimes he used to appear . . . as a raging wild boar, or again as a snake . . . or else horns transformed him into a bull."[27]

In "The Third Expedition," a spaceship from Earth lands near what appears to be a small Martian town. The commander of the ship is Captain John Black. A man eighty years old, Black, "through the grace of God and a science that . . . knows how to make *some* old men young again," is as agile and alert as the chronologically younger men accompanying him. Nearing the town, he and two of his men hear someone "softly, drowsily," playing "Beautiful Dreamer" on a piano. Minutes later, exploring the "dreaming" afternoon streets of the town, the Earthmen find that it appears to be in every way identical to the small, Midwestern towns of their youth; and shortly, in an "amazing dream of reality," Black is happily reunited with his long-dead "brother," "father," and "mother."[28]

But during the night, lying beside his "brother" in a bedroom like the one they shared as children, Black begins to awaken from his "dreaming hypnosis": "Suppose these houses are really some *other* shape, a Martian shape, but, by playing on my desires and wants, these Martians have made this seem like my old home town, my old house. . . . Sometime during the night, perhaps, my brother here on this bed will change form, melt, shift, and become another thing, a Martian. It would be very simple for him just to turn over in bed and put a knife into my heart." By morning, the Martians have, in fact, killed all sixteen men from the rocket ship. At their funeral, the "mayor" of the town, "his face sometimes looking like the mayor, sometimes looking like something else," makes a sad speech, while the faces of Black's crying "relatives" melt from familiar shapes "into something else."[29]

The transformations witnessed by Captain Williams and his crew in a different story, "The Earth Men," are even more bizarre than those encountered by Captain Black in "The Third Expedition." Taken for a hallucinating psychotic because he claims to have come from Earth,

Williams, along with his crew, is locked in a Martian insane asylum, where he must spend the night surrounded by constantly metamorphosing "paranoids":

> A man squatted alone in darkness. Out of his mouth issued a blue flame which turned into the round shape of a small naked woman. . . .
> The captain nodded at another corner. A woman stood there, changing. First she was embedded in a crystal pillar, then she melted into a golden statue, finally a staff of polished cedar, and back to a woman.
> All through the midnight hall people were juggling thin violet flames, shifting, changing, for nighttime was the time of change and affliction. . . .
> Little demons of red sand ran between the teeth of sleeping men. Women became oily snakes. There was a smell of reptiles and animals.[30]

Convinced that Williams is a highly imaginative Martian who has transformed himself into a startlingly effective image of an Earthman, a Martian psychologist excitedly envisions a scientific paper on Williams's feat: "I'll write this into my greatest monograph! I'll speak of it at the Martian Academy next month! *Look* at you! Why, you've even changed your eye color from yellow to blue, your skin to pink from brown. And those clothes, and your hands having five fingers instead of six! Biological metamorphosis through psychological imbalance!"[31] Finally, having judged Williams's case incurable, the Martian psychologist resorts to euthanasia, only to find that, even after the death of Williams, his supposed hallucination, his Earthman's body, continues to exist.

An exhaustive account of the many kinds of transformation taking place in the other stories in *The Martian Chronicles* would require more space than I have been allotted for the rest of this essay, but perhaps I can at least suggest their variety and number before turning to similar materials in Lem's *Solaris*. In the stories and the bridges between the stories, a frosty Ohio winter is transformed into a brief summer by the heat from the exhausts of a rocket ship; Spender, a sensitive archaeologist, is (in spirit, at least) transformed into a Martian; Benjamin Driscoll, a latter-day Johnny Appleseed, turns a Martian desert into a green paradise; Pikes, a man of ten thousand faces, is able to transform himself into "a fury, a smoke, a blue fog, a white rain, a bat, a gargoyle"; Stendahl's guests, after being forced to don masks, are "transformed from one age into another"; a Martian woman, slain by the vulgar and crass Sam Parkhill, turns into "ice, snowflake, smoke," and is blown "away in the wind"; and, at the end of the book, the Hathaway family, having destroyed the rocket ship which brought them to Mars, become

"Martians."[32] This list might be considerably extended, but it should suffice.

Finally, before leaving *The Martian Chronicles*, I must say something about the book's special use of metaphor and simile. All metaphors and similes are, of course, by their very nature transformational. If I, for example, say that "my love is a soft, soft cloud," I am, at *some* level of understanding, for a brief moment at least, transforming her. What is unusually interesting about the metaphors and similes of *The Martian Chronicles*, however, is the high frequency of what I shall call "biomorphic" figures of speech—metaphors and similes with inanimate tenors and animate vehicles. And among the many biomorphic figures of the book, those of greatest interest to me are the figures in which the tenors are machines. Here are a few examples: "the . . . house . . . turned and followed the sun, flowerlike"; "From [the evil weapon] hordes of golden bees could be flung out with a high shriek"; "Up and down green wine canals, boats as delicate as bronze flowers drifted"; "the rocket had bloomed out great flowers of heat and color"; "[the rocket] had moved in the midnight waters of space like a pale sea leviathan"; "The rockets came like locusts"; "It was a machine like a jade-green insect, a praying mantis, delicately rushing through the cold air"; and "the great ships turned as lightly as moon thistles."

In interviews during the 1950s, 1960s, and 1970s, Bradbury repeatedly stated that he had never flown in an airplane, that (whenever possible) he avoided riding in automobiles, and that he disliked telephones and television sets.[34] Consistent with Bradbury's openly negative attitude toward machines, Mr. Hathaway at the end of *The Martian Chronicles* says of life during the last half of the twentieth century, "Science ran too far ahead of us too quickly, and the people got lost in a mechanical wilderness. . . ."[35] Only last year in an interview, Bradbury insisted, "We must learn to humanize the machine."[36] In light of his general mechanophobia, it is not, I think, therefore surprising to find in *The Martian Chronicles* and in Bradbury's other works numerous, probably unconsciously generated, biomorphic figures of speech.

According to Jung, fantasy thinking, although mainly a spontaneous product of the unconscious, contains elements of consciousness. The degree of influence an individual will allow his unconscious is dependent on the degree of rationalism prevailing in his immediate environment. Today, the countries officially most committed to a rationalist position are the socialist states of Europe and Asia, and the most read and most admired socialist writer of fantasy and science fiction is Stanislaw Lem of Poland. In recent public statements about his stories,

Lem has revealed that, although he is officially a staunch rationalist, his attempts to rationalize the creative process have hitherto met with failure:

> I have tried all thinkable, rational, optimization procedures (tactics of writing). All in vain. I do not know where my ideas come from. . . . They come in dreams, but this is very rare; sometimes while reading scientific papers, especially mathematical ones. But then, there is no evidence of a rational linkage between a new idea and the said paper. . . . And truly I never know what I am writing—if it will be a short story, a novel, a serious thing or something grotesque—what problems may emerge, and so on. This is one hell and damnation, especially since I AM a rationalist, but it is so.[37]

Of even greater relevance to the concerns of this essay, though, are Lem's statements about the composition of his best novel, *Solaris*:

> I had no knowledge, not an atom of it, when I wrote the first chapter, what Kelvin would encounter on Solaris Station. I went forward in the same way that Kelvin went, and spoke for the first time with Snow, not knowing what was going on. Then, as I approached the end, again I did not know how to end the story, and it took a whole year—one day there came this illumination, and so it was. I do not like this kind of creative work, because I am myself a rationalist, and I would prefer to write in a planned, "rationalistic" way. . . . There were no plans, no elaborated preconceptions, no tactics, no nothing. . . .[38]

Surprisingly enough, then, Lem's metaphysical masterpiece appears to have been just as much the product of fantasy thinking as Bradbury's less intellectually challenging *Martian Chronicles*. All the extrinsic evidence supports that conclusion.

In addition, considerable intrinsic evidence can be marshaled in support of the same proposition. To begin—throughout *Solaris*, as throughout *The Martian Chronicles*, a dreamlike atmosphere prevails. Kelvin has, in fact, hardly set foot upon Solaris Station when he exclaims, "I must be dreaming. All this could only be a dream!"[39] Shortly thereafter, he encounters Gibarian's nightmarish mistress in a corridor of the space station and his long-dead wife, Rheya, in his own room. At first, he is convinced that he is only dreaming of Rheya, but little by little he begins to entertain the possibility that she is real:

> My first thought was reassuring: I was dreaming and I was aware that I was dreaming. . . . I closed my eyes and tried to shake off the dream. . . . I thought of throwing something at her, but, even in a dream, I could not bring myself to harm a dead person. . . .the room, Rheya,

everything seemed extraordinarily real. A three-dimensional dream. . . .
I saw several objects on the floor. . . . When I wake up, I told myself, I
shall check whether these things are still there or whether, like Rheya, I
only saw them in a dream. . . . We kissed. . . . Was it possible to feel
so much in a dream, I wondered. . . . Was it then that I began to have
doubts? I went on telling myself that it was a dream, but my heart tight-
ened.[40]

To further complicate matters for Kelvin, Rheya herself begins to
dream doubtful dreams: "I have dreams. . . . I don't know whether
they really are dreams. Perhaps I'm ill."[41] And then, ironically, Kelvin,
who had earlier tried to convince himself that he was dreaming, now
dreams of Gibarian trying to convince him that he is awake: "Oh, you
think you're dreaming about me? As you did with Rheya? . . . No, I
am the real Gibarian. . . ."[42]

While Kelvin sleeps, the sentient ocean which inhabits Solaris
probes his unconscious, and its invasive presence is reflected in the
erotic, terrifying imagery of his nightmares. Two of these nightmares
are vividly transformational. The first comes approximately halfway
through the novel: "The night transfixed me; the night took possession
of me, enveloped and penetrated me. . . . Turned to stone, I had ceased
breathing. . . . I seemed to be growing smaller. . . . I tried to crawl
out of bed, but there was no bed; beneath the cover of darkness there
was a void. I pressed my hands to my face. I no longer had any fingers
or any hands. I wanted to scream. . . ."[43] Even more horrifying is the
dream near the end of the book:

> Out of the enveloping pink mist, an invisible object emerges, and touches
> me. . . . I feel this contact like a hand, and the hand recreates me. . . .
> Under the caress of the hesitant fingers, my lips and cheeks emerge from
> the void, and as the caress goes further I have a face, breath stirs in my
> chest—I exist. And recreated, I in my turn create: a face appears before
> me. . . . This creature—a woman?—stays near me and we are motion-
> less. The beat of our hearts combines, and all at once, out of the sur-
> rounding void. . . . steals a presence of indefinable, unimaginable cru-
> elty. The caress that created us . . . becomes the crawling of innumerable
> fingers. Our white, naked bodies dissolve into a swarm of black creeping
> things, and I am—we are—a mass of glutinous coiling worms . . . and
> I howl soundlessly, begging for death and for an end.[44]

In these nightmares, Kelvin undergoes transformations symbolic
of the painful transformation he must in reality suffer on Solaris. That
transformation begins when he first steps from his space capsule, which
resembles a "burst cocoon," onto the space station.[45] After a series of

tense encounters with Snow, Sartorius, and the "visitors" sent to the station by the ocean, Kelvin expresses his doubts and fears to Rheya in language not unlike that which he employs in describing his frightening transformational dreams: "After what has happened already, we can expect anything. Suppose tomorrow it turns me into a green jellyfish! It's out of our hands."[46] Much later, at the end of the novel, a more subdued Kelvin stands on the shore of the ocean and repeatedly reaches out to the waves which, without actually touching them, envelop his hand and his feet. Eventually, the ocean tires of this "game," but Kelvin, having undergone a kind of baptism, has been radically changed. His attitude has now become one of complete and total acceptance: "Although I had read numerous accounts of it, none of them had prepared me for the experience as I had lived it, and I felt somehow changed. . . . I . . . identified myself with the dumb, fluid colossus; it was as if I had forgiven it everything, without the slightest effort of word or thought."[47]

While Kelvin dreams his transformational nightmares and slowly metamorphoses into the sadly wise man who at the end of the novel waits patiently for another chance, for another "time of cruel miracles," the ocean itself is "engaged in a never-ending process of transformation, an 'ontological autometamorphosis.'" This "Polytherian form" of the category "Metamorph," this "mass of metamorphic plasma," is capable of infinitely varied "matter transformations."[48] Most of the time it busies itself with the shaping and unshaping of unique forms, for which a Solarist had in the past created the broad taxonomic categories of "extensor," "mimoid," "symmetriad," and "asymmetriad"; but, in the course of the novel, the protean ocean also at one time or another assumes the shape of a garden, a huge building, an enormous child, distorted tools, and, most important of all, the "visitors."

Of the last group, the "visitors," only two are ever very fully revealed to the reader—Gibarian's giant, steatopygic Negress and Rheya. Near the beginning of the novel, Kelvin characterizes the former as a "monstrous Aphrodite," and near the end of the book, Snow partially repays the compliment (or insult?) when in the presence of Kelvin he sardonically addresses Rheya as "fair Aphrodite, child of Ocean."[49] Both applications of the name are apt. Aphrodite, the Greek goddess of sexual love and beauty, was literally born from the sea, and the myths about her all exemplify the power of love.

Also apt are the names of the spaceships which figure in the novel. The *Laakon* and the *Ulysses*, for example, remind us of ancient myths about the sea. In one, Laocoön, a priest of Poseidon, the god of the sea, angers Apollo, who sends two huge sea serpents to kill Laocoön and his sons. In another, Ulysses, sailing a troubled sea, frequently runs afoul of Poseidon, Lord of Proteus, the old shape changer. In light of these and other mythic resonances within the novel, Kelvin's speculative question near the end seems particularly acute: "Are we to grow used to the idea that every man relives ancient torments, which are all the more profound because they grow comic with repetition?"[50]

Although in many ways very different, *The Martian Chronicles* and *Solaris* are, then, alike in at least one demonstrable way. Both incorporate significant amounts of dreamlike and mythlike transformational materials. An obvious question now comes to mind: are such transformational elements ubiquitous in works of fantasy and science fiction? Certainly, additional examples are easily adduced—the transformation of the animals into beast men and back into animals in *The Island of Dr. Moreau*, the transformation of the robots into human beings in *R. U. R.*, the transformation of individual Gethenians alternately into "males" and "females" in *The Left Hand of Darkness*, the transformation of Mrs. Grales into Rachel in *A Canticle for Leibowitz*, the transformation of the Mark IV computer into Mike in *The Moon Is a Harsh Mistress*, the transformation of the world's children into the Overmind in *Childhood's End*, the transformation of David Bowman into the Star Child in *2001*, the transformation of matter into various forms in *Cosmicomics*, and on, and on. A definitive answer to this intriguing question would obviously, however, require the transformation of this essay into a monograph, and, for the time being at least, I shall let it rest *in embryo*.

JACK P. RAWLINS

Confronting the Alien: Fantasy and Anti-Fantasy in Science Fiction Film and Literature

What is the matter with science fiction films? Year after year studios make them, and science fiction fans go to them, often enjoy them, and leave the theater muttering, "But it's not science fiction." Science fiction films are *not* science fiction, in a way we generally recognize but have trouble explaining. Why are they not? What are they? What is science fiction, this thing they are not?

Of course, we know what these films are—they are "fantasy." We know that fantasy and science fiction are two different things which are always found in each other's company, but no one seems to know what the relationship between them is. Is one a subgenre of the other, and, if so, which one? Unsure of the labels, we usually waffle by using both names together, "fantasy and science fiction," until the phrase becomes a single word, fantasyandsciencefiction. There are, for instance, no "science fiction film" conventions—there are only "fantasy and science fiction film" conventions. Would anyone among us dare claim that he could take a stack of "fantasy and science fiction" films and separate the "fantasy" from the "science fiction"? Hopeless of doing so, we often abandon the terminology and find a label for the aggregate—we speak of "speculative literature" or "imaginative literature," and then solve all our problems by adding, "Of course, all literature is really speculative (or imaginative)."[1]

My question is, are the conventional terms—"science fiction," "fantasy," and the implied other, "mainstream" literature—any good at all, and will they help us account for the acknowledged difference between science fiction on the page and on the screen? I shall begin inductively, by examining classic examples of filmed and written science fiction: Don Seigel's *Invasion of the Body Snatchers* (1956) and John

W. Campbell's "Who Goes There?" The differences will be made more apparent by the sameness of the dramatic situation in each case: an alien thing is taking over people and replacing them with perfect replicas—how may the creature be defeated?

In *Body Snatchers* Dr. Miles Bennel (Kevin McCarthy) returns from a medical convention to his typical American small town (Santa Mira) to find that the universe contains more than he thought possible. He is faced with the essential science fiction challenge: expand the boundaries of your imagined universe to cope with the new knowledge or be destroyed by it.

A work of art instructs its audience in how best to experience it—how does *Body Snatchers* teach us to cope with the alien? Bennel is offered to us as a spokesman for the rational view of the world—he is *sure* everything makes sense. He has the paternal smugness of one who knows all things in heaven and earth already, and knows that all things in both places are knowable through reason. Anyone who thinks otherwise is either sick or crazy. Of course Uncle Ira is Uncle Ira! Bennel starts here, and the movie educates him out of his blind reason. There are kinds of knowledge his rational intellect cannot reach, and he learns to listen to new voices. He begins to honor his instinctual wisdom when he sets out to save his girl, Becky Driscoll (Dana Wynter), from a danger which he knows exists but cannot name, and he apologizes for doing so, saying, "I don't know what it was. Call it a premonition." Soon he is acting without apology from that new source of wisdom: "There was evil in the house," he says simply, irrationally, and accurately.

By the end of the movie, the man of reason is responding from a part of himself daytime life never exercised. He runs up endless, surrealistic flights of steps; he fights to save Becky from symbolic rape; he runs, she falls, they run to exhaustion but keep on running. They roll in the mud. Bennel screams at passers-by, but cannot make himself heard.

In short, Bennel realizes that he is in a dream, where dream responses are called for. *Body Snatchers* instructs us to have a nightmare response to the alien by offering us a spokesman for the rational intellect and showing us his disintegration, his inability to synthesize the new apparition within his rational definition of the universe. In the nighttime, reason will not work.

Other works that want to instruct us to respond with our nonrational selves use this device of offering us a spokesman for the opposition and documenting his failure—*Alien* being a recent, brilliant example. The voice of reason is Ash, the Science Officer (Ian Holm). Our last, desperate hope that the rule of reason will triumph is dashed when he tries to stuff a rolled magazine down Ripley's (Sigourney Weaver's) throat and is revealed to be a machine, indifferent to human survival. Our defense against the nightmare proves to be another nightmare. We run to daddy, the mask comes off in our hands, and we stare into the death's head. Ripley and the audience know then that it is time to scream and run, and run harder.

Bennel and Ripley learn a lesson we reaffirm every night: that our rational experiencing of the world is only one of our sources of knowledge. *Body Snatchers* and the genre it represents—which I will call "fantasy" for the moment—remind us, like our dreams, that the other sources of wisdom deserve our attention and respect: sources such as tarot, ancient curses, spells, dreams, premonitions, talismans, and gypsies' mutterings.

"Fantasy," then, honors the emotive side of the self, what I call the nighttime perspective. The extreme alternative is literature devoted to the exercise of the daytime powers of the intellect. Here my quintessential specimen is John Campbell's "Who Goes There?" The dramatic situation is much like that of *Body Snatchers*, but the art teaches us a very different response. Again, an alien thing capable of swallowing humans and making perfect replicas has gotten loose. Some members of the population have already been processed; some have not. How can the thing be stopped?

The scientists of "Who Goes There?" respond, not with screams (or at least the first screams are immediately frowned upon and regretted as counterproductive), not with pell-mell running, but with a cool, scientific determination to gather data, learn the physical properties of the monster, and thus control it. This time the representatives of the race of Ash (whose job it is to do this in *Alien*) are not monsters; the laws of physics and chemistry prove all-powerful, and the scientific method marches surely and inevitably to a solution: the data produce hypotheses that are systematically tried, the results are used to form better hypotheses, and finally a test is devised to discriminate human from nonhuman. The test is applied to all members of the population, the monsters among us are killed, and the danger is thwarted.

I have tried to suggest by my dry prose the tone of all this—more like a dissection than a drama. The nightmare is very present—in fact, Campbell stresses that the monster looks *just like* a bad dream—and this likeness allows Campbell to state his theme, the theme of all works of this genre: that the nightmare is *not* best met by running, screaming, and shouting, but by logic, the scientific method, and hard, unsentimental sense. Those who respond with emotionalism are gently locked up so that cooler heads may get on with the job at hand.

Campbell's people are quite aware that they live by the scientific method and that in the method lies their salvation. Listen to them *discuss* the likelihood of their comrade Connant's having been swallowed, in Connant's presence:

> "What about Connant in the meantime?" Kinner demanded. . . .
>
> "He may be human—," Copper started.
>
> Connant burst out in a flood of curses. "Human! *May* be human, you damned saw-bones! What in hell do you think I am?"
>
> "A monster," Copper snapped sharply. "Now shut up and listen. . . . Until we know—you know as well as we do that we have reason to question the fact, and only you know how that question is to be answered—we may reasonably be expected to lock you up."[2]

Connant realizes his incarceration is the logical course, and he submits. Time and again Campbell's people are put into situations that invite an emotional response in this way, and we witness them rejecting the emotional response for a more constructive alternative—as opposed to *Body Snatchers*, where the "reasonable" people are simply those who deny the instinctive wisdom of others. All the people who sense that Uncle Ira is not really Uncle Ira are merely crazy, by Bennel's "reasoning." "Fantasy" sees reason as an inflexible commitment to normalcy as the only reality; "science fiction" sees reason as the ultimate flexibility—if the data say you may be a monster, you may be, however much like Connant you look.

And in Campbell's world reason does not fail us, because the universe is thoroughly reasonable. When it becomes apparent that there is a monster on the loose, Campbell's people gather for a lecture from Blair, the biologist, and he says it plainly: "This isn't wildly beyond what we already know. It's just a modification we haven't seen before. It's as natural, as logical, as any other manifestation of life. It obeys the same laws."[3] And the implication is carried as much by Campbell's tone as by his plot: if we know our biology well enough, we *need not fear*. Fear, like all other emotional responses, is counterproductive to the business of understanding and controlling the universe. "Who Goes There?" is not really scary. Readers who come looking for a monster-movie "kick" feel as though they walked in on an anatomy lesson. Campbell's characters are not emotionally engaging, and he does not want them to be. They strike us as the ultimate engineers—dull in the face of wonders. This genre is full of manifestations of its prototype personality, the Galactic Seabee: "Can do"—build a bridge, fly through space warps, outthink a monster. No problem.

"Sense of wonder" is a conventional phrase describing a basic science fiction energy, but I am suggesting that Campbell's mode—which I will call for the moment "science fiction," in quotation marks—trains us in the opposite point of view: far from encouraging us to wonder at alien experience, it suggests we move through wonder as quickly as possible and get down to work, analyzing the alien with the same dispassionate curiosity we would give to any other new lab specimen. If we assume that "science fiction" strives to maximize wondrousness, we shall often think it misfires. "Who Goes There?" seems to squander opportunities for awe. But the monster is not a mind-trip; it is a problem in chemistry. Those who are sensitive to the wondrousness are useless to others who are trying to get a complex task (saving the world) done in a short time.

Written science fiction has always advertised itself as "astounding," "amazing," and the like, yet it has always been populated by heroes who, like the heroes of "Who Goes There?" are strong because they are immune from the debilitating power of imagination. The *non plus ultra* of this character is Charles Raymont, hero of Poul Anderson's *Tau Zero* (1970). Raymont is constable (read: chief of police) of a spaceship on an interstellar voyage. The ship suffers mechanical failures and is forced to fly faster and faster in the slight hope of reaching a place to make repair. As the ship increases speed, earth time speeds up relative to ship's time, until the ship is flashing through entire galaxies in moments, and real-time millennia roll by with each tick of the ship's clock. As the novel's scope grows geometrically, each member of the crew reaches a point where he can no longer conceive of his own reality—what they are doing is simply too big to comprehend—and he becomes incapacitated. Except Raymont, who alone functions efficiently because he does not let his imagination get in the way—he turns his off when he sees that it is an obstacle to problem solving. He simply does not think about it, and the ship is saved by his dullness. Finally, he leads his ship through a new Big Bang and out the other side to a virgin universe and safety, an act the rest of the crew finds too blasphemous or awe-inspiring to contemplate. "Science fiction," purveyor of wonders, paradoxically celebrates the soul who can gaze at wonders and not be too stirred.

For these reasons Terry Carr has called science fiction "the most rigorously rational form of literature we have ever had."[4] People unfamiliar with science fiction and familiar only with its reputation for won-drousness often give the title "most rational" to detective fiction in the Sherlock Holmes tradition, but wrongly. Holmes and his descendants are indeed dedicated to the principle that *all* worldly experience can be fully known via the rational intellect—that any human experience, no matter how apparently "fantastic," is capable of rational analysis. But literature from Campbell's perspective is the Holmsian principle taken a logical step further: *any* experience, whether in a far galaxy or on another spacetime continuum, is obedient to the laws of logic and sci-ence and is therefore fully knowable by the scientific method. We see Holmes' methods effective out beyond the Dog Star, as well as in Lon-don's back streets.

"Who Goes There?" and its genre, then, are more than an alter-native to *Body Snatchers*'s endorsement of the nighttime response; they are an indictment of it. They are *anti*fantastic—a polemic against the notion of fantasy per se, as *Body Snatchers* is a polemic against rea-son's claim to all knowledge. Campbell argues that the fantastic is never really fantastic at all when fully known—it is only the familiar laws of nature repackaged. The sense of fantasy, in these terms, is a juvenile indulgence of our emotional selves. Campbell asks us to grow up.

Two kinds of art instruct us to respond with two different parts of ourselves, the emotive and the rational, and each kind sees responding to the alien with the other side of the self to be counterproductive. And the status of objects in the two universes is correspondingly different. In "fantasy," objects have primarily figurative status, whereas in "sci-ence fiction," the thing is *a thing*, a literal object. And again, each genre presents the alternative as a fundamental error: in "fantasy," people often have to be taught that the object is an externalization of their internal reality—it is, in short, a metaphor—whereas, in "science fiction," to see the object as a projection of the self is next to madness.

For instance, in *Body Snatchers*, to make the point that Bennel's experience is vaguely allegorical, Bennel himself tells us it is, during his infamous exposition of theme while he is hiding in his office. The coming of the pod people, he says, is really symbolic, symbolic of our creeping tendency to dehumanize ourselves bit by bit these days, be-cause being human is hard work. We do not disagree, but we dislike Bennel's underlining it, because it is so obvious: we know we are in a dream, and we need not be told that dream objects are symbols.

"Who Goes There?" is constructed to disabuse us of any tendency to read figuratively; the work of art teaches us how to read it best. The monster is purposely made to look as much like a metaphor as possible; it looks like a conventional nightmare, and its way of operating perfectly matches the central myth of our paranoid age: I am surrounded by things that look like people but really are not, and they are trying to steal my soul. Campbell's people are thus invited to misinterpret the monster as a metaphor, a manifestation of their emotive selves. But it is not. The monster is an external, objective fact—those who lose sight of that go quickly mad. For Campbell, the fundamental act of sanity is to recognize that the furniture of the world does not *represent* anything beyond itself. "Science fiction," however densely populated with mind-boggling products of the imagination, is paradoxically the most extreme form of realistic art there is.

A classic "fantasy" object is the monster in *Alien*. We are never allowed to see it clearly, nor are we allowed to understand how it works or why it acts as it does. We are not encouraged to know it as external object, but we are encouraged to project onto it as much of our inner nightmares as we can. Most audiences, trained by most art literature to assume figurative status, never ask to understand, in rational terms, why the monster is killing these people, for instance—obviously, it does so because it is a nightmare.[5] A classic "science fiction" object is the Jupiter probe Discovery in *2001: A Space Odyssey*. When the ship first appears on the screen, the camera lingers with an endless curiosity about the spaceship as spaceship, a thing fascinating in the Spockian sense, as an object of intellectual examination. Audiences are often puzzled by the lingering camera, and by the way *2001* loves to look at hardware generally, because they assume that the value of the object must be in its status as symbol. They wonder what *the point* is; they wonder why nothing is happening. The hard science fiction fans stare and stare, in sympathy with Kubrick's sense of the thing as valuable as literal object.

The New Wave of science fiction writers devoted much energy to arguing that science fiction is "really" just like mainstream literature, because it shares mainstream's sense of the figurative status of the fictional object. Robert Silverberg put it this way:

> The science fiction writer, in the final analysis, is never really writing of other worlds and other times. Behind the futuristic trappings of his stories lies a more earthbound core. . . . What [the science fiction writer] writes about, comes from within. . . . Science fiction, at its best, illuminates our own time by turning a mirror towards the future.[6]

Ursula Le Guin expresses the same idea by saying the science fiction writer's object of examination is not *outer* but *inner* space. So the monster is really us. Silverberg's and Le Guin's idea in action is the plot of *Forbidden Planet* (1956). Dr. Morbius (Walter Pidgeon) is the Campbellian archetype, the dispassionate scientific investigator of externals, forced to grant Silverberg's and Le Guin's premise. He has spent the last several years of his life studying a machine, a mysterious power plant in the shape of a cube twenty miles on a side, the last artifact of an alien race called the Krell. So closely does he examine the external object that he cannot see its function: The machine is a projector and amplifier of the imagination, designed to materialize the thoughts of its creators—in other words, a metaphor for the fantasy art object. Morbius is so sure that the truth lies outside himself, in the machine, that he is blind to his own existence as fantasizing being—thus he cannot see that the invisible monster ravaging the countryside is his own Id, amplified by the machine. Morbius grows to wisdom when he admits the metaphorical status of the monster outside his walls. The monster literally is he, as Commander Adams (Leslie Nielsen) shouts at him during the finale.

To return, finally, to the problem of terminology: how many kinds of things are we dealing with when we talk of "science fiction and fantasy" and an implied "mainstream" other? I am suggesting that there are only two kinds of things, two ends of a spectrum perhaps. One end looks at the fictive landscape and encourages us to examine it rationally as literal object; the other looks at the same scene and encourages us to relate to it emotively as a manifestation of our inner selves. I hesitate to offer names for these alternate orientations, because I know that historically the terminologist is a seller with no buyers, but if pressed I would say that "science fiction" and "fantasy" are reasonably good labels. More important than fixing labels is to notice the new relationship between "fantasy and science fiction" and "mainstream" that the spectrum implies. The "mainstream" metaphor suggests that somewhere there is a strong current of artistic activity, separate from the concerns of "fantasy and science fiction," which may be one thing or two, but which are definitely in some other drainage. Not so. In general, literature and film look at the fictive landscape and encourage us to experience it with a particular part of our selves. Each individual work chooses to be somewhere on this spectrum. I have not yet found the metaphor for the new classification, but perhaps our genres are fish swimming in the same stream, one group heading upstream to spawn and the other heading for salt water. The vast majority of the world's literature is emotively oriented (is heading downstream?), and there is a tendency to do what Silverberg does—assume that science fiction "at its best" turns around and joins it. But why celebrate one end of the spectrum only? I prefer to admire those science fiction fish, a hardy and irreverent finny tribe, daring to go against the flow of the many.

In fact, the science fiction fish delights in asking those other fish why they are going the other way. For example, one day I was watching Walt Disney's *Pinocchio* again, and an insidious question popped into my head: Why does Pinocchio want to be a real boy? After all, mortality is obviously counterproductive; as a living puppet he is, we may suppose, immortal and impervious to pain or disease. Made flesh, what has he gained? Runny noses, failing faculties, lost beauty, and finally death. Why rejoice?

It was definitely a science fiction fish of a question. In *Body Snatchers* the pod people ask Dr. Bennel the same thing: what is so good about being human, about having feelings? In reason, why resist a life of thoughtless contentedness? Dr. Bennel does not bother to answer, and I suspect Pinocchio would not understand the question, but, in the context of fantasy, the answer is clear: being human is an unquestionable goodness. *Of course* one swims downstream!

But in science fiction emotional truisms do not count, and questions like mine and the pod people's must be dealt with. Have you really considered the alternatives to humanity? Why is it so bad to be a Jovian autochthon, as Poul Anderson asks in "Call Me Joe"? Why do we cringe at the thought of losing our bodies and being transplanted into a strong, clean, efficient machine, as Damon Knight asks in "Masks"? Sounds great, once we grow beyond our enfeebling human perspective. Our feelings hobble us, Campbell says; but go further— our humanity hobbles us. In all reason, consider the fascinating alternatives.

In fantasy, reason cuts us off from the instinctive wisdom of the irrational. In science fiction, reason liberates us from the narrowness of our humanity. So fantasy and science fiction, inseparable companions though they may be, are more than different—they are natural enemies.

While written science fiction is well stocked with works representing all points on the "fantasy-to-science-fiction" spectrum, science fiction films are almost unanimously in the "fantasy" camp.[7] And we know this is intentional, because, since most science fiction films are made from written science fiction, we repeatedly watch the studios choose to remove the rational focus of the written original and replace it with an emotive one. At its worst it is the familiar Hollywood vivisection—excise the brain, graft on the love interest, and send the wretched mutant out to ravage Saturday matinees. But, even when the refocusing produces a valuable result, science fiction fans find themselves denied exactly what they came to see, what they rightly saw as the central value and power of the original.

A familiar example of this change of focus when written science fiction is filmed is *The Thing* (1951), Howard Hawks's film version of "Who Goes There?" However good *The Thing* is, it has none of the virtues of the original—it is a good something else. Campbell's paean to the ratiocinative powers of the scientist becomes Hawks's paean to the physical vitality and courage of the military. Campbell's lengthy sessions of group problem solving are replaced by violent physical activity—barricading doors, running, screaming—and we experience the alien not as an unknown to be analyzed and comprehended, but as a large, strong lug that throws people around. The scientists are represented by Dr. Carrington, who is at best a fool and probably mad. Screaming "I'm not your enemy, I'm a scientist," he tries to establish an intellectual dialogue with the nightmare, and is killed by it. The military is then free to fight the Thing with dream weapons (fire, for instance), and the monster is finally outmuscled, not outthought, when our boys find a big enough bang.

If we look only at film versions of written science fiction, we usually see loss and despoliation, and we might conclude that the fantasy orientation is an inferior version of the science fiction orientation—a brainless, "action-packed" emasculation of the "real thing." But there are fantasy films that are not ersatz rationality, but the "real thing" in their own terms—such as *Body Snatchers*. The masterpiece of the genre is Stephen Spielberg's *Close Encounters of a Third Kind*.

A student in one of my science fiction classes—a student proud that he read only literature of the rational daytime perspective—went to see *Close Encounters* and returned hating it. Why? Because, he explained, it kept not answering the questions that it raised. Why were the aliens coming here? What did they want from us? Why did mailboxes and glove compartments fly open when the aliens were near? What did they want with Neary (Richard Dreyfuss), and why did they choose to call *him* to them? What was the significance of the five-note musical phrase, and how did the aliens learn Kodaly's sign language for musical notation? Why, when the aliens are trying to break into a house, can they unscrew the fastenings on the floor vents, but cannot undo latches or break glass windows? On and on goes the list of questions without answers. My student, beginning from the premise that all science fiction asks to be comprehended through the rational intellect,

assumed that the discovery of such answers was "the point" of the
movie, and tautologically concluded that the movie failed to pay off.
But the movie is doing something else, and teaches us how to watch it
best. As the questions without answers multiply and as we despair of
ever explaining what is happening, we watch Neary seek similar answers and then learn not to ask for them, and we study Lacombe
(François Truffaut), who is supposedly a scientist but in fact is not—he
is a believer, what Neary learns to become. Lacombe accepts. Without
needing permission from his reason, he accepts the message of his
heart, and simply *knows* that the aliens are benign and that their coming
is a blessing. What is happening makes sense—this Lacombe knows
surely, this Neary must learn to rely on a new part of himself to accept—and the audience, like Neary, is offered an opportunity to exercise a new source of knowing. My student passed the opportunity by;
he watched with science fiction eyes, saw nothing, and called *Close
Encounters* bad science fiction. It is, rather, the apotheosis of the nighttime perspective, the finest expression of Sense of Wonder on film, and
the archetypal statement of one of my central premises: that wonder
and analysis are antitheses.

The litmus test of any attempt to generalize about science fiction
and film is *2001*, the triumph and enigma of the genre. It has been
called many things: the ultimate "hard" science fiction movie, the best
science fiction film of all time, a modern myth, and an exercise in
pointlessness, vague mysticism, and tedium. Every viewer recognizes
that the movie requires a new way of seeing, but many viewers never
find that way. Is the newness, which some viewers find uniquely re-
warding and which some find frustrating and inaccessible, something
we can by our new terminology call "science fiction"?

We have established two questions for distinguishing "science fiction" from "fantasy": Which side of the human psyche, rational or
emotive, proves effective in encountering the unknown? and What is
the reality status, literal or figurative, of the furniture of this imagined
world? If we ask these questions of *2001*, we do not get simple answers. Dr. Heywood, Bowman, and Poole seem perfect representatives
of the Campbellian perspective—until Bowman (Keir Dullea) reaches
the Star Gate, at which point he, and we with him, are jerked violently
from a world completely comprehensible by reason—where in fact we
have been drilled in the use of the daytime perspective—into a world
experienced with guts and blunt senses, where thinking profits us nothing and we grope for a new means to process an utterly new kind of
data.

The status of objects changes in like manner. In the beginning the world of *2001* is a world of literal objects, as we mentioned before. The spaceships are spaceships, and millions of dollars have been budgeted to make them, the lunar telephones, and the like worthy of our acceptance and attention as literal objects. Again, when we reach the Star Gate, the status of all objects becomes moot. We are not sure, but we strongly suspect that these light shows, blood-red landscapes, Louis XVI hotel suites, and space embryos are symbolic of *something*.

The movie *2001* would seem then to be like other works we have discussed, in that it rhetorically leads us from a rational experiencing of the external world as objective phenomena, through the failure of that perspective to comprehend the alien, to some kind of nonrational alternative, but it is clearly different from the others, and the difference accounts for the rage with which some audiences respond to it. I know many people who are madder at *2001* than at any other movie they have ever seen—people who have waded through the murkiest of foreign art films, the flimsiest efforts of the avant-garde. So surely it is not merely obscurity or badness that breeds such feeling.

Audiences rage because *2001* seems to betray them in two ways. First, *Body Snatchers* shows us a rational character who must be re-educated to handle the new unknown, and the movie sets out reorienting him, and us, immediately. Dr. Bennel is immediately informed that his old perspective is not working, and he can begin opening himself up to the emotive alternative as soon as he is willing. We see where he is headed, and arrive there ahead of him. However, *2001* seems to give no such rhetorical guidance, and in fact trains us to use the orientation that will abruptly and violently prove bankrupt. We have been set up.

Second, the Star Gate catapults us into a world where neither of our alternative perspectives brings understanding. If reason and literalism fail us at *2001*'s conclusion, the apparent alternative fares no better. This makes *2001* unique in our paradigm, because in every other work we have considered, one of the two sides of the human psyche was the "right" side. Not so here. If Bowman's hotel suite is symbolic, what can it possibly be symbolic of? If it is literal, why in heaven's name would Bowman make a mind-wrenching voyage across space and time and end up in a velvet dressing gown eating meat and potatoes in a Louis XVI hotel suite with Watteau paintings on the walls? Many viewers understandably feel as though they have read most of a captivating mystery novel, only to discover the final chapter written in Sanskrit.

This rhetorical structure is intended to shock, but it is not a betrayal, because we have been warned—we have been in fact promised a conclusion beyond our human comprehension. Once before, we witnessed man at one stage in his evolution encounter the monolith and be catapulted into a new world, one incomprehensible to the old ways of seeing. The man-ape tosses his new weapon into the air, and we find ourselves instantly in a world of space stations and lunar rockets. From which side of the man-ape's psyche can he comprehend such things? Clearly, no side. He must transcend himself. The second time, we are the man-apes, glimpsing a future unknowable by any of the forms of wisdom we now possess. Remember the Pinocchio principle: our humanity hobbles us. The failure of our rational wisdom to comprehend the universe beyond the Star Gate is not an invitation to our emotive wisdom to do better; rather, what we need is a superhuman logic. Thus *2001* is the quintessential science fiction film, and the audiences' confusion and rage are a testament to their lack of practice with science fiction modes of seeing in film.

Thus all objects in *2001* are literal, and reason is an infallible guide to comprehending the alien. The monolith is not representative of anything but itself—it is simply an alien machine designed to be discovered by man and to accelerate his evolution toward ultimate wisdom. Similarly, the hotel suite is a hotel suite, and the embryo floating in space is an embryo floating in space. Film audiences and critics find it difficult to believe that grownups could even temporarily ask other grownups to accept these things literally, so they search desperately for the film's "meaning," while the "meaning" is transparently there all the time: a race of superintelligent aliens is hastening our evolution for purposes beyond human comprehension. That is what it means. Really.

Why then can we not rationally understand the movie's conclusion? Because we are not rational *enough*. Since audiences are so practiced in the wrong orientation to the alien and since Stanley Kubrick seems unwilling to provide explicit rhetorical direction, Arthur C. Clarke must do it; he writes a novelization of the movie, to put our response right. In the novel *2001*, he explains painstakingly that Bowman's experience beyond the Star Gate, like his experience before it, is completely literal and accessible to reason.

He begins with a foreword that states his thesis and purpose in writing: this story is *not* symbolic. Given the size of the universe, Clarke says, it is statistically inevitable that some day we shall meet our masters. Thus *2001* is one possible scenario of that literal experience.

Clarke, who sports the polar opposite of Lacombe's faith beyond explanation, sets out to answer all possible logical questions that might remain unanswered after a viewing of the film: who the aliens are, what they want, how the monolith works, what it does to the man-apes, and so on, right up to who the Star Child is and why and how he is made. Clarke explains and explains, until our intellectual curiosity is satisfied, then glutted—he even manages to explain how and why the alien has built Bowman's hotel suite: the alien, in order to make Bowman feel "at home" when he arrives, has monitored Earth television broadcasts and duplicated the set of a popular soap opera.[8] But notice, to make it make sense, Clarke must abolish the really troublesome details of the scene—the ominous sterility, the Watteau paintings, and the like. What Clarke cannot explain, the Star Child can, though our reason is inadequate to comprehend. The proportions of the monolith, which before seemed arbitrary or symbolic, are now revealed to be logically inevitable, if one's logic embraces multitudinous dimensions.[9] Far from valuing man's emotive side, Clarke triumphantly evolves it out of existence.

Thus it seems that science fiction films are so committed to the emotive orientation that the masterpiece of rational science fiction movies needs a novel-length manual to teach audiences how to watch it. Why is this so? Logically, one might expect film to embrace the Campbellian perspective, because of film's ability to glorify the object as object. But film has not done this, and I offer only the most obvious and superficial of explanations: film works emotively. Thomas R. Atkins has said, "Because its potential is chiefly visual and emotional rather than intellectual, the SF film usually communicates to the instinctive child in us instead of the reflective adult."[10] That does not mean that science fiction films are for those who cannot think; Lacombe and the aliens he greets are both childlike, but not from a failure to mature.

The reading process seems inherently analytical, in a way that film perhaps can never be. The issue transcends science fiction films. For instance, we see the same shift in focus when detective novels are filmed. Similarly, television documentaries traditionally find themselves driven to choose between being analytical (a choice that usually produces a static image of faces talking to the audience or to each other) and being interesting (a choice that leads to an emphasis on drama and personality and to inevitable charges of sensationalizing, personalizing, or overdramatizing the news).

For whatever reason, science fiction films have always been overwhelmingly of the nighttime orientation, and they are getting more so. We are in the midst of an explosion of science fiction moviemaking, but the renaissance is emphatically emotive. *Close Encounters*, *Star Wars*, *Alien*, *Star Trek*—we are making better and better "fantasy" films. Is anyone interested in attempting the alternative any more?

GARY KERN

The Search for Fantasy: From Primitive Man to Pornography

So full of shapes is fancy
That it alone is high fantastical.

Shakespeare, *Twelfth Night, or What You Will*

The birth of fantasy took place, I imagine, among primitive men. Not so primitive as to lack a language, even a complicated one, with subtle terms, concepts, and an oral narrative tradition, but primitive enough to hunt for food, live in the dirt, and sit around the fire scraping hides. One night, after the usual account by the chief storyteller, one of the tribe got an idea which had never entered a human head before. Either because he was bored with the story, which repeated point for point something that had happened, or he envied the exploits of the story- teller, or doubted the words of the gods, or simply he was a trouble- maker, or half-crazy, or sick and feverish, for whatever reason, he de- cided to tell the story differently. And so, without going anywhere or doing anything, he altered the story in his head—cut out old things, added new things, made it better. Then he told this new version to his clan. Their heavy brows knitted, their uncouth mouths dropped open: they were disturbed. Something magical was happening: the mind was separating from brute matter, becoming independent of fact. By its own force it was changing words, changing the pictures in the thick skulls, and dimly making itself felt.

What happened after this is hard to imagine. The new storyteller may have gained power, become a medicine man, a soothsayer, a priest. He may have become a leader, a hero in his own stories and after his death—a god. He may have become an idiot, whose inven- tions were stolen by the first storyteller and everybody else, while he himself was ridiculed. Or he may have been stoned, driven out, or eaten. Since great discoveries are usually repeated by individual experimenters, I assume that all of these possibilities were realized with different tribes. In one way or another, however, the achievement was retained. The first storyteller had resisted the flow of time, tried to hold it with his words, but he was still a slave to events—internal and external. The second storyteller resisted the shape of events and arranged them to suit his purpose. He was their master, he made them exist. Before him, there was only reproduction.

Having dreamed up this little theory, I decided to apply it to various works I had read in my life, perhaps skimming a few new ones where necessary. Not so much to prove the theory correct, as to see if it could order what scattered knowledge I had. I would sail in my theory in search of fantasy, beginning as far back as I could. Creation myths seemed a good starting place, and of their ancient sources, Egypt and Mesopotamia, I chose the latter, understanding that by this time men had risen from the dirt, spread over the earth, developed agriculture in accordance with floods, founded cities, mined ores, invented writing, and institutionalized religions. Fade out campfire, fade in Babylon.

Babylon

> *When there was no heaven,*
> *no earth, no height, no depth, no name,*
> *when Apsu was alone,*
> *the sweet water, the first begetter; and Tiamat*
> *the bitter water, and that*
> *return to the womb, her Mummu,*
> *when there were no gods*[1]

The Babylonian Creation begins before time, when there are only Apsu—the abyss, the bottomless gulf, the sweet water, desiring only to sleep in peace—and Tiamat, his mate, formlessness, chaos, inertia, seeking nothing. Apsu is masculine, a mindless begetter; Tiamat is feminine, with eyes, nostrils, paps, a moist monster whose bitter waters can flood and cause destruction. Their offspring is Mummu, a mist or cloud, desiring return to the womb. From these amorphous spirits creation begins in a manner dialectical: the sweet and bitter waters mingle, forming silt—the masculine Lahmu and the feminine Lahamu; the silt forms a line between earth and heaven—the masculine horizon Anshar and the feminine Kishar; this leaves Anu, the empty heaven, who from long-lasting boredom, it seems, creates Ea, the god of intellect and wisdom. Meanwhile, in Tiamat's prolific belly, new babies are teeming, making noise, disturbing Apsu, who with the counsel of Mummu decides to kill them. Thus begins life and the possibility of death.

The Babylonian Creation is therefore a cosmogony—an explanation of the birth of the cosmos. It is also a theogony—the birth of the gods. And, from what follows, a polisogony—the creation of the city of Babylon. Finally, it is a hero myth—the triumph of the god Marduk. The murderous plan of Apsu is foiled by Ea, who drowns him and takes away his crown; Mummu is led away by the nose. Then, having filled the abyss with intelligence, Ea begets Marduk: "His body was beautiful; when he raised his eyes great lights flared; his stride was majestic; he was the leader from the first."[2] Tiamat, roused by her complaining children, plots revenge for Apsu, spawns enormous serpents with poisonous fangs:

> *She made the Worm,*
> *the Dragon*
> *the Female Monster*
> *the Great Lion*
> *the Mad Dog*
> *the Man Scorpion*
> *the Howling Storm*
> *Kulili (the flying dragon)*
> *Kusariqu (the wild bison)*[3]

And she chooses the clumsy laborer Kingu as her war captain. In alarm the gods—Tiamat's original offspring—attempt to counteract her, but they are terrified by her aspect. Only Marduk, combining intelligence with will, is able to vanquish her: "When the mouth gaped open to suck him down he drove in Imhullu (the tumid wind), so that the mouth would not shut but wind raged through her belly; her carcass blown up, tumescent, she gaped—And now he shot the arrow that split the belly, that pierced the gut and cut the womb."[4] The Terrible Mother explodes. As for Kingu, her dull slave, Marduk sends him into the underworld to be the god of death. The hero stands clear of the absorbing feminine unconscious and—for this moment in history—of its destructive remnant, death.[5] Having rescued the gods, he now assumes supreme command, acquires all their qualities, creates man as their servant from the blood of Kingu, and founds Babylon as his residence.

To those who knew and recited this account, it was reality. The recitation was made in the second millennium during the New Year festival, each part on successive days, before the idol of Marduk. The ritual insured the legitimacy of the kingship as well as its subordination to Marduk and official religion; the city itself was arranged so as to accommodate the temples; the skies were read as divine signs. So it would seem that in *The Babylonian Creation* there were no fiction, no fantasy, no history even—everything is divine truth. Even so, there is proto-fiction: a poetic line with a caesura, two beats, and insistent assonance; a mixture of narration and dialogue; a use of refrain helpful for memorization, but also pleasing to the listener; a recapitulation at the beginning of each section before the action continues; and the perspective of the omniscient author, the priest mentioned at the end of the liturgy: "the wise teacher to whose words we listen; he wrote it down, he saved it for time to come."[6] There is proto-fantasy: the conquering god, leading to monotheism, who later becomes the conquering hero, leading to individuality. And there is proto-history: Marduk was the god of Babylon, and as the city rose in stature, so rose its god.

More obviously poetical, yet still connected with ritual, is the work known as *Inanna's Descent into the Underworld*. Fragments are spread over a thousand years of Sumerian and Akkadian clay tablets, yet a firm poetical structure is felt throughout. One version begins:

> *This lady left earth and heaven*
> > *and went down into the pit,*
> *power and titles she left,*
> > *she went down into the pit,*
> *left Emushkalamma in Badtibira,*
> > *she went down into the pit,*
> *left Zabalam in Giguna,*
> > *she went down into the pit;*
> *Esharra she left in Adab,*
> > *she went down into the pit.*[7]

Inanna, possibly wishing to conquer hell, or to learn about death, puts on seven insignia; these same seven are enumerated as she takes them off one at a time at each gate of hell; they are enumerated again when she leaves (Akkadian version).[8] She gives instructions to her servant before her descent; he fulfills them in order after her descent. And so on, an elaborate series of parallels and refrains is put together, and while the seven gates may mirror the seven celestial bodies—sun, moon, and five visible planets[9]—the act of connecting a narrative account with the cosmic order was at some point in time a creative act, even if unconscious. The story of Inanna is also filled with themes repeated in myths the world over: mythic pairs (Inanna, goddess of heaven—her sister Ereshkigal, goddess of the underworld), seven stages of initiation (the gates), water of life and water of death, mother's lament, sister's lament, terrible woman (Inanna sacrifices her husband to escape hell). The whole thing relates to the return of spring (Inanna from hell) and the renewal of kingship (the king of Uruk each year was ritually resurrected and married to Inanna).[10] Parallels are found in the Egyptian Osiris and Isis, the Greek Persephone, and the Syrian Thammuz, later Adonis. Inanna herself reappears as Ishtar, Astarte, Aphrodite, and Venus.

Another Sumerian-Akkadian text, *Adapa: The Man*, gives a curious twist to one of these themes. Inanna was rescued from hell because her servant, following her orders, refused Ereshkigal's offer of water—the water of death. Adapa is advised by Ea to refuse proffered water when called to heaven to account for some curses he has uttered. Adapa obeys, only to learn that he has renounced the water of eternal life, thereby bringing suffering and death to all mankind. Here no ritual seems to be involved, only a theological explanation of mortality. And perhaps a proto-joke.

The Epic of Gilgamesh is the earliest preserved epic, antedating Homer by fifteen hundred years. Probably first written in the third millennium, its oldest tablets (Sumerian) date from the early second millennium, its latest (Akkadian) from the seventh century B.C. In the composition of the story, scholars are able to trace various historical layers. The earliest include myths of creation, fertility, and nature; then comes the story of primeval man and his civilization (Enkidu); there follows the story of the builder-king and his search for immortality (Gilgamesh); into this story is inserted the myth of the flood; and attached to the whole are words of wisdom provided by later Akkadian priests. Since there is no one recension of the epic which is complete, our conception of the work is of necessity a collation of materials, an ideal version of Gilgamesh. And since many authors took part in its composition, we must posit a continuous literary intelligence from first to final recension.

The chief source of the epic was secular. We know that Gilgamesh was a historical personage, fifth king of Uruk after the flood, reigning around 2700 B.C., famous as the builder of city walls and a temple to Inanna. There was a certain king of Lagash who obtained precious cedarwood from distant mountains; Gilgamesh is credited in the epic with the same achievement.[11] Enkidu probably was a historical figure who, like Gilgamesh, conquered Uruk.[12] The ill-fortuned lovers of the goddess Inanna (Ishtar) mentioned in the epic may refer to the kings of

Uruk who took part in the ritual marriage.[13] Everything in the epic may derive from something factual, so it is tempting to locate fantasy in mere exaggeration: Enkidu spends six days and seven nights in coitus with the harlot; Enkidu and Gilgamesh break the doorposts and shake the walls when they grapple; they carry axes of nine score pounds, swords with blades of six score pounds, with pommels and hilts of thirty pounds.[14] Yet heroic hyperbole was also part of the historical record: the Sumerian King List written at the beginning of the second millennium states that Gilgamesh reigned 126 years, while kings after him are listed for normal life terms.[15] Probably people believed it, but later they doubted. Tablets have been recovered from the eighth century B.C., that is, about a century before the latest Akkadian recension of the epic and about the time of Homer, which make fun of the schoolbook Gilgamesh. They present a letter from Gilgamesh to a king demanding outlandish amounts of livestock and metal as gifts for Enkidu. This appears to be a primitive piece of fantasy, anticipating Lucian, and the four copies suggest that there was already a tradition of parody.[16]

A more likely area for fantasy seems to me the descriptions of Gilgamesh's journeys, for here he took leave of the known world and traveled lands seen mainly by imagination. In his search for Dilmun, where the Noah figure Utnapishtim enjoys eternal life, Gilgamesh traveled eastward through mountain passes inhabited by lions, past twin mountains guarded by scorpion men, through twelve leagues of darkness into the blazing sun, then across Ocean, which to the ancient Sumerians lay somewhere out beyond the Persian Gulf, and finally to Dilmun—the garden of paradise and heaven. The author moved with him into the unknown, marking the path with signposts available in his time, but also tracing the course of his mind through myth.

"Myth," writes the theologian John Dunne, "is an interpretation of mystery."[17] At the time of its creation it may not be entirely conscious, but it is a step toward consciousness. Gilgamesh is the hero—his name means "father-man" or "father-hero" (in our terms, "super-hero").[18] Such a hero will return with Odysseus, Aeneas, Parsifal, and Faust.[19] Gilgamesh is made by the gods two-thirds divine and one-third human, and like a baby or a primitive he regards himself and the world as one: he takes sons from their fathers, he leaves no girl a virgin.[20] To check his hubris, the people appeal to the gods, who in response shape Enkidu out of moistened clay—the name means "Enki is good" (Enki being the Sumerian water god, associated with fertility).[21] Scholars may see here a simple fusion of two legendary heroes into one story, but something psychologically profound is involved. Enkidu, although of divine creation, is earthy, primitive, savage; he is weakened by intercourse with a woman (or harlot) and civilized;[22] when he comes before Gilgamesh, he is almost indistinguishable from him. The roles of the two seem to interchange in the epic, and in portrayals of the time they are well-nigh identical. This is because they are the same man. In Jungian terms, Enkidu is the shadow of Gilgamesh, made known to him first through a dream, then through the medium of the harlot—the anima. The shadow is a demonic and surprising part of the psyche, overwhelming at first to the naive subject. Thus it is interesting that Enkidu grapples with Gilgamesh, brings him down to earth. (In one reading of the Babylonian recension, Enkidu in fact defeats Gilgamesh.)[23] After their struggle, the two become united in friendship and function as twins— the motif is repeated with Castor and Pollux, Romulus and Remus, Cain and Abel, and our own movie heroes with their faithful sidekicks. Now the sly Enkidu makes Gilgamesh face mortality, interpreting a dream from the gods, who decree that Gilgamesh is destined to rule, but not to live forever. Death is the mystery to be interpreted by myth.

Where then is fiction? Where then is fantasy? I can't really find it, but I think it is being born. In the author's choice of materials, his shaping of the story, his mythmaking. In this multilayered, many-centuried epic, Gilgamesh is made to seek different types of immortality— the perpetual growth of the evergreen forest, the timelessness of paradise, the eternal rejuvenation of nature. In his quest he must thrice overcome destructive powers—the monster guardian of the evergreens Humbaba, the murderous lover-goddess Inanna (Ishtar), the worldly wise, coy innkeeper Sabitum.[24] Each offers a different form of self-obliteration for the emerging masculine consciousness. Yet at the end, Gilgamesh does not find immortality, rather the knowledge of mortality. He returns home, engraves his story in stone, dies, and is buried with full ceremony. His reward would seem to be understanding, acceptance of his humanity, and we may presume the author who shaped the story earned the same reward. Besides this, the story which Gilgamesh engraved in stone brought him another type of immortality, even as the author of the epic invades the mind of each reader. The walls of Uruk, built by the historical Gilgamesh, were intentionally razed by the conquering Akkadian king Sargon, but the words of the epic, though obliterated in places, were not confined to stone: they took root in the more enduring substance of the mind.

Athens

Having stayed a while in Babylon, I proceeded in my search for fantasy directly to Athens, skirting warily past the Scylla of Homer and the Charybdis of the Old Testament. In Athens I found history already invented as a work of narrative prose, with a chronicle of facts, an interpretation of motives, and a description of barbarian customs. Thucydides, who heard Herodotus recite in public, is busy recording the Peloponnesian War, purging from his account everything that cannot be verified, yet feeling free in invent the opposing sides of an argument at which he was not present. His purpose is to compose a record of truth—an "everlasting possession" for the reflective mind.[25] Lyrical poetry flourishes in Athens, evidently much more so than in Egypt and Mesopotamia. And people can be heard telling tales about talking animals—an ant and a grasshopper, a fox and a crow: fables attributed to Aesop, who according to legend was brought as a slave to Athens and instructed his masters discreetly by means of moral tales. Actually, such tales were told a hundred years before Aesop by Archilochus, who in the seventh century B.C. observed, "The fox knows many tricks, the hedgehog only one. / One good one."[26] And scholars say animal tales came to Greece from ancient Babylon. Is this fantasy? The animal talks, but never betrays his nature—the fox is wily, the ant industrious—and he always proves a moral. This fantasy, for all of its variety, seems to be held on a leash.[27]

In the theater tragedies are presented which mine the material of the myths, now consciously understood as such. And comedies, with a well-established form: a prologue, setting the situation; a parodos, marking the entry of the chorus; episodes, set off by fixed choral elements; a parabasis, or address, to the audience, with six subsections and fixed poetic meters; and an exodos, or triumphant marching-away song.[28] The material as well, though perhaps not so strict, is established by tradition, deriving from the Attic κῶμος, or popular procession of revelers in masks and animal costumes singing and dancing in honor of Dionysus. Yet it is here, in the comedies of Aristophanes, that I find the first great burst of fantasy, though he had precedents, notably Magnes, who is believed to have written plays called *The Birds*, *The Flies*, and *The Frogs*. I must assume that within severely imposed limits Aristophanes did something very imaginative, since he caused the audience to laugh and won the first prize most often. Within his plays, most of which make a satiric comment upon the Peloponnesian War, I would distinguish two types of fantasy: the improbable and the impossible. An Athenian tired of the war concludes his own private peace by offering a wineskin to the enemy, and then sets up a profitable trade *(The Acharnians);* the women of both sides, tired of the war, go on a sex strike and force their male members to make peace *(Lysistrata):* these are improbable actions, perhaps psychologically impossible, but not physically so. Physically impossible are Socrates suspended aloft in the heavens *(The Clouds),* jurists transformed into wasps *(The Wasps),* a man flying to Mt. Olympus on a giant dung beetle in order to recover Peace *(Peace),* birds building a perfect state in the sky *(The Birds).* All of these impossibilities are in some measure realized metaphors: Socrates must "suspend judgment" and raise his thoughts to celestial matters; the jurists run around buzzing in wasp costumes because the hero has "stirred up a wasp's nest," and also the Greek word ἐγκεντρίς signified both a voting stylus and a sting; Trygaeus mounts the dung bettle because it is "the only living thing with wings, so Aesop says, that ever reached the gods"; and the birds can build Cloudcuckooland because they rule the skies, Zeus appears with an eagle in pictures, people swear by the birds and write winged poetry, and also because νόμος means both law and melody, πόλος means firmament, and πόλις means city.[29] Of course, Aristophanes mixes the improbable and the impossible, so that Pisthetaerus leaves Athens a man, takes a magic root which transforms him into a bird, and by building Cloudcuckooland rises to the level of the gods. By such fantasy, Aristophanes set his vision, his creative mind, and himself in opposition to the political direction of his society. He created absurdities to match the absurdities of the war, and within the created absurdities everything proceeds according to its own logic, as it does in the external world. Thus he separated reality and fantasy, using the latter to produce a "counter-image" which questions, criticizes, and condemns the former.[30]

Thus fiction and fact have become quite distinct and found expression in appropriate genres. But fact is not limited to external events; there is also the mind which apprehends them and tries to go beyond them. The genre for this mode of thought is represented by the Platonic dialogue, which might be called speculative fiction. For we know that Plato could not possibly have recorded all the conversations of his departed master: Socrates became a literary figure for him who participated in ideal dialogues. Their beauty consists not only in their understated drama, intellectual excitement, and moral purity, but also in their self-reflective nature: When Socrates advises self-control, he himself demonstrates it *(Charmides);* when he investigates friendship, he gives a model conversation of one friend with another *(Lysis)*; when he inquires into words, his speech becomes fanciful *(Cratylus)*; when he speaks for the laws, he himself observes them *(Crito)*; when he postulates the ideal state, he himself establishes it with his friends *(The Republic)*. When he speaks of something beyond normal human experience, he invokes myth as a legendary or invented tale which may lack historical verification, yet reveal philosophical or religious truth. Thus the story of Er, a man who died and came back to life with an account of the Isle of the Blessed and the judgment of souls. Socrates tells Callicles (in The *Gorgias*) that though it may seem like a fable *(muthos)*, he himself regards it as the truth *(logos)*. And on the same point, he tells Phaedo: "This or something like it at any rate is what happens in regard to our souls and their habitations—that this is so seems to me proper and worthy of the risk of believing; for the risk is noble."[31] The aging Cephalos gives a different slant to tales of life after death: when you are young you laugh at them, but when you are old and nearer to death they torment your soul *(The Republic)*. In various ways, then, myth is believed to impart truth, if not a specific description of things. It is an "interpretation of mystery," and Plato's art is its conscious representation.

It is from the Greeks that we get the word *fantasy*. Generally speaking, they understood φαντασία to refer to images retained in the mind after perception: these might appear haphazardly (what we would call *daydreaming*) or intentionally (what we would call *imagining*). In either case the images are presented before the mind's eye. For the Greeks this was a matter of epistemology, not of literary genre.[32] They didn't know that I would be coming back to them in search of fantasy. Still, their approach enables me to distinguish the object of my search: *aesthetic fantasy*—images not allowed to appear haphazardly, but consciously shaped into artistic form. Random daydreams or reveries of wish-fulfillment don't count.

Around the year A.D. 165, an important event occurred in the history of aesthetic fantasy. A successful lecturer moved his family from the banks of the Euphrates to Athens, broke off his career, and began writing fanciful stories and dialogues. In the introduction to one story, he marked his change of direction:

> Since I'm vain enough myself to want to leave something behind to posterity and since I have nothing true to record—I never had any experiences worth talking about—in order not to be the only writer without a stake in the right to make up tall tales, I, too, have turned to lying—but

much more honest lying than all the others. The one and only truth you'll hear from me is that I *am* lying; by frankly admitting that there isn't a word of truth in what I say, I feel I'm avoiding the possibility of attack from any quarter.

Well, then, I'm writing about things I neither saw nor heard from another soul, things which don't exist and couldn't possibly exist. So let all readers beware: don't believe any of it.[33]

What follows is the famous *True Story*, in which Lucian, writing in the first person, tells of his voyage to an island with a river of wine and women-vines who grow clusters of grapes from their fingers; his flight to the moon where a buzzard cavalry wages war with an ant cavalry from the sun; his sighting of Cloudcuckooland, which really exists; his experience inside a whale 150 miles long and his escape by lowering the ship from ropes tied to its teeth; and his stopover at the Isle of the Blessed, where Socrates is threatened with banishment unless he gives up his irony and Plato is absent, being consigned to live in the republic he had invented. Such things could not possibly exist, but the sources of their non-existence are fairly obvious: the exploits of Odysseus, the fabulous lands of Herodotus, the myths of Plato. Details are filled out by hyperbole, transposition of human and animal parts, and realized metaphors. Further, Lucian may have seen or heard some of these things from another soul, notably Menippus, whose satires are lost, and in any event, once Lucian hits on an idea, he retells it in endless variation according to the rules of rhetoric and models well known to him.[34] More than one scholar has approached Lucian as an original genius and ended up branding him an industrious hack. All the same, however much he may tire after a few works, Lucian marks an important advance in the evolution of fantasy. When Apsu and Tiamat mingle and separate the sweet and bitter waters, this is divine truth, immediate to the people in ritual before a god. When Gilgamesh crosses Ocean and learns the story of the flood, this is legend, remote yet still felt by the people of the two rivers. When Er returns from the dead with his story of the judgment of souls, this is myth and known as such. When Trygaeus flies to Mt. Olympus on a dung beetle, this is fantasy, albeit politically motivated and, within the impossible premise, fairly realistic. But when Lucian flits from moon to sun to Cloudcuckooland to whale to Isle of the Blessed amid an assortment of half-human, half-animal figures, this is fantasy pure and simple. True, he delights in ridiculing the classics, not without philosophic purpose. But he's no philosopher, and as a satirist he's not very current: the classics primarily give him material for a self-sufficient play of fantasy. The delight is in creating and varying the fantastic images and in making an amusing adventure, whatever the subject or source.

Departure from Athens

At this point I wanted to move quickly from Lucian to modern fantasy and make a neat scheme while doing so. Accordingly, I drew two lines on my literary map, following the charts of various navigators. The first line, utopian literature: Sir Thomas More, Montaigne, Bacon, Campanella, Samuel Johnson, Voltaire, Jules Verne, H. G. Wells, our modern utopias and anti-utopias. The second line, the somewhat amorphous genre known as the Menippean satire: Erasmus's *In Praise of Folly*, Rabelais, Grimmelshausen, Cyrano de Bergerac, Swift, Voltaire's *Micromegas*, Diderot's *Rameau's Nephew*, Jean Paul Richter, E. T. A. Hoffmann, Dostoevsky.[35] These lines, of course, do not start from Lucian, but pass through him and sometimes intersect each other, always aware of the distance traversed. This is particularly true of the utopian line, where each author is conscious of the tradition before him and struggles with it while attempting to advance it. A third line, that of pure adventure, might be drawn through Lucian as a divergence from fantasy. As for fantasy itself, the two most important points after Lucian seem to me the science fiction of Jules Verne and H. G. Wells, which not only presented counterimages to their societies, but also turned the reader's gaze toward the future; and the grotesqueries of E. T. A. Hoffmann, which presented paradoxes to his society and turned the reader's gaze inward. By now, the nineteenth century, aesthetic fantasy has become so multifarious that, like the word "game" in Wittgenstein's *Sprachspiele*, no one definition would seem to encompass it: it has become a world of relationships and possibilities which permits a number of definitions dependent on one's point of view and one's specific need.

St. Petersburg

My space-time machine carried me swiftly to a fantastic city created in the marshes of the Neva River on the bones of exhausted slaves. St. Petersburg, the pinnacle of rationalism, with its straight streets and glittering prospekts, its tables of ranks and bureaucracies, yet seems like a mirage when the mists roll off the river, or the river overflows, or the white snow fills the air and the river freezes solid, or the summer sun never goes down and the sky is white all night. Nevsky Prospekt runs the length of the mainland as a grand processional way, and here everything is bright, intoxicating, and deceitful. "Oh, do not trust that Nevsky Prospekt!" declaims a strange little man with a big nose. "I always wrap myself up more closely in my cloak when I walk along it and do my best not to look at things I pass. For all is deceit, all is a dream, all is not what it seems."[36] And, sure enough, over there, emerging from a carriage, wearing a uniform embroidered in gold with a high-standing collar and buckskin breeches with a sword at the side, indicating the rank of state councillor, is a nose. And there, running after him, is a collegiate assessor without a nose. The assessor accosts the councillor and exclaims, "Why, you are my own nose!" To which the councillor replies, "You are mistaken, my good sir. I'm on my own. Furthermore there cannot be any close relations between us. Judging by the buttons on your uniform, you must work in another department."[37]

Not only is the nose disconnected, but the logic. One critic has catalogued seven kinds of comic illogicality in the works of Nikolai Gogol: absurd speculations, abrupt digressions, arbitrary associations, fractured speech, false leads, non-sequitur dialogue, and unmotivated action.[38] For my purpose, I would say that fantasy has invaded logic. Some examples from "The Nose":

> Ivan Yakovlevich, like every decent Russian workman, was a terrible drunkard.

> "Today, Praskovya Osipovna, I will not drink coffee," said Ivan Yakovlevich, "but instead would like to eat a bit of hot bread with onion." (That is, Ivan Yakovlevich would have liked both the one and the other, but knew that it was quite impossible to ask for two things at once: for Praskovya very much disliked such whims.)

> Ivan Yakovlevich was a great cynic, and when the collegiate assessor Kovalyov would say to him as usual while he was being shaved: "Ivan Yakovlevich, your hands always stink!" Ivan Yakovlevich would reply with the question: "Why shouldn't they stink?" "I don't know, brother, only they stink," the collegiate assessor would say, and Ivan Yakovlevich, having taken a pinch of snuff, would soap him for this both on the cheek and under the nose and behind the ear and under the beard, in a word, wherever he wanted.[39]

And from *"The Overcoat"*:

> The tailor Petrovich . . . despite his one eye and the pockmarks all over his face, engaged rather successfully in the repair of clerks' and all other sorts of trousers and tailcoats, of course, when he was in a sober state and not nourishing some other notions in his head.[40]

With such verbal grotesquerie—verbal fantasy, if you will—Gogol produces a world which not only could not possibly exist, it could not possibly be comprehended. "It's true," cries one confused character, "if God wanted to punish us, then first he'd take away reason." Another: "How this happened, I can't for the life of me explain. It's like some kind of fog dumbfounded us, the devil mixed things up!"[41] And this is the author's view: he draws us into a game of illogic, a world mixed up by the devil, then catches us with a sudden shift, a reminder of a better world (the pathetic moment in "The Overcoat," the conclusion of *The Inspector General*). But despite this purpose, he often delights in illogicality for its own sake—that is, for its comic, mind-boggling possibilities: "But all the same, when you think about it, there is something, really, in all this. No matter what anyone says, such things happen in the world: rarely, but they happen."[42]

In fantastic St. Petersburg there are many fantasists: they themselves become suitable material for fantasy. "In natures which are avid for activity, avid for immediate life, avid for reality, but which are weak, feminine, tender," writes the young Dostoevsky, "little by little there grows something which is called dreaminess, and a man becomes at last not a man, but some kind of creature in between—*a dreamer.*"[43]

Such a creature is the hero of *White Nights*, who romanticizes his relationship to a young woman and loses her to another man, whom she herself romanticizes. But he does not mind: he experienced a moment of bliss, which he can repeat in his thoughts, as he revisits the places of the romance. A different sort of dreamer is the hero (or antihero) of *Notes from Underground*, a man of "acute consciousness" who holds lofty ideals of the beautiful and the sublime while nurturing his rancor against mankind in his mouse hole of reflection. His sickness, as Kierkegaard described it, is the "sickness unto death"—the fear of acting and losing infinite potential, the self-glorification of untried dreams and ideals. With this subject Dostoevsky created a new form within the broad Menippean satire—part philosophy, part romantic story (parody), the whole convoluted by the thought of the fantasist, just as Kierkegaard independently created a new philosophical-literary genre with *Either/Or* and his other "aesthetic" works. To make a neat formula, I would say that with Dostoevsky fantasy becomes its own subject. (Both of his dreamers, please note, write notes—they are aesthetic, not random fantasists.)

Toward the end of his career, Dostoevsky gave an explanation of fantastic literature which his readers would hardly have expected. He published three fantastic stories at this time in his *Diary of a Writer* (1876–1881). In "Bobok," a morose man visits the graveyard and hears the conversations of decomposing corpses. In "The Dream of a Ridiculous Man," a would-be suicide dreams of flying to a paradisical double of the earth, which he corrupts, yet from which he returns with the message of brotherly love. In "The Gentle One," a man reflects to himself just after his wife has committed suicide. This third story would seem the least fantastic of the set, and the author appends a preface by way of explanation. The story, he says, is called fantastic and yet is in the highest degree real; the fantastic element consists in the form, in supposing that the thoughts of such a man could be captured and put to paper, as if by a stenographer, just as, for example, Victor Hugo made his hero keep a diary of his last day before execution—up to the last moment. It is not fantastic, Dostoevsky implies, that corpses should talk, but that they should be heard and recorded. Not fantastic that a failed suicide should fly to paradise in his dream, but that the dream should be presented to us on paper. The act of literature, of capturing thought and giving it artistic form—this is what Dostoevsky found to be fantastic. The mind, with all of its unpredictable, compulsive, even insane thoughts, was reality.

Thus Andrei Belyi's novel *Petersburg* (1911) is able to reverse the usual order of reality. The mind which imagines now produces phenomena, from an imaginary point to a dot on a map, to the concentric circles forming the city, to the circular wheels of carriages rolling down the prospekts and the circulars announcing revolution, to the black dots on the page, producing a surge of words, straight lines describing the straight prospekts down which square boxes of carriages move bearing characters with circular heads. The characters themselves are infected by the flood of images, which the author calls *mozgovaya igra* ("cerebral play"), which are ephemeral, yet real, begetting words and names from mere sounds, characters from mental images, conflicts from the opposites of circles and lines, red and green, East and West. The mighty structure, St. Petersburg, rises up as the novel's chief character, with all its dreams, nightmares, illusions, and literary traditions. The city conceives itself.

And the author conceives himself and all of existence in another experiment, *Kotik Letaev* (1916). Retracing the origin and growth of his consciousness from before birth to the age of five, Kotik creates psychology—the infant's impressions and attempted interpretation; myth—the images of mankind repeated by the child; linguistics—the formation of language and meanings; structure—the emergence of literary form out of chaos; autobiography—the material of Belyi's childhood; religion—the discovery of memories before memories, life after life, Christ. Belyi wrote the work in insomniac fits while working on a temple for the founder of Anthroposophy, Rudolf Steiner. I am not sure how closely Belyi followed this philosophy in his work, but I am struck by its precise parallels to a work by a Jungian psychologist, Erich Neumann, entitled *The Origins and History of Consciousness* (1949). Both the writer and the psychologist proceed from the same premise: the development of the individual reproduces the evolution of the race, not only physically, but psychically. Thus the child moves through the same myths—uroboros, creation, separation of the world parents, emergence of the hero, his quest, and victory in consciousness—both in the novel and in the psychological study without any contact between the two.[44]

In Evgeny Zamyatin's *We* (1920), I find a synthesis of the preceding moments in fantasy. Belyi's *mozgovaya igra* is complemented by *myslennyi yazyk* ("thought language")—a telegraphic style of dots, dashes, and broken-off thoughts; circles and squares are complemented by mathematical imagery and mock formulas for freedom and happiness; Dostoevsky's rejection of the crystal palace and his story of the Grand Inquisitor are transformed into a glass city ruled by a Benefactor, the underground man into a disturbed true believer; Gogol's grotesquerie is represented by metonymic imagery and a reversal of values; Wells's projection into the future, carrying the present "to the last rung of the logical ladder," is repeated with the projection of the Soviet State one thousand years ahead; Plato's republic is represented by the Bureau of the Guardians; Aristophanes' counterimage is seen throughout, but also in details, such as the numbering of citizens; myths are repeated—Adam and Eve, St. George and the dragon; the archetypes are realized—D-503 = the persona; his "shaggy self" = his shadow (also R-13); I-330 = his anima; his conversion to the revolution = conscious awakening; his fight for I-330 and the cause = individuation. And it is clear that Zamyatin was conscious of his achievement in fantasy, for the rigid monolith of the One State believes itself endangered precisely by an epidemic of fantasy and so devises an operation for its excision. D-503 is lobotomized and afterward asserts that "reason will conquer," but meanwhile the reader has been infected by fantasy and discounts the ironic ending, which Zamyatin called "a falsely positive statement."[45]

All of the fantasy I have considered has to a greater or lesser degree been communicable, that is to say, has retained a sufficient amount of the conventional language and concepts to make its difference felt and possibly understood. In the terms of psychology, the primary process (unconscious creation, paleological thinking) has fused with the secondary process (the conscious conventions of society) to form a tertiary or artistic process.[46] In schizophrenics or intensely subjective thinkers, connection with the secondary process may not be made, or be fairly tenuous. The imagination may be extremely fertile, yet produce only cryptic signs. Such, for the most part, are the works of Velimir Khlebnikov, considered by some Russia's most imaginative poet, by others—a hopeless idiot. Among other things, he kept lists of dates, trying to find the mathematical laws of history; he made lists of words, trying to find the primary meaning of each consonant in the aim of creating a universal language, which itself would establish understanding and peace; he wrote poems on the basis of such considerations. He also expressed something like the "riot of identifications" common to schizophrenics, so that the distinctions between first, second, and third person may be lost in the course of a poem and each person become the other. He wrote entire poems generated out of one word, such *laugh (smekh)* or *love (lyubov')*, which with prefixes, infixes, suffixes, and inflections practically exhausted the possibilities of meaning. He wrote palindromic poems—as many as four hundred lines. He wrote a play with reverse chronology—from grave to cradle. Without enumerating all of his inventions, it is safe to say that he exploded words, meanings, literary forms—and yet, as one critic noted, he left behind nothing that could be called an unqualified masterpiece. What then could be the value of his scraps and fragments, many of which are partly, if not wholly, indecipherable? For myself, there are three answers. First, they are simply fascinating—they cause me to wonder. Second, they show how the primary process works—how it makes connections in an autonomous way, even an autistic way, and this informs us about the mind. Finally, they reveal unsuspected possibilities for art—in a sense, offer an Ur-art, which writers with a firmer hold on convention can exploit. The word inventions of Stanislaw Lem's *Futurological Congress*, for example, seem straight out of Khlebnikov's notebooks.[47] So do the word games of Oulipo—the Ouvroir de Littérature Potentielle (Workshop of Potential Literature), which specializes in perverbs, novels with missing letters, and palindromes.[48] Khlebnikov may not have been read by these people, but he lit the way and left his track in many a region of twentieth-century literature, including, no doubt, recesses impossible to trace.

Résumé

Nearing the end of my search, I am not certain what I have discovered. Perhaps I had best draw up a résumé—not exactly a definition of the creature fantasy, but a record of some of its movements. Fantasy is born as the possibility of giving experience a literary form, telling things not as they come, but as they make a meaningful form (Babylonian works). Guided by this sense of form, perhaps not entirely consciously, the author may select materials from other literary works and combine them into a new whole *(Gilgamesh)*. As the literary process becomes conscious, it may be set against the external world in the form of moral tales (Aesop), ideal dialogues (Plato), or satires (Aristophanes). It may also delight in its own inventions, pretty much as an end-in-itself (Lucian). With science fiction (Wells) it may investigate potentials of human thought and invention; with philosophical fantasy (Hoffmann) it may question the nature of reality and knowledge. By destroying logic, it may question the reason of the world (Gogol). By turning on itself, it may prove its own reality, but also its flight from reality (Dostoevsky). By re-creating myth, it may demonstrate its generative power, as well as its palingenesis (Belyi). By an act of synthesis, it may consummate all of these acts (Zamyatin). By creating its own systems, even if insane, it may reveal its autonomy (Khlebnikov), suggesting new types of creation (Lem). And all of these things, it seems possible to me, may be experienced by the individual fantasist as he prepares to write.

Fantasyland
Coming back to my own time, by means of thought-warp, I am suddenly baffled. There, in the past, I could pick and choose; here, in the present, I am swamped with hundreds of novels, plays, movies, television programs, illustrations, comic books, all called fantasy. There I could see progress, a series of monuments marking the extension of fantasy; here I see stasis, a reproduction of the same form, the same idea, only with new materials. For example, the phenomenon of *Jaws*. Its sources: a newspaper clipping, *The Old Man and the Sea*, *Moby Dick*, *An Enemy of the People*. Its story: man-eating shark, beach town which tries to squelch news of the shark, hero who opposes the town authorities and hunts the shark. Its fantasy: magnification of the shark. Its success with the public: enormous. Others decide to cash in on the idea. In place of the shark—killer bees, fire ants, savage dogs, cats, snakes, rats and other vermin. Just when it seems no animals are left, the entertainment industry returns to the scene of the killing: *Jaws II*. And all of this is called "fantasy."

The situation is similar in science fiction. We have any number of robots, aliens, anti-utopias, strange worlds, none of them marking an advance in form or thought on their original creators: Wells, Čapek,

Zamyatin, Huxley, Orwell. Rather, it seems only that new bugaboos are put into the old story, fresh disasters drawn from our own time. When Wells and his followers wrote their anti-utopias, the dangers seemed remote but real, the horrible futures seemed possible. But now the dangers are with us every day, shown on television, and their use in novels and films merely fictionalizes them; the multiplicity of horrible futures invented by science-fiction writers cancel themselves out. New ways of thinking are needed, new fantasy, but we have only new technology. The novels are converted into films, the films into novels. And all of this is called "fantasy."

Clearly, fantasy has entered a new phase. The genres are standardized, therefore not even perceived. Such are the novels-films of disasters (overturned ships, flaming skyscrapers, crashed jets), the novels-films of supernatural powers (demonic possession, mind over matter, ghosts, ESP), the novels-films of space (Buck Rogers brought up to date, Star Trek repeated, new special effects), the novels-films of aliens (Frankenstein brought up to date, yucky monsters), the novels-films of fantasyland (cute little goblins, Thors and Amazons). Since the form is basically the same for all of these "genres," critics have stopped looking at it and switched to a different track. The tide of pulp is not examined as art with intrinsic worth, but rather as an indicator of "popular culture." And so it can still be called "fantasy."

I regard it all as *dead fantasy*. Save for some works by Lem and the brothers Strugatsky, and even these with reservation, I believe the fantastic strain has a better chance of survival in the metaphysical games of Borges, the absurdities of Ionesco, the bizarre rituals of Gombrowicz. But these works are already fairly old. I must confess my incompetence: either from ignorance, or confusion within the present, I cannot find today any striking new idea, any challenging new form, any flash of fantasy to startle my mind and propel it into a future of exciting possibilities. Perhaps the future itself is closed, and fantasy has been reduced to a pastime.

And so my search ends for the moment, amid the dead forms. In such a sorrowful state, I take a look at pornography. This is often called "adult fantasy," though the "fantasy" here is more random than aesthetic. The form is standard, the material stock, the combinations known in advance. Yet, due to its short life, pornography may prove useful in the laboratory. Its effect can be measured, not only mentally, but also physically. And when it loses effect, it must change quickly to survive—invent novel details within the well-worn form. Pornography is the fruit fly of fantasy: through its transparent body may be seen a dialectic of reality and unreality. The reader (or viewer) is presented with an unreality—the hired sexual object—which he must strive hard to believe, knowing all the while it is false. The unreality must not be too extreme, or he will not be able to achieve his half-belief. In this state of half-belief, he can enjoy sex with another person without the inconvenience of that person's presence. On the other hand, should he try to carry his fantasy into real life and find a partner willing to follow his scenario, the partner must take care not to assert her (or his) actual presence, lest the unreality be spoiled. In short, the pornographical, like Todorov's fantastical, must hesitate between the plausible and the impossible.[49] Too much unreality makes it ludicrous, too much reality makes it pathetic. Whether this dialectic can be observed in the other genres of dead fantasy, and whether the public can maintain this tight balance, I leave to the experts on pop culture. I cannot stay here: there is too much deceit, too much of the whore. The term "pornography" originally referred to a realistic portrayal of whores—either in painting or in writing.[50] There was little fantasy involved. Today, there is little reality involved: pornography is written by whores, who offer a pretense of reality in exchange for real money.

Real fantasy overcomes restrictive notions of reality, dead forms and whores. The fantasist feels constrained by what is accepted: he is bored, skeptical, or half-crazy, but he must make an innovation, perhaps not extreme, so that conventional minds will accept it, yet substantial, so that eventually these minds will overturn. I think one innovation needed today is the abolition of the single, objective point of view (i.e., the omniscient author). Fantasy may claim its place in the twentieth century of Einstein, Heisenberg, Bohr, and Gödel, not by packing topical materials into dead forms, but by admitting that the gods did not give us immortality, nor did they give us omniscience— they did not even give us certainty. A severe limitation, yet with ample room for imagination and the search for new forms.

Notes
Biographical Notes
Index

Notes

Form, Formula, and Fantasy: Generative Structures in Contemporary Fiction

1. Jorge Luis Borges, "The Library of Babel," *Ficciones*, no trans. (New York: Grove Pr., 1962), p. 80.
2. Italo Calvino, *The Castle of Crossed Destinies*, trans. William Weaver (New York: Harcourt, 1979), p. 97.
3. W. R. Irwin, *The Game of the Impossible: A Rhetoric of Fantasy* (Urbana: Univ. of Illinois Pr., 1976), p. 9.
4. Eric S. Rabkin, *The Fantastic in Literature* (Princeton: Princeton Univ. Pr., 1976), p. 15.
5. See, for example, Vladimir Propp, *Morphology of the Folktale* (Austin: Univ. of Texas Pr., 1968); Roland Barthes, *S/Z*, trans. Richard Miller (New York: Hill and Wang, 1974); A. J. Greimas, *Sémantique structurale* (Paris: Larousse, 1966); Tzvetan Todorov, *Grammaire du Décameron* (The Hague: Mouton, 1969); and Claude Brémond, *Logique du récit* (Paris: Seuil, 1973).
6. Tzvetan Todorov, *Introduction à la littérature fantastic* (Paris: Seuil, 1970); in English, *The Fantastic: A Structural Approach to a Literary Genre*, trans. Richard Howard (Cleveland: Case Western Reserve Univ. Pr., 1973), p. 7. See also Propp's contrast of the "amazing multiformity, picturesqueness, and color" of the Russian folktale with "its no less striking uniformity, its repetition" (p. 21).
7. JoAnn Cannon discusses this role of debunking the Romantic myth in her analysis of Calvino's *Castle*, "Literature as Combinatory Game: Italo Calvino's *The Castle of Crossed Destinies*," *Critique* 21, no 1 (1979): 88.
8. Cited by Roland Barthes in "Introduction to the Structural Analysis of Narrative," *Image—Music—Text*, trans. Stephan Heath (New York: Hill and Wang, 1977), p. 177.
9. Jorge Luis Broges, *Other Inquisitions*, trans. Ruth L. C. Simms (Austin: Univ. of Texas Pr., 1964), p. 164; cited by Cannon, p. 88.
10. Cited by Cannon, p. 88.
11. Barthes, "Introduction," pp. 123–24.

12. "Interview with Robert Coover," conducted by Larry McCaffery, to appear in the summer 1981 issue of *Genre*.

13. Barthes, "Introduction," p. 117.

14. Robert Scholes, *Fabulation and Metafiction* (Urbana: Univ. of Illinois Pr., 1979).

15. Darko Suvin, *Metamorphoses of Science Fiction* (New Haven: Yale Univ. Pr., 1979), p. 12.

16. Ibid., p. 12.

17. Ibid., p. 67.

18. Ibid., p. 66.

19. In the dedication to *Pricksongs and Descants* (1969; reprint ed., New York: Plume, 1970), Robert Coover comments that "great narratives remain meaningful as a language-medium between generations, as a weapon against the fringe-areas of our consciousness, and as a mythic reinforcement of our tenuous grip on reality. The novelist uses familiar mythic or historical forms to combat the content of those forms" (pp. 78–79).

20. Samuel R. Delany, *The Einstein Intersection* (1967; reprint ed., New York: Ace, 1973), p. 147.

21. Ibid., p. 127.

22. Ibid., pp. 39, 85.

23. Eric Gould, "Condemned to Speak Excessively: Mythic Forms and James Joyce's *Ulysses*," *Sub-Stance*, 22 (1979): 71.

24. Delany, p. 94; Donald Barthelme, *Snow White* (1967; reprint ed., New York: Bantam, 1968), p. 6.

25. Delany, p. 132.

26. As Robert Scholes has suggested, one of the problems faced by current writers who wish to use myth is precisely our increased self-consciousness about it. Scholes notes that "Once so much is known *about* myths and archetypes, they can no longer be used innocently. Even their connection to the unconscious finally becomes attenuated as the mythic materials are used more consciously" (p. 100).

27. Roland Barthes, "Myth Today," *Mythologies*, trans. Annette Lavers (New York: Hill and Wang, 1972), p. 155.

28. Steven Katz, *Creamy and Delicious* (New York: Random, 1970), p. 19.

29. Ibid., p. 29.

30. Ibid., pp. 32–33.

31. Coover, p. 93.

32. See Larry McCaffery, "Robert Coover's Cubist Fictions," *Par Rapport* 1 (1978): 33–40.

33. Coover, pp. 64, 65, 74, 62.

34. Cannon's phrase.

35. Calvino, p. 127.

36. Ibid., p. 105.

37. Ibid., p. 6.

38. Ibid., p. 41. Although this passage refers to the operations of the first novella, "The Castle of Crossed Destinies," an analogous process occurs in the second novella, "The Tavern of Crossed Destinies."
39. Cannon, p. 85.
40. Calvino, p. 126.
41. Ibid., p. 48.
42. Ibid., p. 75.
43. Ibid., p. 81.
44. Barthes, *Image—Music—Text*, p. 124.

A View from Inside the Fishbowl: Julio Cortázar's "Axolotl"

1. Julio Cortázar, "Axolotl," *Final del jeugo* (Buenos Aires: Editorial Sud-americana, 1964), pp. 161–68.
    I am indebted to Fredric Jameson for his interest in my initial analysis of "Axolotl." He provided valuable comments leading toward preliminary drafts of this essay. I would also like to thank the people who gave me thoughtful suggestions that influenced the development of ideas presented here. They include Susan Kirkpatrick, Michel deCerteau, Carlos Blanco, Donald Wesling, Adolfo Prieto, Michael Davidson, Mary Prose and Roy Harvey Pearce. My thanks also to Leo Chavez and Paul Espinosa for readings of the manuscript.
2. Tzvetan Todorov, *Introduction à la littérature fantastique* (Paris: Seuil, 1970); in English, *The Fantastic: A Structural Approach to a Literary Genre*, trans. Richard Howard (Cleveland: Case Western Reserve Univ. Pr., 1973). In his last chapter, Todorov looks for examples of a twentieth-century fantastic and concludes that there are none: "Why does the litera-ture of the fantastic no longer exist?" (p. 166). Franz Kafka's "Metamor-phosis" is the closest example he finds to the fantastic of the nineteenth century.
3. Some of Todorov's examples of fantastic works are Gérard de Nerval's *Aurélia*, Prosper Mérimée's *Venus d'Ille*, Philippe Villiers de l'Isle-Adam's *Véra*, Matthew Gregory Lewis's *Monk*, and Edgar Allan Poe's horror stories.
4. Ultimately, I think the structural features of Todorov's and Cortázar's fan-tastic, asserted in the following paragraph above, are linked to sociologi-cal-historical phenomena. The linearity and irreversibility of Todorov's fantastic narratives imply a rising social group's confidence and optimism in the powers and energies of the individual, in the discoveries of modern science, and in the development of the nation-state; whereas the schizo-phrenic quality of the consciousness, and the nonlinear, reversible quali-ties of Cortázar's fantastic works suggest regressive movement, a lack of confidence and pessimism about the future, and an undermining of prog-ress and forward expansion.
5. Todorov's two other categories of the fantastic are the "uncanny" and the

"marvelous." The uncanny is the story that presents unbelievable events and resolves them with a rational explanation. Poe's "Fall of the House of Usher" is in this category. See Todorov, pp. 47–48. The marvelous resolves incredible happenings by recourse to supernatural laws. Todorov's example is *"Véra"* (p. 53).

6. Ibid., pp. 37–40.
7. My thanks to Michel deCerteau for suggesting this idea.
8. Todorov, p. 168.
9. The impression of an outside power in control of the individual's destiny is one we derive from many of Cortázar's stories. In "La autopista del sur" (*Todos los fuegos el fuego* [Buenos Aires: Editorial Sudamericana, 1966], pp. 9–42), individuals become victims of an outside agent that seems to function like a huge lottery device or a giant computer controlling the stop-and-go of the freeway machine. In "Continuidad de los parques" (*Final del juego*, pp. 9–11), the implications of the individual's lost centrality reverberate into our own world: just as the man who thought he was reading a novel turns out to be a character in that novel about to be assassinated, so we readers of this story may also be vulnerable to the manipulations of some sinister and stronger power.
10. See *Langages* (Mar. 1970), Tzvetan Todorov, "Problèmes de l'énonciation," *Langages*, no. 17: 3–11. See also Jean Dubois, "Énoncé et énonciation," *Langages* (Mar. 1969): 100–10.

   David Lagamanovich, in "Rasgos distintivos de algunos cuentos de Julio Cortázar," *Hispamérica* 1, no. 1 [July 1972]: 5–15, adopts specific categories from linguistic theory in an attempt to formulate a model of general traits whose presence or absence characterize Cortázar's short stories. While I think the combination of his general characteristics (*literaturización, transformación, desrealización, ambiguación, duplicación*) suggests an interesting model to be tested on Cortázar's stories, I disagree that "Axolotl" is marked by an absence of his first and broadest category, *literaturización*. Works marked by a presence of this trait in Lagmanovich's model are texts which emphasize the act of narrating (*estructura del contar*) as opposed to those emphasizing the objects of narration (*estructura de lo contado*). The novelty of my interpretation rests on the idea that "Axolotl" is not so much concerned with the *what* of narration as it is with the *form* or *how* of narration (pp. 7, 14–15).
11. Roman Jakobson, *Shifters, Verbal Categories, and the Russian Verb*, Russian Language Project (Harvard Univ., 1957). The "shifter" as a linguistic phenomenon is also mentioned by Dubois, (p. 103), and by Fredric Jameson (*Prison-House of Language* [Princeton: Princeton Univ. Pr., 1973], p. 138).

   Antonio Pages Larraya, in "Perspectivas de 'Axolotl,' Cuento de Julio Cortázar," *Nueva narrativa hispanoamericana* 2, no. 2 (Sept. 1972): 8, refers to the personal pronouns in "Axolotl" as "shifters." I agree with Pages Larraya that the shifting of the personal pronouns is crucial to understanding the location of the narrator (p. 13). In the analysis which follows, I describe in concrete terms how the act of narration through the ambiguous usage of the personal pronouns *and* the binary oppositions creates the experience of reading this story.

12. Cortázar, p. 161.

The fact that personal pronouns are dropped in Spanish without any loss in idea-coherence sometimes gives an original Cortázar text an advantage over its English translation, with respect to the issue of ambiguity. This grammatical phenomenon is not as striking in "Axolotl" as it is in "Continuidad de los parques," narrated in third person. The absence of the stated pronoun *él* in strategic places in this story heightens the ambiguity of the referent because it can refer either to the man in the chair reading the novel or to the character from whose perspective we witness the events in the novel. The English must continually state the pronoun *he*, therefore losing some amount of ambiguity.

Another type of linguistic peculiarity of the Spanish pronoun *él* functions in "Axolotl." *Él* can be used to refer to a living person and also to animals whose sex is not determined. Thus *él* can often represent *it* in English. When Cortázar uses *él* to refer to the salamander, he takes advantage of the pronoun's ambiguity to suggest a human quality. Since the context of *él* as fish or man is ambiguous in the story, this linguistic peculiarity heightens the uncertainty. Paul Blackburn, in his English translation of "Axolotl," does not use *he* or *him* to refer to the axolotl until the transformation, when *he* can refer to the actual man outside the tank with the consciousness of the axolotl (*Blow-Up and Other Stories* [New York: Macmillan, 1967], pp. 3–8).

13. Blackburn, p. 4.

14. "Había nueve ejemplares"; "Aislé mentalmente una"; "Vi un cuerpecito rosado" (Cortázar, p. 162).

15. "Es que no nos gusta movernos mucho, y el acuario es tan mezquino; apenas avanzamos un poco nos damos con la cola o la cabeza de otro de nosotros" (ibid., p. 163).

16. "Los axolotl se amontonaban en el mezquino y angosto (sólo yo puedo saber cuán angosto y mezquino) piso de piedra y musgo del acuario" (ibid., p. 162).

17. "Sus ojos, sobre todo, me obsesionaban. Al lado de ellos, en los restantes acuarios, diversos peces me mostraban la simple estupidez de sus hermosos ojos semejantes a los nuestros" (ibid., p. 164).

18. "Dejé me bicicleta contra las rejas y fui a ver los tulipanes" (ibid., p. 161).

19. "La parte más sensible de nuestro cuerpo" (ibid., p. 162).

20. Making this distinction in the transformation is important in my analysis because it marks Cortázar's fantastic as different from Todorov's nineteenth-century fantastic. Pages Larraya, who has done the most detailed analysis I have read of this story (see n. 11 above), does not distinguish between a "material transformation in which the reader must perceive

Cortázar's narrator actually become an axolotl and one that occurs *only* at the level of the narrator's consciousness, as I try to stress.

21. This is certainly true of most of Cortázar's stories. It should be noted, though, that some of his stories do not depend for their "fantastic" effect upon an initial identification between reader and subject narrator, elaborated upon later in the discussion, nor upon pronominal shifting or some other kind of linguistic "sleight-of-hand" device, but which are nonetheless loosely termed "fantastic." An example is "La autopista del Sur." For me, stories such as "Axolotl" and "Continuidad de los parques," whose fantastic effect does rely on reader-subject-narrator identification and innovative linguistic techniques, represent the height of Cortázar's fantastic.

22. I agree with Lagmanovich's classification of "Axolotl" as revealing an absence of what he terms *desrealización* (see n. 10 above). Cortázar's stories marked by a presence of this trait in Lagmanovich's model begin with very real occurrences and transform them in the course of the story into fantastic events. "Axolotl," in this sense, begins with a very unreal event ("Now I am an axolotl") and proceeds to explain it. A key point in distinguishing the presence or absence of this trait is whether the transformation takes place in a present or past moment in the story. Even though "Axolotl" begins with an illogical statement, it nevertheless presents a transformation, but one which already has taken place when the reader begins the story.

23. Fredric Jameson, "Metacommentary," *PMLA* 86, no. 1 (Jan. 1971): 11.

24. A. J. Greimas, "Les Jeux des contraintes sémiotiques" (Interaction of Semiotic Constraints), *Du Sens* (Paris: Seuil, 1970), pp. 135–55. An English translation of this article has appeared in *Yale French Studies*, no. 41 (1968): 86–105.

25. "Era inútil golpear con el dedo en el cristal, delante de sus caras: jamas se advertía la menor reacción" (Cortázar, p. 164).

26. "Me quedé una hora mirándolos y salí, incapaz de otra cosa" (ibid., p. 161).

27. "Me apoyaba en la barra de hierro que bordea los acuarios y me ponía a mirarlos"; "con sus ojos de oro a los que se acercaban" (ibid., p. 162).

28. "Y entonces descubrí sus ojos, su cara. Un rostro inexpresivo, sin otro rasgo que los ojos: dos orificios como cabezas de alfiler, enteramente de un oro transparente, carentes de toda vida pero mirando, dejándose penetrar por mi mirada que parecía pasar a través del punto áureo y perderse en un diáfano misterio interior" (ibid., p. 163).

29. "A ambos lados de la cabeza, donde hubieran debido estar las orejas, le crecían tres ramitas rojas como de coral, una excrecencia vegetal, las branquias, supongo" (ibid.).

30. "No eran animales" (ibid., p. 164).

31. "Su mirada ciega, el diminuto disco de oro inexpresivo y sin embargo

terriblemente lúcido, me penetraba como un mensaje: "Sálvanos, sálvanos'"
(ibid., p. 165).

32. "No eran seres humanos, pero en ningún animal había encontrado una
relación tan profunda conmigo" (ibid.).

33. "que algo infinitivamente perdido y distante seguía sin embargo uniéndonos"
(ibid., 162).

34. "El horror venía . . . de creerme prisionero en un cuerpo de axolotl, trans-
migrado a él con mi pensamiento de hombre, enterrado vivo en un axolotl, condenado a moverme lúcidamente entre criaturas insensibles"
(ibid., p. 167).

35. "Por eso no hubo nada de extraño en lo que occurió" (ibid., p. 166).

36. "Mi cara estaba pegada al vidrio del acuario, mis ojos trataban una vez
más de penetrar el misterio de esos ojos de oro sin iris y sin pupila. Veía
de muy cerca la cara de un axolotl inmóvil junto al vidrio. Sin transición,
sin sorpresa, vi mi cara contra el vidrio, en vez del axolotl vi mi cara
contra el vidrio, la vi fuera del acuario, la vi del otro lado del vidrio.
Entonces mi cara se apartó y yo comprendí (ibid.).

37. "El azar me llevó hasta ellos una mañana de primavera"; "Oscuramente
me pareció comprender su voluntad secreta" (ibid., pp. 161, 163).

38. " . . . la parte más sensible de nuestro cuerpo"; "Es que no nos gusta
movernos mucho" (ibid., pp. 162, 163).

39. Pages Larraya notes the story's circular structure and refers to the idea of
the axolotl as narrator (pp. 12–13). While my analysis coincides with his
on these points, I try to link these structural aspects of Cortázar's fantastic
to a form that represents an inversion of the nineteenth-century fantastic.

40. "Y en esta soledad final, a la que él ya no vuelve, me consuela pensar que
acaso va a escribir sobre nosotros, creyendo imaginar un cuento va escribir todo esto sobre los axolotl" (Cortázar p. 168).

41. For Cortázar's own explication of the *lector-cómplice* and *lector-hembra*
categories, see his *Rayuela* (Buenos Aires: Editorial Sudamericana,
1963), chs. 79, 97, 99, 109.

The Meeting of Parallel Lines: Science, Fiction, and Science Fiction

1. James Clerk Maxwell, *The Scientific Papers of James Clerk Maxwell* (Paris:
Librairie Scientifique, for Cambridge Univ. Pr., 1890), vol. 1, p. 159.

2. Ibid., p. 160.

3. Werner Heisenberg, "The Representation of Nature in Contemporary Physics," in *The Discontinuous Universe*, ed. Sallie Sears and Georgianna W.
Lord (New York: Basic, 1972), p. 125.

4. Ernst Nagel, *The Structure of Science* (New York: Harcourt, 1961), p. 105.

5. Albert Einstein and Leopold Infeld, *The Evolution of Physics* (New York: Simon, 1938), p. 277.
6. Ibid., p. 294.
7. Ibid., p. 295.
8. Nagel, p. 115.
9. Tzvetan Todorov, *The Fantastic* (Ithaca, NY: Cornell Univ. 1975), p. 40.
10. Arlen J. Hansen, "The Dice of God: Einstein, Heisenberg, and Robert Coover," *Novel: A Forum on Fiction* 10, no. 6 (Fall 1976): 38–58.
11. See the provocative work, Robert L. Jacobs, *Understanding Harmony* (London: Oxford University Press, 1958).
12. Douglas R. Hofstadter, *Gödel, Escher, Bach: An Eternal Golden Braid* (New York: Basic, 1979).
13. Isaac Asimov, "Social Science Fiction," reprinted in Dick Allen, *Science Fiction: The Future* (New York: Harcourt, 1971), p. 263.

On Realistic and Fantastic Discourse

1. Eric S. Rabkin, *The Fantastic in Literature* (1976; reprint ed., Princeton, Princeton Univ. Pr., 1977), p. 12.
2. Ibid., p. 215.
3. Ibid., p. 41.
4. "Le fantastique, c'est l'hésitation éprouvée par un être qui ne connaît que les lois naturelles, face à un événement en apparence surnaturel" (Tzvetan Todorov, *Introduction à la littérature fantastique* [1970; reprint ed., Paris: Seuil, 1976], p. 29).
5. See Tynyanov's essay "Literaturnii Fakt" (1924). German trans. in *Russischer Formalismus* ed. Jurij Striedter (1969; reprint ed., Munich: Wilhelm Fink, 1971), pp. 394–431.
6. Robert Scholes, *Structural Fabulation: An Essay on the Fiction of the Future*, University of Notre Dame Ward Phillips Lectures in English Language and Literature, vol. 7 (Notre Dame: Univ. of Notre Dame Pr., 1975), pp. 4–6; Darko Suvin, *Metamorphoses of Science Fiction* (New Haven: Yale Univ. Pr., 1979), pp. 7–10.
7. For a critique of the *cogito* from a structural psychoanalytic point of view, see Jacques Lacan, "L'instance de la lettre dans l'inconscient ou la raison depuis Freud," in *Écrits* (Paris: Seuil, 1966), pp. 493–528.
8. On the concept of the noematic, see Edmund Husserl, *Ideen* I, *Gesammelte Werke*, ed. Walter Biemel (The Hague: Martinus Nijhoff, 1950), vol. 3, pp. 233–37.
9. "Peut-être découvrirons-nous un jour que la même logique est à l'oeuvre dans la pensée mythique et dans la pensée scientifique . . . " (Claude Lévi-Strauss, "La structure des mythes," in *Anthropologie structurale* [1958; reprint ed., Paris: Plon, 1974], p. 255).
10. "Le héros revient à lui, «comme s'il s'éveillait d'un songe,»" (Lévi-

Strauss, *Le Cru et le cuit, Mythologiques* [Paris: Plon, 1964], vol. 1, p. 44).

11. "Le réel supporte le fantasme, le fantasme protège le réel" (Jacques Lacan, *Les quatre concepts fondamentaux de la psychanalyse, Le Seminaire de Jacques Lacan*, [Paris: Seuil, 1973], vol. 11, p. 41).

12. "Hier scheinen die Produkte des menschlichen Kopfes mit eignem Leben begabte, untereinander und mit den Menschen in Verhältnis stehende selbständige Gestalten" (Karl Marx, *Das Kapital*, bd. 1, *Werke* [Berlin: Dietz, 1972], vol. 23, p. 86).

13. William Van O'Connor, "The Grotesque: An American Genre," in *The Grotesque: An American Genre and Other Essays* (Carbondale: Southern Illinois Univ. Pr., 1962), p. 13.

14. Ibid., p. 18.

15. "Die Dissonanz, Signum aller Moderne " (Theodor Adorno, *Ästhetische Theorie, Gesammelte Schriften* [Frankfurt on the Main: Suhrkamp, 1970], vol. 7, p. 29).

16. Jay Martin, *Nathaniel West: The Art of his Life* (New York: Farrar, 1970), p. 324.

17. Nathanael West, *Day of the Locust*, in *The Complete Works of Nathanael West* (New York: Farrar, 1957), p. 262.

18. " . . . la réalité est constituée à partir de l'imaginaire. Ce qui est donné d'abord, c'est l'objet fantasmatique. . . . La réalité n'est jamais qu'un secteur de champ imaginaire auquel nous avons acceptée de renoncer, duquel nous avons accepté de désinvestir nos fantasmes de désir" (Jean-François Lyotard, *Discours, Figure* [Paris: Klincksieck, 1971], p. 284.

19. " . . . l'oeuvre du désir résulte de l'application d'une force sur une texte. Le désir ne parle pas, il violente l'ordre de la parole" (ibid., p. 239).

20. ". . . espace neutre, vide, plan des pures oppositions" (ibid., p. 244).

21. " . . . le mot normal est . . . transparent: sa signification est immédiate, c'est elle qu'on reçoit, le véhicule phonique ou graphique n'est pour ainsi dire pas perçu . . . " (ibid.).

22. " . . . à premiere vue le «langage» du rêve parait n'être pas plus et pas moins que celui de l'art. Il en est au principe, il est peut-être son modèle" (ibid., p. 260).

23. The phrase is Lacan's.

24. Sigmund Freud, *Jokes and Their Relation to the Unconscious* (1905), trans. and ed. James Strachey (1960; reprint ed., New York: Norton, 1963), p. 179.

25. Ibid., p. 179.

26. "Exprimé de façon naïve, ce principe veut simplement dire qu'une chose peut-être presentée tout aussi bien de façon simple que de façon compliquée, qu'un mot simple peut être expliqué par une séquence plus large, et qu'inversement un seul mot peut souvent être trouvé pour designer ce que l'on a d'abord conçu sous forme d'un développment" (Algirdas-Julien Greimas, *Sémantique structurale* [Paris: Larousse, 1966], p. 73).

27. "... ne prend toute sa signification que si une séquence en expansion est reconnue comme équivalente d'une unité de communication syntaxiquement plus simple qu'elle" (ibid., p. 73).
28. "... *condensation* ... doit être comprise comme une sorte de décodage compressif des messages en expansion" (ibid.).
29. "... le discours, conçu comme une hiérarchie des unités de communication s'emboîtant les unes dans les autres, contient en lui la négation de cette hiérarchie, du fait que les unités de communication différentes peuvent en même temps être reconnues comme équivalentes" (ibid., p. 72).
30. Freud, p. 16.
31. This seems to me a less awkward translation of "Verdichtung mit Ersatzbildung" than Strachey's "condensation with formation of composite word."
32. "... das die Schwierigkeit und Länge der Wahrnehmung steigert, denn der Wahrnehmungsprozeß ist in der Kunst Selbstzweck und muß verlängert werden ... " (Viktor Shklovsky, "Kunst als Verfahren," in Striedter, p. 15. German translation of "Izkusstvo kak Priem" [1916]).
33. Freud, p. 44.
34. "Aufklärung ist totalitär" (Max Horkheimer and Theodor Adorno, *Dialektik der Aufklärung, Philosophische Fragmente* (1947; 1969; reprint ed., Frankfurt on the Main: Fischer Taschenbuch, 1971), p. 10.
35. In particular, see "Le stade du miroir comme formateur de la fonction du Je," in Lacan, *Écrits*, pp. 93–100.
36. Rabkin, p. 213.
37. "Maintenant je n'étais plus separé d'elle; les barrières étaient tombées, un fil délicieux nous réunissait" (Marcel Proust, *Du côté de chez Swann, A la recherche du temps perdu*, ed. Pierre Clarac and André Ferré [Paris: Gallimard, 1954], vol. I, p. 30.
38. I have taken this phrase from Max Horkheimer.
39. For the concept of "supplement," see Jacques Derrida, *De la grammatologie* (Paris: Minuit, 1967).
40. Lacan, *Les quatre concepts*, p. 27.
41. On the secularization of art see Walter Benjamin, "Das Kunstwerk im Zeitalter seiner technischen Reproduzierbarkeit," as well as Adorno, *Ästhetische Theorie*.
42. Schreber introduces the description of his collapse with the magisteral sentence: "In dieser ›wundervollen Aufbau "ist nun in neurer Zeit ein Riß gekommen, der mit meinem persönlichen Schicksal auf das engste verknüpft ist" (*Bürgerliche Wahnwelt um Neunzehnhundert: Denkwurdigkeiten eines Nervenkranken von Daniel Paul Schreber*, ed. Peter Heiligenthal and Reinhard Volk [Wiesbaden: Focus-Verlag, 1973], p. 21). Schreber's memoir was first published in 1903.
43. "... pourquoi la littérature fantastique n'existe-t-elle plus?" (Todorov, p. 175).

44. "Allons plus loins: la psychanalyse a remplacé (et par la même a rendu inutile) la littérature fantastique" (ibid., p. 169).
45. ". . . l'ideé même de chercher une traduction directe doit être rejetée, parce que chaque image en signifie toujours d'autres, dans un jeu infini de relations. . . . Nous refusons cette manière de reduire les images à des signifiants dont les signifiés seraient des concepts" (ibid., p. 152).
46. "Le XIXᵉ siècle vivait, il est vrai, dans une metaphysique du réel et de l'imaginaire, et la littérature fantastique n'est rien d'autre que la mauvaise conscience de ce XIXᵉ siècle positiviste. Mais aujourd'hui, on ne peut plus croire à une réalité immuable, externe, ni a une littérature qui ne serait que la transcription de cette réalité" (ibid., pp. 176–77).
47. ". . . nach innen geht der geheimnisvolle Weg. In uns, oder nirgends, ist die Ewigkeit mit ihren Welten—die Vergangenheit und Zukunft. Die Außenwelt ist die Schattenwelt—sie wirft ihren Schatten in das Lichtreich." (Novalis [Friedrich, Freiherr von Hardenberg], "Vermischte Bemerkungen [Urfassung von «Blütenstaub»], 1797–1798, no. 17, *Werke*, ed. Gerhard Schulz [Munich: C. H. Beck, 1969], p. 329).
48. ". . . l'événement étrange ou surnaturel était perçu sur le fond de ce qui est jugé normal et naturel . . . l'événement surnaturel ne provoque plus d'hésitation car le monde décrit est tout entier bizarre, aussi anormal que l'événement même à quoi il fait fond" (Todorov, p. 189).

The Audience in Children's Literature

1. C. S. Lewis, *The Lion, the Witch, and the Wardrobe* (New York: Macmillan, 1950), pp. 54–55.
2. Kenneth Grahame, *The Wind in the Willows* (New York: Scribners 1954), pp. 109–10.
3. Ibid., p. 234.
4. Roger Sale, *Fairy Tales and After* (Cambridge, MA: Harvard Univ. Pr. 1978), pp. 7–21.
5. Wordsworth, *The Prelude*, III, 180–83.
6. Ibid., 178–81.
7. Ibid., 193–94.

The Apparition of This World: Transcendentalism and the American "Ghost" Story

1. I have explored this relationship in a series of related works. See chs. 2 and 7, and the opening sections of chs. 4, 5, 6, of *Poe's Fiction: Romantic Irony in the Gothic Tales* (Madison: Univ. of Wisconsin Pr., 1973); "Romanticism and the Gothic Tradition," the introduction to *The Gothic Imagination: Essays in Dark Romanticism* (Pullman: Washington State

Univ. Pr., 1974); "Gothic Fiction of the Romantic Age: Context and Mode," the introduction to *Romantic Gothic Tales 1790–1840* (New York: Harper, 1979). The present essay is part of a longer work and is closely connected to another essay, "The 'Psychological Ghost Story' and the American Gothic Tradition: The Example of Washington Irving's 'Strange Stories,'" forthcoming in *The Haunted Dusk: American Supernatural Fiction 1820–1920,* ed. Howard Kerr, John W. Crowley, and Charles Crow. In the first section of the present essay, I recapitulate some of my criticism of ghost-story critics offered in the Irving study and in a review in *Modern Fiction Studies* 26 (1981), 714–19, a repetition necessary for this essay to be self-contained. The rest of the present piece develops at length some of the speculations on American literary history offered at the end of the Irving essay; the interested reader may want to read both that essay and this one as one extended argument.

2. Jack Sullivan, *Elegant Nightmares: The English Ghost Story from Le Fanu to Blackwood* (Athens: Ohio Univ. Pr., 1978), pp. 5–6.
3. Ibid., p. 9.
4. Ibid., p. 11.
5. Julia Briggs, *Night Visitors: The Rise and Fall of the English Ghost Story* (London: Faber, 1977); see pp. 143–44 ff.
6. Pamela Search, introduction to *The Supernatural in the English Short Story* (London: Bernard Hanison, 1959), p. 13.
7. Sullivan, p. 11.
8. Representative is a favorite comment of mine by Edward Wagenknecht, who vigorously denounces "psychological" readings of ghostly tales: "Abnormal as he is, the narrator [of "Ligeia"] is a farily conventional type of Poe hero; if we are to assume that we see the whole story in a distorted mind in this instance, why should not the other stories be interpreted on the same basis? . . . there is no reason why we should confine ourselves to misrepresenting Poe; an unlimited field is open up" (*Edgar Allan Poe: The Man Behind the Legend* [New York: Oxford Univ. Pr., 1963], pp. 248–49.
9. National Hawthorne, *Works,* Riverside Edition, ed. George Parsons Lathrop (Boston: Houghton, 1883), vol. 12, pp. 288–91.
10. Ibid., pp. 288–89.
11. For extended discussion, see Thompson, *Romantic Gothic Tales,* esp. pp. 13–32.
12. Tzvetan Todorov, *The Fantastic: A Structural Approach to a Genre,* trans. Richard Howard. (Cleveland: Case Western Reserve Univ. Pr., 1973), pp. 41–57 esp.
13. Thomas Carlyle, *Sartor Resartus,* ed. Charles Frederick Harrold (New York: Odyssey, 1937), p. 197, n. 4.
14. Ralph Waldo Emerson, *Works,* Riverside ed., rev., (Boston: Houghton, 1892,)vol. 1, pp. 9–80.
15. Ibid., p. 65.

16. Ibid., pp. 62–63.
17. Ibid., pp. 66–67.
18. Ibid., p. 68.
19. Ibid., p. 77.
20. F. O. Matthiesson, *American Renaissance* (New York: Oxford Univ. Pr., 1941), pp. xiv–xv, 179.
21. Walt Whitman *Leaves of Grass*, Reader's Comprehensive ed. (New York: Norton, 1965). Quoted lines of Whitman's poems are from this edition.
22. See Henry A. Pochmann's *German Culture in America* (Madison: Univ. of Wisconsin Pr., 1957) for an extensive survey; note the relation between Hedge and Emerson (see p. 171 e.g.).
23. Carlyle, bk. 1, ch. 3, p. 21.
24. Hawthorne, vol. 1, pp. 343–48.
25. *Moby Dick*, ed. Harrison Hayford and Hershel Parker (New York: Norton, 1976), chs. 42 & 36.
26. Emerson, I, p. 21.
27. Carlyle, bk. 3, ch. 8, p. 264.
28. Melville, ch. 42.

Fantasy and "Forestructures": The Effect of Philosophical Climate upon Perceptions of the Fantastic

1. Tzvetan Todorov, *Introduction à la littérature fantastique* (Paris: Seuil, 1970); in English, *The Fantastic: A Structural Approach to a Literary Genre*, trans. Richard Howard (Cleveland: Case Western Reserve Univ. Pr., 1973), p. 160.
2. Eric S. Rabkin, *The Fantastic in Literature* (Princeton: Princeton Univ. Pr., 1976), p. 182.
3. Martin Heidegger, *Being and Time*, trans. John Macquarrie and Edward Robinson (New York: Harper, 1962), p. 190.
4. Ibid., pp. 191, 194, 204–10, 199, 192.
5. Howard Pearce, "A Phenomenological Approach to the *Theatrum Mundi* Metaphor," *PMLA* 95 (1980): 43.
6. Todorov, p. 167; Rabkin, pp. 12, 25, 42 *passim*.
7. Ptolemy *Tetrabiblos* 2.9.
8. Ibid., 2.13.
9. Robert Burton, "Digression of Air," *The Anatomy of Melancholy*, part 2, section 2, member 3 (New York: Empire State Book Co., 1924), p. 328.
10. John Donne, "An Anatomy of the World: The First Anniversary," *Major Poets of the Earlier Seventeenth Century*, ed. Barbara K. Lewalski and Andrew J. Sabol (New York: Odyssey, 1973), p. 111.
11. Sir Walter Raleigh, *History of the World*, quoted in George Williamson, *Seventeenth Century Contexts*, rev. ed. (Chicago: Chicago Univ. Pr., 1969), p. 29.

12. William Drummond of Hawthornden, "Cypresse Grove," quoted in Williamson, p. 35.

13. George Hakewill, *Apologie or Declaration of the Power and Providence of God in the Government of the World . . .* , quoted in Williamson, p. 18.

14. J. B. Leishman, *The Metaphysical Poets* (Oxford: Clarendon, 1934), p. 61.

15. Williamson, p. 10.

16. Cf. Heidegger: "Science is not exact because it makes exact calculations; it must make such calculations because its way of adhering to its sphere [the 'ground plan' of its forestructures] has the character of exactitude" ("The Age of the World View," trans. Marjorie Grene, *Martin Heidegger and the Question of Literature: Toward a Postmodern Literary Hermeneutics* [Bloomington: Indiana Univ. Pr., 1979], p. 4). As a model of "the existent," science forces upon humanistic disciplines the propriety and need for detailed representation.

17. Todorov, p. 25.

18. Ibid., pp. 15, 22, 17, 114–20.

19. Todorov's emphasis on the supernatural may be partly explained as cultural orientation. As Rabkin remarks: "In the world of English speakers, perhaps the paradigmatic Fantasist is Lewis Carroll. For speakers of German and French, the paradigmatic Fantasist is the ghastly Hoffmann" (p. 226).

20. Ibid., pp. 1, 10, 16, 29, 33, 75, 77, 194, 211, 215, 217, 226.

21. Ibid., p. 223.

22. Eugène Ionesco, "From *Notes and Counter Notes*," *Genet/Ionesco: The Theater of the Double.* ed. Kelly Morris (New York: Bantam, 1969), pp. 119–20.

23. Eugène Ionesco, quoted in Martin Esslin, *The Theater of the Absurd* (Garden City, N.Y.: Doubleday, Anchor, 1961), p. 100.

24. Ionesco, "From *Notes and Counter Notes*," p. 122.

25. Randel Helms, *Tolkien's World* (Boston: Houghton, 1974), p. 79.

26. J. R. R. Tolkien, *Tree and Leaf* (Boston: Houghton, 1965), p. 9.

27. Heidegger, *Being and Time*, p. 190.

28. Ibid., p. 194.

29. Ursula Le Guin, *The Farthest Shore* (New York: Bantam, 1975), p. 84.

30. Ibid., p. 120.

31. Ibid., p. 121.

32. Ibid.

33. Ibid., p. 122.

The Logic of Wings: García Márquez, Todorov, and the Endless Resources of Fantasy

1. *Leaf Storm, and Other Stories*, trans. Gregory Rabassa (New York: Harper & Row, 1972), p. 112. The story was originally written in 1968, just after

the completion of *One Hundred Years of Solitude*. Subsequent references to the short story all refer to Rabassa's 1972 translation.
2. George R. McMurray, *Gabriel Garcia Marquez* (New York: Frederick Ungar Publishing Co., 1977), p. 119.
3. C. Hugh Holman, *A Handbook to Literature* (New York: The Bobbs-Merrill Company, 1972) p. 333.
4. W. R. Irwin, *The Game of the Impossible: A Rhetoric of Fantasy* (Urbana: University of Illinois Press, 1976); Eric S. Rabkin, *The Fantastic in Literature* (Princeton: Princeton University Press, 1976); Tzvetan Todorov, *The Fantastic: A Structural Approach to a Literary Genre*, trans. Richard Howard (Ithaca: Cornell University Press, 1973). Todorov's work originally appeared in French in 1970. Marquez has provided his own designation for his story, subtitling it "a tale for children," a not altogether apt attribution, for it is a children's story only in the sense that *Alice in Wonderland* is.

Power Fantasy in the "Science Fiction" of Mark Twain

1. Norman Spinrad, *The Iron Dream* (New York: Avon, 1972).
2. Brian W. Aldiss, *Billion Year Spree: The True History of Science Fiction* (Garden City, N.Y.: Doubleday, 1973); *Anatomy of Wonder: Science Fiction*, ed. Neil Barron (New York: Bowker, 1976). Other "histories" in which Mark Twain does not appear include J. O. Bailey, *Pilgrims Through Time and Space: Trends and Patterns in Scientific and Utopian Fiction* (1947; reprint ed., Westport, Conn.: Greenwood Pr., 1972); and Sam J. Lundwall, *Science Fiction: What It's All About* (New York: Ace, 1971).
3. Darko Suvin, *Metamorphoses of Science Fiction: On the Poetics and History of a Literary Genre* (New Haven: Yale Univ. Pr., 1979), pp. 200–01. It should be noted that, intermittently, from this paragraph onward I have adapted some material that will appear in the introduction to my forthcoming collection *The "Science Fiction" of Mark Twain*.
4. "By 'scientifiction,'" Gernsback wrote, "I mean the Jules Verne, H. G. Wells, and Edgar Allan Poe type of story—a charming romance intermingled with scientific fact and prophetic version" (editorial to the first issue of *Amazing Stories* (Ap. 1926). It was recently discovered, however, that the term "science fiction" seems to have been first used in William Wilson's *Little Earnest Book Upon a Great Old Subject* (that is, poetry) published in 1851. Moreoever, Wilson uses the term in something close to the modern sense. The discovery seems to belong to John Eggeling, owner of Phantasmagoria Books, London, England, who quoted a relevant sentence in his *Catalogue*, for July 1975. Shortly afterward two writer-critics rushed into print with the news almost simultaneously. See Brian Stableford, "William Wilson's Prospectus for Science Fiction:

1951," *Foundation*, no. 10 (June 1976): 6–12; and Brian W. Aldiss, "On the Age of the Term 'Science Fiction,'" *Science-Fiction Studies*, 3 (July 1976): 213. Aldiss mistakenly refers to the author of *A Little Earnest Book . . .* as "William Watson."

5. C. S. Lewis, *An Experiment in Criticism* (Cambridge: At the Univ. Pr., 1961), p. 109; Robert M. Philmus, "Science Fiction: From Its Beginning to 1870," in *Anatomy of Wonder*, pp. 3–16 (this is one of the best attempts at definition to date). For a "heterogeneous" approach which may be related to Philmus's, see Robert Scholes, "Educating for Future Realism," *Alternative Futures* I (Fall 1978): 91–95.

6. On the area of congruence between the "structure" of science fiction and the "structure" of transcendence, see David Ketterer, *New Worlds for Old: The Apocalyptic Imagination, Science Fiction, and American Literature* (New York: Doubleday, Anchor; and Bloomington: Indiana Univ. Pr., 1974).

7. See *Mark Twain's Notebooks & Journals, Volume III (1883–1891)*, ed. Robert Pack Browning, Michael B. Frank, and Lin Salamo (Berkeley and Los Angeles: University of California Press, 1979), pp. 260–61. In my introduction to *The "Science Fiction" of Mark Twain*, Clemens' interest in telepathy, spiritualism, dreams, time travel, and the telephone is treated at length in terms of "instantaneous communication" and the ontological anxiety concordant with such forms of communication.

8. Paul E. Baender, "Mark Twain's Transcendent Figures" (Ph.D. diss., Univ. of California, 1956).

9. *Mark Twain's Notebooks & Journals, Volume I (1855–1873)*, ed. Frederick Anderson, Michael B. Frank, and Kenneth M. Sanderson (Berkeley and Los Angeles: Univ. of California Pr., 1975), pp. 511–16; Edward Wagenknecht, *Mark Twain: The Man and His Work* (1935; 3d ed., Norman: Univ. of Oklahoma Pr., 1967), p. 105.

10. My sources of information regarding "A Murder, a Mystery, and a Marriage" are *Mark Twain's Letters*, ed. Albert Bigelow Paine (New York: Harper, 1917), pp. 257–76, 278–79, 284, 288; "News from the Rare Book Sellers," *Publisher's Weekly* 148 (18 Aug. 1945), pp. 620–21; and *The New Yorker* 25 (29 Jan. 1949), pp. 15–16.

11. Mark Twain, *A Murder, a Mystery, and a Marriage* (New York: Manuscript House, 1945), p. 9.

12. For this special use of the term "apocalyptic" (as distinct from the "mimetic" and the "fantastic"), see David Ketterer, *New Worlds for Old*, pp. 3–25, 38–39.

13. See, for example, Hamlin Hill, introduction to *A Connecticut Yankee in King Arthur's Court* (San Francisco: Chandler, 1963), pp. xi–xiv.

14. An entry made before the end of April 1885 reads as follows: "Have a battle between a modern army, with gatling guns—(automatic) 600 shots a minute, ⟨with one pulling of the trigger,⟩ torpedos, balloons, 100-ton cannon, iron-clad feet &c & Prince de Joinville's Middle Age Crusaders";

see *Mark Twain's Notebooks & Journals, Volume III (1883–1891)*, p. 86. Angle brackets enclose canceled words.

15. Jan Pinkerton, "Backward Time Travel, Alternate Universes, and Edward Everett Hale," *Extrapolation* 20 (Summer 1979), p. 172.

16. *Mark Twain's Mysterious Stranger Manuscripts*, ed. William M. Gibson (Berkeley and Los Angeles; Univ. of California Pr., 1969), p. 117. The following material is relevant to the study of the textual and interpretive complexities these manuscripts give rise to: John S. Tuckey, *Mark Twain and Little Satan: The Writing of "The Mysterious Stranger"* (West Lafayette, IN: Purdue Univ. Pr., 1963); Mark Twain's *"The Mysterious Stranger" and the Critics*, ed. John S. Tuckey (Belmont, CA: Wadsworth, 1968); introduction and apparatus to *Mark Twain's Mysterious Stranger Manuscripts*; and Sholom J. Kahn, *Mark Twain's Mysterious Stranger: A Study of the Manuscript Texts* (Columbia: Univ. of Missouri Pr., 1978).

17. *Mark Twain's Notebooks & Journals, Volume III (1883–1891)*, p. 56.

18. For an excellent account of the omnipotent individual segueing into solipsism, see H. Bruce Franklin, *Robert A. Heinlein: America as Science Fiction* (New York: Oxford Univ. Pr., 1980).

19. See "The Symbols of Despair," in Bernard DeVoto, *Mark Twain at Work* (Cambridge, MA: Harvard Univ. Pr., 1942), pp. 105–30; reprinted in *Mark Twain: A Collection of Critical Essays*, ed. Henry Nash Smith (Englewood Cliffs, NJ: Prentice-Hall, 1963), pp. 140–58.

The Unconscious, Fantasy, and Science Fiction: Transformations in Bradbury's Martian Chronicles *and Lem's* Solaris

1. Poul Anderson, quoted in Jeffrey M. Elliot, "Poul Anderson: Seer of Far-Distant Futures," in *Science Fiction Voices #2*, ed. Jeffrey M. Elliot (San Bernardino, CA: Borgo Pr., 1979), pp. 44–45.

2. Poul Anderson, "Poul Anderson Talar Om Science Fiction," *Algol* 15, no. 3 (1978): 14.

3. Lester del Rey, quoted in Darrell Schweitzer, "An Interview with Lester del Rey," *Science Fiction Review* 5, no. 3 (1976): 8.

4. L. Sprague de Camp, quoted in Darrell Schweitzer, "L. Sprague de Camp," in *Science Fiction Voices #1*, ed. Darrell Schweitzer (San Bernardino, CA: Borgo Pr., 1979), p. 60.

5. Gregory Benford, quoted in Nancy Mangini and Jim Purviance, "Interview with Nebula Nominee Gregory Benford," *SF & F 36: A Science Fiction Fanzine*, no. 6 (1978): 8, 7.

6. "In dreams and fantasies the sea or a large expanse of water signifies the unconscious" (C. G. Jung, *Symbols of Transformation: An Analysis of the Prelude to a Case of Schizophrenia*, 2d ed. [1956; reprint ed., Princeton: Princeton Univ. Pr., 1974], p. 219).

7. Joe Haldeman, "Great Science Fiction About Artichokes & Other Story Ideas," *Algol* 15, no. 3 (1978): 21.

8. Ibid.

9. A. E. Van Vogt, quoted in Jeffrey Elliot, "Interview: Van Vogt," *Galileo*, no. 8 (1978): 11.

10. Ibid., p. 10.

11. Ibid., pp. 8–9.

12. Stephen R. Donaldson, quoted in Neal Wilgus, "An Interview with Stephen R. Donaldson," *Science Fiction Review* 8, no. 2 (1979): 29.

13. Ibid.

14. Richard Lupoff, quoted in Jim Purviance and Nancy Mangini, "Interview with Nebula Nominee Richard Lupoff," *SF & F 36: A Science Fiction Fanzine*, no. 6 (1978): 14, 15.

15. Jung, *Symbols of Transformation*, pp. 11, 21.

16. Ibid., p. 17.

17. C. G. Jung, "The Psychology of the Child Archetype," in C. G. Jung and C. Kerényi, *Essays on a Science of Mythology* (New York: Pantheon, 1949), pp. 102, 103.

18. Ray Bradbury, "How Not to Burn a Book; or, 1984 Will Not Arrive," *Soundings* 7, no. 1 (1975): 19, 22, 13.

19. Ray Bradbury, quoted in Jeffrey M. Elliot, "Ray Bradbury: Poet of Fantastic Fiction," in *Science Fiction Voices #2*, ed. Jeffrey M. Elliot (San Bernardino, CA: Borgo Pr., 1979), pp. 21, 24.

20. Jung, "The Psychological Aspects of the Kore," in Jung and Kerényi, p. 241.

21. Ibid., p. 235.

22. Ibid., p. 238.

23. Nietzsche and Freud quoted by Jung. Jung, *Symbols of Transformation*, p. 24.

24. Ray Bradbury, *The Martian Chronicles* (New York: Bantam, 1975), p. 108.

25. Ibid., p. 126.

26. Ibid., p. 130.

27. Ovid, *Metamorphoses* (Baltimore: Penguin, 1967), p. 198.

28. Bradbury, *The Martian Chronicles*, pp. 35, 39, 43.

29. Ibid., pp. 46, 47, 47–48.

30. Ibid., pp. 26, 27.

31. Ibid., p. 29.

32. Ibid., pp. 110, 112, 138.

33. Ibid., pp. 2, 11, 14, 32, 78, 80, 140.

34. See, for example, Richard Donovan, "Morals from Mars," *The Reporter*, 26 June, 1951, pp. 38–40; Matt Weinstock, Los Angeles *Mirror-News*, 11 July, 1955, p. 10; Lawrence Lipton, "The Illustrated Man: Ray Bradbury," *Intro Bulletin* 1, nos. 6,7 (1956): 9; Maggie Savoy, "Ray Bradbury

Keeping Eye on Cloud IX," Los Angeles *Times*, 15 Mar., 1970, sec. E, p. 1.

35. Bradbury, *The Martian Chronicles*, pp. 179–80.
36. Bradbury, quoted in Elliot, p. 26.
37. Stanislaw Lem, quoted in Daniel Say, "An Interview with Stanislaw Lem," *The Alien Critic* 3, no. 3 (1974): 8.
38. Stanislaw Lem, "Stanislaw Lem, Krakow Poland," *S F Commentary* 24 (1973): 28.
39. Stanislaw Lem, *Solaris*, trans. Joanna Kilmartin and Steve Cox (New York: Berkley Medallion Books, 1971), 16.
40. Ibid., pp. 60, 61, 62.
41. Ibid., p. 117.
42. Ibid., p. 141.
43. Ibid., p. 99.
44. Ibid., pp. 187–88.
45. Ibid., p. 11.
46. Ibid., p. 153.
47. Ibid., p. 210.
48. Ibid., pp. 17, 24, 26, 30, 82, 211.
49. Ibid., pp. 37, 192.
50. Ibid., p. 211.

Confronting the Alien: Fantasy and Antifantasy in Science Fiction Film and Literature

1. Throughout this paper I shall use the term "literature" to include film. I have found no happy label for the category of "books and movies."
2. John W. Campbell, "Who Goes There?" in *The Science Fiction Hall of Fame*, ed. Ben Bova (Garden City, NY: Doubleday, 1973), vol. 2, p. 54.
3. Ibid., p. 49.
4. Terry Carr, *An Exaltation of Stars: Transcendental Adventures in Science Fiction* (New York: Simon, 1973), p. 7.
5. Interestingly, the alien originally had good reasons for his actions, reasons removed from the story line during the film's shooting. Scenes and dialogue explaining that the creature was using the crew of the Nostromo in its reproductive process were edited out by director Ridley Scott because he realized that rational understanding is an obstacle to terror. Thinking blunts feeling.
6. Robert Silverberg, *Earthmen and Strangers* (New York: Dell, 1966), p. 8.
7. *Andromeda Strain* and *Destination Moon* I would place among the rare exceptions.
8. Arthur C. Clarke, *2001: A Space Odyssey* (New York: New American Library, 1968), p. 214.

9. Ibid., p. 219.
10. Thomas R. Atkins, *Science Fiction Films* (New York: Monarch Pr., 1976), p. 6.

The Search for Fantasy: From Primitive Man to Pornography

1. *Poems of Heaven and Hell from Ancient Mesopotamia*, ed. and trans. N. K. Sandars (Harmondsworth: Penguin, 1971), p. 73.
2. Ibid., p. 75.
3. Ibid., p. 77.
4. Ibid., p. 91.
5. The interpretation of myth as the development of masculine consciousness is made by Erich Neumann, *The Origins and History of Consciousness* (1949), trans. R. F. C. Hull (Princeton: Princeton Univ. Pr., 1973).
6. *Poems*, p. 111.
7. Ibid., p. 135.
8. *The Ancient Near East*, ed. James B. Pritchard (Princeton, NJ: Princeton Univ. Pr., 1958), pp. 84–85.
9. Joseph Campbell, *Myths to Live By* (New York: Bantam, 1972), pp. 55–56.
10. John S. Dunne, *The City of the Gods: A Study in Myth and Mortality* (New York: Macmillan, 1965), pp. 8–14.
11. *The Epic of Gilgamesh*, An English Version with an Introduction by N. K. Sandars (Harmondsworth: Penguin, 1972), pp. 13–16.
12. Morris Jastrow and Albert T. Clay, *An Old Babylonian Version of the Gilgamesh Epic* (New Haven: Yale Univ. Pr.,1920), p. 46.
13. Dunne, pp. 8–9; Jastrow, p. 48.
14. *The Epic of Gilgamesh*, p. 73.
15. Ibid., p. 20.
16. Ibid., p. 16.
17. Dunne, p. 1.
18. Jastrow, pp. 28–29; the possible meaning of "axe of Mash" is discussed in idem., p. 31.
19. Ibid., p. vi.
20. The stage of the uroboros, described by Neumann, pp. 5–38.
21. Jastrow, p. 24.
22. The fact that the harlot does not take Enkidu immediately to Gilgamesh, but spends some time civilizing him, argues persuasively for a separate work about a primitive man, Enkidu; see Jastrow, pp. 32–47.
23. Jastrow's reading, p. 68. Other readings have Gilgamesh toss Enkidu by bending his own knee down to earth; see Alexander Heidel, *The Gilgamesh Epic and Old Testament Parallels* (Chicago: Univ. of Chicago Pr., 1963), p. 32.

24. The name Sabitum indicates an innkeeper, public woman or harlot; she therefore offers herself to Gilgamesh (Jastrow, p. 102). Thus interesting parallels arise between Gilgamesh and Enkidu: Enkidu sleeps with a harlot at the beginning of the epic—Gilgamesh rejects one at the end; Enkidu kills lions at the beginning—Gilgamesh toward end; Enkidu first fears Humbaba—then Gilgamesh; Enkidu is a new man in the beginning—Gilgamesh visits the new Adam (first man of the new world, Utnapishtim) at end; both flaunt Ishtar and kill the bull in the middle.

25. *Hobbes's Thucydides*, ed. Richard Schlatter (New Brunswick, NJ: Rutgers Univ. Pr., 1975), pp. 40–41.

26. *Greek Lyrics*, trans. Richard Lattimore (Chicago: Univ. of Chicago Pr., 1960), p. 4.

27. See Oliver Goldsmith, "The Life of Aesop" and "An Essay Upon Fable," in *Bewick's Select Fables of Aesop and Others* (London, 1886), pp. xxx–xl.

28. Kenneth J. Dover, *Aristophanic Comedy* (Berkeley and Los Angeles: Univ. of California Pr., 1972), pp. 49–53; Moses Hadas, introduction to *The Complete Plays of Aristophanes* (New York: Bantam, 1978), pp. 5–6.

29. In ancient Egyptian literature, "realized metaphors" and "puns" are used to explain creation, but in ernest—not satirically. Thus, in my opinion, they are not really metaphors and puns. Cf. James B. Pritchard, *Ancient Near Eastern Texts*, 3rd ed. (Princeton: Princeton Univ. Pr., 1969), esp. pp. 3–11.

30. The term belongs to Cedric H. Whitman, *Aristophanes and the Comic Hero* (Cambridge, MA: Harvard Univ. Pr., 1964), esp. ch. 8, "Discourse of Fantasy," pp. 259–80.

31. *The Great Dialogues of Plato*, trans. W. H. D. Rouse (New York: Mentor, 1956), p. 518.

32. The term does not occur in Aristotle's *Poetics*.

33. *Selected Satires of Lucian*, ed. and trans. Lionel Casson (New York: Norton, 1962), p. 15.

34. Graham Anderson, *Lucian: Theme and Variation in the Second Sophistic* (Leiden, the Netherlands: E. J. Brill, 1976), p. 26.

35. The case for Menippean satire as a continuing genre is made by Mikhail Bakhtin, *Problems of Dostoevsky's Poetics*, trans. R. W. Rotsel (Ann Arbor: Ardis, 1973), pp. 92–122.

36. Nikolai Gogol, "Nevsky Prospekt," trans. David Magarshack, in *Tales of Good and Evil* (New York: Doubleday, 1957), p. 201.

37. Nikolai Gogol, "The Nose," trans. Priscilla Meyer, in *Dostoevsky and Gogol: Texts and Criticism* (Ann Arbor: Ardis, 1979), p. 26.

38. Aleksandr Slonimsky, *Tekhnika komicheskogo u Gogolya* (Petrograd, 1923; reprinted, Providence: Brown Univ. Pr., 1963), pp. 35–56.

39. Meyer, pp. 22, 21, 22.

40. Ibid., p. 45. Many more examples, and their interpretations, may be found in Dmitry Chizhevsky, "On Gogol's 'The Overcoat,'" in Meyer, pp. 137–61.
41. Quoted by Slonimsky, p. 61.
42. Conclusion to "The Nose," in Meyer, p. 40.
43. Quoted from a feuilleton of 1847 in F. Dostoevsky, *Polnoe sobranie sochinenii*, vol. 2 (Leningrad: Nauka, 1972), p. 486.
44. Insofar as both Anthroposophy and Analytical Psychology seek to define psychic structures, some similarities (with different terminology) may be expected. Yet the correspondence between Belyi and Neumann is so remarkable as to argue for independently discovered truth.
45. Zamyatin, as Belyi, did not know the works of Jung. A number of studies on Zamyatin appear in *Zamyatin's WE: A Collection of Critical Articles* (Ann Arbor: Ardis, in press).
46. This is the basic idea of Silvano Arieti, *Creativity: The Magic Synthesis* (New York: Basic, 1976).
47. See especially the passage on "morphological forecasting," in Stanislaw Lem, *The Futurological Congress*, trans. Michael Kandel (New York: Avon, 1976), pp. 106–10. (I cannot read the original Polish.) Velimir Khlebnikov's works are available in *Snake Train: Poetry and Prose*, ed. and trans. Gary Kern (Ann Arbor: Ardis, 1976).
48. See "Mathematical Games," *Scientific American* (Feb. 1977), pp. 121–26, and Howard W. Bergerson, *Palindromes and Anagrams* (New York: Dover, 1973).
49. Tzvetan Todorov, *The Fantastic: A Structural Approach to a Literary Genre*, trans. Richard Howard (Cleveland: Case Western Reserve Univ. Pr., 1973), esp. ch. 2.
50. The word *pornographos* is first noted in Athenaeus, ca. A.D. 192; see *The Deipnosophists*, trans. Charles Burton Gulick (Cambridge, MA: Harvard Univ. Pr., 1950), vol. 6, p. 63 (original ch. 13, p. 567). The English word *pornography* comes to us through the French *pornographie*, based on the Greek roots *porne* ("whore," "purchased slave") plus *graph* ("writing," "painting").

Biographical Notes

HAROLD BLOOM, De Vane Professor of the Humanities at Yale University is the author of *The Anxiety of Influence* and *The Flight to Lucifer*.

DAVID CLAYTON teaches comparative literature at the University of California, San Diego.

ROBERT A. COLLINS teaches in the Department of English at Florida Atlantic University and is coordinator of the annual Swann Conference on the Fantastic.

JOHN GERLACH teaches in the Department of English at Cleveland State University.

GEORGE R. GUFFEY, Professor of English at the University of California, Los Angeles, writes on seventeenth-century literature and science in literature.

ARLEN J. HANSEN teaches English at the University of the Pacific and is specialized in the interactions of science and contemporary literature.

GARY KERN has published on early Soviet literature and Solzhenitsyn, and has translated Eichenbaum, Khlebnikov, and, most recently, Lev Kopelev.

DAVID KETTERER is Professor of English at Concordia University and has written on science fiction, Poe, and Mark Twain.

LARRY MCCAFFERY teaches English and comparative literature at San Diego State University and writes on contemporary fiction.

ERIC S. RABKIN is Professor of English at the University of Michigan and writes on fantasy, narrative theory, and science and literature.

JACK P. RAWLINS is Associate Professor of English at California State University, Chico, and has a long-standing interest in science fiction film.

ROGER SALE is Professor of English at the University of Washington and the author of *Fairy Tales and After*.

MARTA E. SÁNCHEZ teaches in the Department of Literature at the University of California, San Diego.

ROBERT SCHOLES is head of the Semiotics Program at Brown University and the author of *Structural Fabulation*.

GEORGE E. SLUSSER is Curator of the Eaton Collection at The University of

California, Riverside, and writes on nineteenth-century literature and science fiction.

G. RICHARD THOMPSON is Professor of English at Purdue University and writes on nineteenth-century American literature.

Index

Abgrund, 117–19
Abrams, Meyer, 97
Acharnians, The (Aristophanes), 183
Adapa: The Man, 179
Adonais (Percy Shelley), 10
Adorno, Theodor, 65, 205n; *Dialectic of Enlightenment* (with Max Horkheimer), 70, 206n
"Adventure of the German Student" (Irving), 95
Aesop, 182, 192, 216n
Aesthetic fantasy, 184
Aesthetic Movement, the, 7
Alastor (Percy Shelley), 10, 13, 16
Aldiss, Brian; *Billion Year Spree*, 131, 211–12n
Algol, 144
Algren, Nelson, 64
"Alice Doane's Appeal" (Hawthorne), 90, 103
Alice in Wonderland (Carroll), 1, 10, 17, 80, 85
Alien, 161–62, 166, 174
Allegory: The Theory of a Symbolic Mode (Fletcher), 18
Ambassadors, The (Henry James), 71
Anatomy of Wonder (Barron), 131, 211n, 212n
Andersen, Hans Christian, 2, 17
Anderson, Poul, 143–44, 149, 213n; "Call Me Joe," 168; *Tau Zero*, 164
Anderson, Sherwood, 64
Anthroposophy, 190, 218n
Antifantastic, 160, 165
Arcadia (Sir Philip Sidney), 112

Archilochus, 182
Aristophanes, 182–83, 190, 192, 216–17n; *The Acharnians*, 183; *The Birds*, 183; *The Clouds*, 183; *Lysistrata*, 183; *Peace*, 183; *The Wasps*, 183
"As I Ebb'd with the Ocean of Life" (Whitman), 100
As I Lay Dying (Faulkner), 65
Asimov, Isaac, 53, 58, 204n
Atkins, Thomas R., 173, 216n
Atlantic Monthly, The, 135
At the Back of the North Wind (Macdonald), 17
Augustine; *The City of God*, 118
Aurélia (Nerval), 39, 199n
Austen, Jane, 62
"Axolotl" (Cortázar), 38–41, 44, 49–50, 199–203n

Babylonian Creation, The, 176–78
Bacon, Francis, 186; *Novum Organum*, 113
Bach, Johann Sebastian, 56–57
Baender, Paul, 134, 212n
"Balloon Hoax, The" (Poe), 134
Barron, Neil; *Anatomy of Wonder*, 131, 211n
Barth, John, 27, 57; *Chimera*, 30; *Giles Goat Boy*, 30
Barthelme, Donald; *Snow White*, 30, 198n
Barthes, Roland, 21, 24–26, 31, 37, 197–99n
Baum, L. Frank, 85

Beardsley, Aubrey, 6
Beckett, Samuel, 57
Belyi, Andrei, 192, 218n; *Kotik Letaev*, 189–90; *Petersburg*, 189
Benford, Gregory, 144, 213n; *In the Ocean of Night*, 145
Beyond the Pleasure Principle (Freud), 4
Bible, The, 79, 82
Billion Year Spree (Aldiss), 131, 211n
Birds, The (Magnes), 182; (Aristophanes), 183
Black, Joseph, 53, 57
"Black Cat, The" (Poe), 95
Blake, William, 13, 17, 64; *Jerusalem*, 12
Bloom, Harold; *The Flight to Lucifer: A Gnostic Fantasy*, 6, 12, 18; *The Lost Traveller's Dream*, 18
"Bobok" (Dostoevsky), 188–89
Bohr, Niels, 55–57, 194
Boltzmann, Ludwig, 57
Borges, Jorge Luis, 17, 57, 193; "The Garden of Forking Paths," 33; "The Library of Babel," 21, 23–24, 36–37, 197n; "Pierre Menard, Author of Don Quixote," 35
Bradbury, Ray; *The Martian Chronicles*, 142, 149–50, 152–56, 159, 214–15n
Brahe, Tycho, 110
Brémond, Claude, 24, 197n
Briggs, Julia, 93, 208n
Bring the Jubilee (Moore), 137
Brown, Charles Brockden, 91; *Wieland*, 92
Browne, Sir Thomas, 111
Browning, Robert; *Childe Roland to the Dark Tower Came*, 1, 14
Buck Rogers, 193
Bunyan, John, 112; *Pilgrim's Progress*, 64, 79, 111
Burgess, Anthony, 57
Burton, Robert, 111, 209n

Cain and Abel, 181
Calder, Nigel, 51

Caldwell, Erskine, 64
"Call Me Joe" (Poul Anderson), 168
Calvino, Italo, 23–27, 198n; *The Castle of Crossed Destinies*, 22, 34–36, 197n, 199n; *Cosmicomics*, 159
Campanella, Tommaso, 186
Campbell, John W.; "Who Goes There?", 160–66, 215n
Canticle for Leibowitz, A (Miller), 159
Capek, Karel, 192; *R.U.R.*, 159
Carlyle, Thomas, 1, 8,13, 19, 98, 208–9n; Natural Supernaturalism, 97, 106; *Sartor Resartus*, 2, 7. 9, 97, 103, 106
"Carmilla" (Le Fanu), 66
Carr, Terry, 164, 215n
Carroll, Lewis (pseudonym of Charles L. Dodgson), 1–3, 5, 10, 17, 57, 180, 210n; *Alice in Wonderland*, 1, 10, 17, 80, 85; *Through the Looking Glass*, 1, 19
Cartesian *cogito*, 61
Castle of Crossed Destinies, The (Calvino), 22, 34–36, 197n, 199n
Castle of Otranto, The (Walpole), 96
Castor and Pollux, 181
Cather, Willa, 53
Cat in the Hat (Dr. Seuss), 79
Cavell, Stanley; *The Claim of Reason*, 11
"Celestial Railroad, The" (Hawthorne), 105
Chairs, The (Ionesco), 115–16
Charlotte's Web (White), 81
Charmides (Plato), 184
Chaucer, Geoffrey, 82
Childe Roland to the Dark Tower Came (Browning), 1
Childhood's End (Clarke), 159
Chimera (Barth), 30
City of Dreadful Night, The (Thomson), 9
City of God, The (Augustine), 118
Claim of Reason, The (Cavell), 11
Clarke, Arthur C., 172–73, 215n; *Childhood's End*, 159

Clausius, Rudolf, 57
Clemens, Samuel L. (pseudonym Mark Twain), 134, 140, 211n, 212n
Clinamen, 1–2, 10, 16
Close Encounters of a Third Kind (Spielberg), 169–70, 174
Clouds, The (Aristophanes), 183
Coleridge, Samuel Taylor, 103
Condensation, 68–69, 206n
Confidence Man, The (Melville), 65, 105
Connecticut Yankee in King Arthur's Court, A (Twain), 133, 136, 138
Cooked and the Raw, The (Lévi-Strauss), 62, 205n
Coover, Robert, 26–27, 34–35, 37, 204n; "The Gingerbread House," 33; *Pricksongs and Descants*, 32, 198n
Copernicus, Nicolaus, 110, 120
Cortázar, Julio, 43, 48; "Axolotl," 38–41, 44, 49–50, 199–203n
Cosmicomics (Calvino), 159
Crane, Stephen, 64
Cratylus (Plato), 184
Creamy and Delicious (Katz), 30–31, 198n
Crito (Plato), 184
"Crossing Brooklyn Ferry" (Whitman), 98, 101
Crying of Lot 49, The (Pynchon), 65
Cuchulain of Muirthemme (Lady Gregory), 13
Cuentos fantásticos, 43, 49
Cyrano de Bergerac, 186

Dana, Richard Henry (elder); *Paul Felton*, 96
Dante, 1
Dasein, 109–10, 119
Day of the Locust, The (West), 65, 205n
Dead fantasy, 193
de Brunhoff, Jean, 85
de Camp, L. Sprague, 144, 149, 213n; *Lest Darkness Fall*, 133–34
De La Mare, Walter, 93

Delany, Samuel R., 29–31; *The Einstein Intersection*, 27–28, 34, 36–37, 198n
del Rey, Lester, 144, 149, 213n
De Quincey, Thomas, 91
Derrida, Jacques, 206n
De Voto, Bernard, 140, 212n; "Eseldorf" manuscript, 137; "The Great Dark," 138
Dialectic of Enlightenment (Adorno and Horkheimer), 70
Diaphaneite (Pater), 7
Diary of a Writer (Dostoevsky), 188–89
Dick, Philip K.; *The Man in the High Castle*, 137
Dickens, Charles, 91
Diderot, Denis; *Rameau's Nephew*, 186
Directed thinking, 148–49
Discours, Figure (Lyotard), 67–68, 205n
Disney, Walt; *Pinocchio*, 168
"Divinity School Address, The" (Emerson), 106
Dodgson, Charles L. *See* Carroll, Lewis
"Dolph Heyliger" (Irving), 95
Don Quixote, 10
Donaldson, Stephen R., 149, 214n; *The Power That Preserves*, 147
Donne, John, 111, 209n
Dos Passos, John, 76
Dostoevsky, Fyodor, 186, 190, 192, 218n; "Bobok," 188–89; *Diary of a Writer*, 188–89; "The Dream of a Ridiculous Man," 189; "The Gentle One," 189; *Notes from Underground*, 188; *White Nights*, 188
Dracula (Stoker), 77
"Dream of a Ridiculous Man, The" (Dostoevsky), 189
Dreiser, Theodore, 76
Drummond of Hawthornden, William, 111, 210n
Dryden, John, 64, 142
Dumas, Alexandre, 84
Duneka, Frederick A., 137

Dunne, John, 180, 215–16n

Earthsea, 116–19
Eddison, E. R., 84
Einstein, Albert, 51, 55, 57, 194, 204n; *The Evolution of Physics* (with Leopold Infeld), 54, 204n
Einstein Intersection, The (Delany), 27–28, 34, 36–37, 198n
Either-Or (Kierkegaard), 188
Eliot, George, 3
Elliot, Robert C., 59
Emerson, Ralph Waldo, 2, 6, 97, 105, 208–9n; "The Divinity School Address," 106; "Experience," 90, 100, 102; "Montaigne; or, the Skeptic," 100; *Nature*, 98–99
Enemy of the People, An (Ibsen), 192
Epipsychidion (Percy Shelley), 10
Erasmus, Desiderius; *In Praise of Folly*, 186
Escher, N. C., 56–57, 115
"Eseldorf" manuscript. *See* De Voto
Essays on a Science of Mythology (Jung), 150–51
Euphues (Lyly), 112
Evolution of Physics, The (Einstein and Infeld), 54, 204n
"Experience" (Emerson), 90, 102

Faerie Queene, The (Spenser), 64, 87, 112
"Fair-Haired Eckbert, The" (Tieck), 96
"Fall of the House of Usher, The" (Poe), 72–73, 93, 200n
Fantasmatic, 62–63, 66–67, 70–76
Fantastic in Literature, The (Rabkin), 59, 204n, 209n, 211n
Fantasy thinking, 148–49, 155–56
Faraday, Michael, 51, 53
Farmer, Philip José; "Sail On, Sail On," 138
Farthest Shore, The (Le Guin), 117–18
Feldman, Lew D., 135
Fichte, Johann Gottlieb, 103
Filial Piety, 79
Finnegan's Wake (Joyce), 57

Fitzgerald, F. Scott, 56
Five Weeks in a Balloon (Verne), 134
Fletcher, Angus; *Allegory: The Theory of a Symbolic Mode*, 18
Flies, The (Magnes), 182
Flight to Lucifer, The (Bloom), 6, 12, 19
Forbidden Planet, 167
Foucault, Michel; *Science humaine*, 27
Frankenstein (Mary Shelley), 10–11, 193
Freud, Sigmund, 2, 5–6, 18–19, 66, 70, 150–52, 204n, 206n; *Beyond the Pleasure Principle*, 4; *The Interpretation of Dreams*, 67–68; *Jokes and Their Relation to the Unconscious*, 68–69, 205n; Pleasure/Pain Principle, 3–4, 10, 13; Reality Principle, 3–4, 12; *Das Unheimliche*, 5
Frogs, The (Magnes), 182
Frye, Northrop, 114
Futurological Congress (Lem), 191, 217

Galileo, 52, 110
García Márquez, Gabriel; "A Very Old Man with Enormous Wings," 121–29
"Garden of Forking Paths, The" (Borges), 33
Garland, Hamlin, 53
Gaskell, Elizabeth, 91
"Gentle One, The" (Dostoevsky), 189
Gernsback, Hugo, 132, 211n
Gibbon, Edward, 118
Giles Goat Boy (Barth), 30
Gilgamesh, The Epic of, 179–81, 192, 216n
"Gingerbread House, The" (Coover), 33
Gnosticism, 2, 9, 18
Gödel, Escher, Bach: An Eternal Golden Braid (Hofstadter), 57, 204n
Gödel, Kurt, 57, 194
Gogol, Nikolai, 190, 192; *The Inspector General*, 188; "The Nose,"

187, 217n; "The Overcoat," 187–88, 217n, 218n
Gombrowicz, Witold, 193
Gorgias (Plato), 184
"Gospel of Self, The" (Twain), 139
Gould, Eric, 29, 198n
Grahame, Kenneth, 84, 207n; *The Wind in the Willows*, 80, 83
Grapes of Wrath, The (Steinbeck), 79
"Great Dark, The" (Twain), 138
"Great Good Place, The" (James), 111–12
Greene, Robert; *Pandosto*, 111
"Greene Tea" (Le Fanu), 93
Greimas, A. J., 24, 197n, 202n; condensation, 68, 73; semantic rectangle, 44–45; *Sémantique structurale*, 68, 205n
Grimmelshausen, Hans Jacob Christoph von, 186
"Grotesque: An American Genre, The" (O'Connor), 64, 205n

Haldeman, Joe, 145–46, 149, 213n
Handbook to Literature, A (Holman), 122, 211n
Harlowe, Jean, 28
Harrold, Charles Frederick, 97
"Haunted Mind, The" (Hawthorne), 103
Hawkes, John, 27
Hawks, Howard; *The Thing*, 169
Hawthorne, Nathaniel, 91, 96, 99–100, 102, 107, 208–9n; "Alice Doane's Appeal," 90, 93–94, 103; "The Celestial Railroad," 105; "The Haunted Mind," 103–4; "The Hollow of the Three Hills," 94; "The Legends of the Province House," 93–94; "Prophetic Pictures," 95; "Wives of the Dead," 94; "Young Goodman Brown," 94, 103, 106
Hedge, Frederic Henry, 103, 209n
Hegel, G. W. F., 70
Heidegger, Martin, 108–9, 117, 209–10n
Heine, Heinrich; *Reisebilder*, 68
Heinlein, Robert A., 66, 139; *The Moon Is a Harsh Mistress*, 159;

Stranger in a Strange Land, 140
Heinrich von Ofterdingen (Novalis), 9
Heisenberg, Werner, 52, 55, 194, 203–4n
Helms, Randel, 117, 210n
Hemingway, Ernest; *The Old Man and the Sea*, 192
Hind and the Panther, The (Dryden), 64
Hirsch-Hyacinth, 69
Hitler, Adolf; *Lord of the Swastika* (see Spinrad, *The Iron Dream*), 130–31, 139
Hobbit, The (Tolkien), 81
Hoffmann, E. T. A., 2, 186, 192, 210n; "The Sandman," 5, 96
Hofstadter, Douglas R.; *Gödel, Escher, Bach: An Eternal Golden Braid*, 57, 204n
Hogg, James, 91
Hollander, John, 12
"Hollow of the Three Hills, The" (Hawthorne), 94
Holman, C. Hugh; *A Handbook to Literature*, 122, 211n
Hooker, Richard; *Laws of Ecclesiastical Polity*, 113
Horkheimer, Max, 70, 206n
Howells, William Dean, 135
Hoyle, Fred, 110, 115, 144
Huckleberry Finn (Twain), 65
Hugo, Victor, 189
Husserl, Edmund, 61, 204n
Huxley, Aldous, 193
Huygens, Christian, 53
Hyman, Allan, 135
Hymns to the Night (Novalis), 10

Ibsen, Henrik; *An Enemy of the People*, 192
Inanna's Descent into the Underworld, 178–79
Infeld, Leopold (see Einstein), 54, 204n
Inklings, The, 15
In Praise of Folly (Erasmus), 186
Inspector General, The (Gogol), 188
Interpretation of Dreams, The (Freud),

67–68

In the Ocean of Night (Benford), 145

Introduction à la littérature fantastique (Todorov), 38, 108, 197n, 199n, 204n

Invariance theory, 55

Invasion of the Body Snatchers (Siegel), 160–63, 165, 168–69, 171

Ionesco, Eugene, 117–18, 193, 210n; *The Chairs*, 115–16; *Rhinoceros*, 115

Iron Dream, The (Spinrad), 130, 211n

Irving, Washington, 91, 93, 96, 99; "Adventure of the German Student," 95; "Dolph Heyliger," 95; "The Legend of Sleepy Hollow," 95; "The Spectre Bride-groom," 95; "Strange Stories by a Nervous Gentleman," 95; *Tales of a Traveller*, 95; *Tales of the Alhambra*, 95

Irwin, W. R., 23, 126, 197n

Island of Dr. Moreau, The (Wells), 159

Jakobson, Roman, 41, 200n

James, Henry, 66, 71–72; "The Great Good Place," 111–12; *The Turn of the Screw*, 93

Jaws, 192

Jerusalem (Blake), 12

Joachim of Flora, 1

Johnson, Samuel, 64, 186

Jokes and Their Relation to the Unconscious (Freud), 68–69, 205n

Jung, C. G., 152; Directed thinking, 148–49; *Essays on a Science of Mythology*, 150–51; Fantasy thinking, 148–49, 155–56; Jungian, 115, 145, 147; "Psychology of the Child Archetype," 148, 214n; *Symbols of Transformation*, 148, 214n

Jungian, 115, 145, 147

Just-So Stories, The (Kipling), 85

Kafka, Franz 17, 19, 66; "The Metamorphosis," 76–77, 199n

Katz, Steve, 32, 37; *Creamy and Delicious*, 30–31, 198n

Kelvin, Lord, 53, 55, 57

Kepler, Johannes, 111

Khlebnikov, Vlemir, 191–92, 217n

Kierkegaard, Soren; *Either-Or*, 188

King Lear (Shakespeare), 89

Kipling, Rudyard, 84, 113; *The Just-So Stories*, 85

Klingsohr's Fairy Tale (Novalis), 9

Knight, Damon; "Masks," 168

Kodaly, Zoltan, 169

Kotik Letaev (Belyi), 189–90

Kubrick, Stanley; *2001: A Space Odyssey*, 166, 170–73, 215n

Kuhn, Thomas S., 51

Lacan, Jacques, 63, 67, 70, 74, 204n–6n

Lady Gregory; *Cuchulain of Muirthemme*, 13

Lafferty, R. A., 145

Larousse Encyclopedia of Mythology, 147

Laws of Ecclesiastical Polity (Hooker), 113

Lavoisier, Antoine Laurent, 51

Lector cómplice, el, 49, 203n

Lector hembra, el, 49, 203n

Lee, Sophia; *The Recess*, 96

Le Fanu, Sheridan, 208n; "Carmilla," 66; "Green Tea," 93

Left Hand of Darkness, The (Le Guin), 189

"Legend of Sleepy Hollow, The" (Irving), 95

"Legends of the Province House, The" (Hawthorne), 93

Le Guin, Ursula, 116, 119, 166–67, 210n; *The Farthest Shore*, 117–18; *The Left Hand of Darkness*, 159

Lem, Stanislaw, 155, 192–93; *Futurological Congress*, 191, 218n; *Solaris*, 142, 149, 154, 156–59, 215n, 218n

Lévi-Strauss, Claude, 29; *The Cooked and the Raw*, 62–63, 204–5n

Lewis, C. S., 15, 17, 81–83, 85, 87, 132, 207n, 210n, 212n

Lewis, Matthew G., 91; *The Monk*, 96, 199n

"Library of Babel, The" (Borges), 21, 23–24, 36–37, 197n
Liddell, Alice, 80
"Ligeia" (Poe), 93, 103
Lilith (Macdonald), 17, 87
Lindsay, David; *A Voyage to Arcturus*, 1, 5–17, 19, 84
Lodge, Thomas; *Rosalind*, 112
Longinus, 9
Lord of Light (Zelazny), 30
Lord of the Rings, The (Tolkien), 81
Lord of the Swastika, The (Hitler). See Spinrad, Norman
Lost Traveller's Dream, The (Bloom), 18
Lucian, 186, 192, 217n; *A True Story*, 185
Lu Ki; *Wen-fu*, 142
Lupoff, Richard, 149, 214n; *Sword of the Demon*, 147
Luther, Martin, 120
Lyly, John; *Euphues*, 112
Lyotard, J. F.; *Discours, Figure*, 66–68, 205n
Lysis (Plato), 184
Lysistrata (Aristophanes), 183

McCullers, Carson, 65
MacDonald, George, 84; *At the Back of the North Wind*, 17; *Lilith*, 17, 87; *Phantastes*, 17
McMurray, George, 121–23, 127
Magnes; *The Birds*, 182; *The Flies*, 182; *The Frogs*, 182
Mallarmé, Stéphane, 75
Man in the High Castle, The (Dick), 137
"MS. Found in a Bottle, A" (Poe), 95
Martian Chronicles, The (Bradbury), 142, 149–50, 152–56, 159, 214–15n
Martin, Jay, 65, 205n
Marvell, Andrew, 152
Marx, Karl, 64, 70, 205n
"Masks" (Knight), 168
Mather, Cotton, 94
Matthiessen, F. O., 100, 208n
Maxwell, James Clerk, 51–53, 55, 57, 203n

Maxwell's Demon, 55–56
Medusa (Visiak), 12
"Mellonta Tauta" (Poe), 105
Melville, Herman, 99–100, 149, 209n; *The Confidence-Man*, 105; *Moby-Dick*, 34, 105, 192
Menippean Satire, 186, 188, 217n
"Mental Telegraphy" (Twain), 134
"Mental Telegraphy Again" (Twain), 134
Metamorphoses (Ovid), 151–52, 214n
Metamorphoses of Science Fiction (Suvin), 61, 198n, 204n, 211n
"Metamorphosis, The" (Kafka), 76–77, 199n
"Metzengerstein" (Poe), 95
Micromégas (Voltaire), 186
Middle Earth, 116, 119
Miller, Walter M., Jr.; *A Canticle for Leibowitz*, 159
Milne, A. A., 85
Milton, John, 11, 120, 151–52; *Paradise Lost*, 111
Miss Lonelyhearts (West), 18
Moby-Dick (Melville), 34, 105, 192
Moebius Strip, 57
Moon Is a Harsh Mistress, The (Heinlein), 159
Moore, Ward; *Bring the Jubilee*, 137
Monk, The (Lewis), 96, 199n
Montaigne, Michel de, 186
"Montaigne; or, the Skeptic" (Emerson), 100
More, Sir Thomas, 186
Morris, William, 84
Mozgovaya igra, 189–90
"Murder, a Mystery, and a Marriage, A" (Twain), 134–36, 212n
Myslennyi yazyk, 190
"Mysterious Balloonist, The" (Twain), 134
Mysterious Stranger manuscripts (Twain), 136–38

Nagel, Ernst; *The Structure of Science*, 53–54, 203–4n
Narcissus as Narcissus (Tate), 18
Narcissism, 10–11, 15
Nashe, Thomas; *The Unfortunate*

Traveller, 18
Natural Supernaturalism (Carlyle), 97, 106
Nature (Emerson), 98
Naturphilosophie, 97
Nerval, Gérard de; *Aurélia*, 39, 199n
Neumann, Erich; *The Origins and History of Consciousness*, 190, 216n
"Never Bet the Devil Your Head" (Poe), 105
Newton, Sir Isaac, 51
Nietzsche, Friedrich, 4, 75, 152
Niven, Larry, in *Science Fiction Voices #2*, 142
Noematic, 61–64, 66–67, 70–75
"Nose, The" (Gogol), 187, 217n
Novalis, 2, 75; *Heinrich von Ofterdingen*, 9; *Hymns to the Night*, 10; *Klingsohr's Fairy Tale*, 9
Novum Organum (Bacon), 113
Notes from Underground (Dostoevsky), 188
"No. 44" manuscript (Twain), 137–39

O'Connor, William Van, 65; "The Grotesque: An American Genre," 64, 205n
Ode to the Confederate Dead (Tate), 18
"Of the Terrible Doubt of Appearances" (Whitman), 100
"Old Comrades" (Twain), 139
Old English Baron, The (Reeve), 96
Old Man and the Sea, The (Hemingway), 192
Origins and History of Consciousness, The (Neumann), 190, 215n
Orwell, George, 192
Ouvroir de Littérature Potentielle (Oulipo), 191
"Overcoat, The" (Gogol), 187–88, 217n
Ovid, 10, 13, 19; *Metamorphoses*, 151–52, 214n

Paine, Albert Bigelow, 137, 212n
Pandosto (Greene), 112
Paradise Lost (Milton), 111

Pater, Walter, 2, 8, 14–15, 19; *Diaphaneite*, 7
Paul Felton (Dana), 96
Peace (Aristophanes), 183
Pearce, Howard, 109, 209n
Penrose, Roger, 52
Petersburg (Belyi), 189
"Petrified Man" (Twain), 136–37
Phantastes (Macdonald), 17
Philmus, Robert M., 132, 211n
"Pierre Menard, Author of Don Quixote" (Borges), 35
Pilgrim's Progress" (Bunyan), 64, 79, 111
Pinocchio (Disney), 168
Pinkerton, Jan, 137, 212n
"Pit and the Pendulum, The" (Poe), 95
Plato, 60, 149, 190, 192, 217n; *Charmides*, 183; *Cratylus*, 184; *Crito*, 184; *Gorgias*, 184; *Lysis*, 184; *The Republic*, 184
Pneuma, 15
Poe, Edgar Allan, 66, 76, 91, 94, 96, 99–100, 102, 132, 199n, 207–8n, 211n; "The Balloon Hoax," 134; "The Black Cat," 95; "The Fall of the House of Usher," 72–74, 93, 200n; "Ligeia," 93, 95, 103; "A MS. Found in a Bottle," 95; "Mellonta Tauta," 105; "Metzengerstein," 95; "Morella," 93, 95; *The Narrative of Arthur Gordon Pym*, 34; "Never Bet the Devil Your Head," 105
Pornography, 175, 193–94, 218n
Potter, Beatrix, 80; *Squirrel Nutkin*, 85
Pound, Ezra, 7
Power That Preserves, The (Donaldson), 147
Pricksongs and Descants (Coover), 32, 198n
Principia Mathematica (Russell and Whitehead), 57
Prometheus Unbound (Percy Shelley), 10
Prometheanism, 11, 15
Propp, Vladimir, 24, 197n

Proteus, 153, 159

Proust, Marcel; *Swann's Way*, 71, 206n

"Psychology of the Child Archetype, The" (Jung), 148, 213n

Ptolemy, 115, 120; *Tetrabiblos*, 110, 209n

Pynchon, Thomas, 27, 30; *The Crying of Lot 49*, 65

Rabelais, François, 186

Rabkin, Eric S., 1, 23, 60, 64–66, 70, 108–10, 114–17, 126–27, 197n, 206n, 210n; *The Fantastic in Literature*, 59, 204n, 209n

Radcliffe, Ann; *The Mysteries of Udolpho*, 96

Raleigh, Sir Walter, 111, 209n

Rameau's Nephew (Diderot), 186

Recess, The (Lee), 96

Reeve, Clara; *The Old English Baron*, 96

Reisebilder (Heine), 68

Republic, The (Plato), 184

Rhinoceros (Ionesco), 115

Richter, Jean-Paul, 186

Romulus and Remus, 181

Rosalind (Lodge), 112

Rothschild, Baron Salomon, 69

R.U.R. (Capek), 159

Ruskin, John, 8

Russell, Bertrand, 57

"Sail On, Sail On" (Farmer), 138

"Sandman, The" (Hoffmann), 5, 96

Sartor Resartus (Carlyle), 2, 7, 9, 97, 103, 106, 208n

Schlegel, Friedrich von, 8–9

Scholes, Robert, 26, 61, 198n, 204n, 212n

Schreber, Daniel Paul, 74, 206n

Science Fiction Review, 144

Science Fiction Voices #2, 142

Science humaine, 27

Scientifiction, 132

Scott, Sir Walter, 91

Search, Pamela, 93, 208n

"Secret History of Eddypus, the World-Empire, The" (Twain), 139

Sémantique structurale (Greimas), 68, 205n

Sendak, Maurice, 84

Seuss, Dr., 85; *Cat in the Hat*, 79

Shakespeare, William, 78, 87, 89, 142, 151; *Twelfth Night*, 175

Shelley, Mary; *Frankenstein*, 10–11

Shelley, Percy, 9, 11–12, 17, 19; *Adonais*, 10; *Alastor*, 10, 13, 16; *Epipsychidion*, 10; *Prometheus Unbound*, 10; *The Triumph of Life*, 10

Sherlock Holmes, 165

Shklovsky, Viktor, 67, 69–70, 206n

Sidney, Sir Philip; *Arcadia*, 112

Siegel, Don; *Invasion of the Body Snatchers*, 160–63, 165, 168–69, 171

Silverberg, Robert, 166–67, 215n

Solaris (Lem), 142, 149, 154, 156–59, 214n

"Song of Myself" (Whitman), 98

"Spectre Bride-groom, The" (Irving), 95

Spenser, Edmund, 19; *The Faerie Queene*, 64, 87, 112

Spielberg, Stephen; *Close Encounters of a Third Kind*, 169–70

Spinrad, Norman; *The Iron Dream*, 130, 139, 210n

Sprachspiele, 186

Squirrel Nutkin (Potter), 85

Stapledon, Olaf, 132

Star Trek, 174, 193

Star Wars, 19, 174

Steinbeck, John; *The Grapes of Wrath*, 79

Steiner, Rudolf, 190

Stevens, Wallace, 7, 17

Stevenson, Robert Louis, 84

Stoker, Bram; *Dracula*, 77

Stranger in a Strange Land (Heinlein), 140

"Strange Stories By A Nervous Gentleman" (Irving), 95

Structure of Science, The (Nagel), 53–54, 203n

Strugatsky, the Brothers, 193

Stuart Little (White), 81

Sullivan, Jack, 92–93, 208n
Suvin, Darko, 26, 31, 131; *Metamorphoses of Science Fiction*, 61, 198n, 204n, 211n
Swann's Way (Proust), 71, 206n
Swift, Jonathan, 186
Swinburne, Algernon, 7
Sword and Sorcery, 130
Sword of the Demon (Lupoff), 147
Symbols of Transformation (Jung), 148, 213n

Tale, Allan; *Narcissus as Narcissus*, 18; *Ode to the Confederate Dead*, 18
Tales of a Traveller (Irving), 95
Tales of the Alhambra (Irving), 95
Tau Zero (Poul Anderson), 164
Territorial Enterprise, The, 136
Tetrabiblos (Ptolemy), 110, 209n
"There Was a Child Went Forth" (Whitman), 98
Thing, The (Hawks), 169
Thomson, James; *The City of Dreadful Night*, 9
Thoreau, Henry David; *Walden*, 98, 100
"Three Thousand Years Among the Microbes" (Twain), 138
Through the Looking Glass (Carroll), 1, 19
Tieck, Ludwig; "Fair-Haired Eckbert," 96
Tin Drum, The, 5
Todorov, Tzvetan, 5, 24, 39–40, 43–44, 53, 59, 74–77, 96, 109–10, 113–16, 120–22, 126–27, 129, 194, 200–201n, 206n–11n, 218n; *Introduction à la littérature fantastique*, 38, 108, 197n, 199n, 204n
Tolkien, J. R. R., 15, 37, 84, 87, 116–17, 119, 210n; *The Hobbit*, 81; *The Lord of the Rings*, 81
Tractatus (Wittgenstein), 25
Traherne, Thomas, 142
Triumph of Life, The (Percy Shelley), 10
True Story, A (Lucian), 185

Truffaut, François, 170
Turn of the Screw, The (James), 93
Twain, Mark, 130–32, 140, 210–11n, 212n; *A Connecticut Yankee in King Arthur's Court*, 133, 136, 138, 212n; "The Gospel of Self," 139; "The Great Dark," 138; "Mental Telegraphy," 134; "Mental Telegraphy Again," 134; "A Murder, a Mystery, and a Marriage," 134–36, 212n; "The Mysterious Balloonist," 134; the Mysterious Stranger manuscripts, 136–38; "No. 44" manuscript, 137–38; "Old Comrades," 139; "Petrified Man," 136–37; "The Secret History of Eddypus, the World-Empire," 139; "Three Thousand Years Among the Microbes," 138; *What Is Man?*, 139
Twelfth Night (Shakespeare), 174
2001: A Space Odyssey (Kubrick), 166, 170–73, 215n
Tynyanov, Yuri, 60, 204n

Unfortunate Traveller, The (Nashe), 18
Unheimliche, Das (Freud), 5

Valentinus the Gnostic, 1
Valéry, Paul, 21, 24
Van Vogt, A. E., 146, 149, 214n
Verne, Jules, 8, 66, 132, 135, 186, 211n; *Five Weeks in a Balloon*, 134
"Very Old Man with Enormous Wings, A" (García Márquez), 121–29
Visiak, E. H.; *Medusa*, 12
Vision, A (Yeats), 12
Voltaire; *Micromégas*, 186; *Zadig*, 137
Voyage to Arcturus, A (Lindsay), 1–2, 6–12, 17, 19

Walden (Thoreau), 98, 100
Walpole, Horace, 91; *The Castle of Otranto*, 96
Wasps, The (Aristophanes), 183
We (Zamyatin), 190, 217n

Weber, Max, 70
Wells, H. G., 132, 186, 192–93, 211n; *The Island of Dr. Moreau*, 159
Wen-fu (Lu Ki), 142
West, Nathanael, 64; *The Day of the Locust*, 65, 205n; *Miss Lonelyhearts*, 18
What Is Man? (Twain), 139
Whistler, James MacNeil, 7
White, E. B.; *Charlotte's Web*, 81; *Stuart Little*, 81
Whitehead, Alfred North; *Principia Mathematica*, 57
White Nights (Dostoevsky), 189
Whitman, Walt, 97, 105; "As I Ebb'd With the Ocean of Life," 100–101; "Crossing Brooklyn Ferry," 98, 101; "Of the Terrible Doubt of Appearances," 100, 102; "Song of Myself," 98, 100; "There Was a Child Went Forth," 98, 100

"Who Goes There?" (Campbell), 161, 215n
Wieland (Brown), 92
Wilde, Oscar, 2, 7–8, 14, 16
Williams, Charles, 15
Williamson, George, 111, 209n–10n
Wind in the Willows, The (Grahame), 80, 83
Wittgenstein, Ludwig, 186; *Tractatus*, 25
"Wives of the Dead" (Hawthorne), 94
Wordsworth, William, 86, 207n

Yeats, William Butler, 7; *A Vision*, 12
"Young Goodman Brown" (Hawthorne), 94, 103

Zadig (Voltaire), 137
Zamyatin, Evgeny, 192–93; *We*, 190, 218n
Zelazny, Roger, 27; *Lord of Light*, 30
Zeno, 56